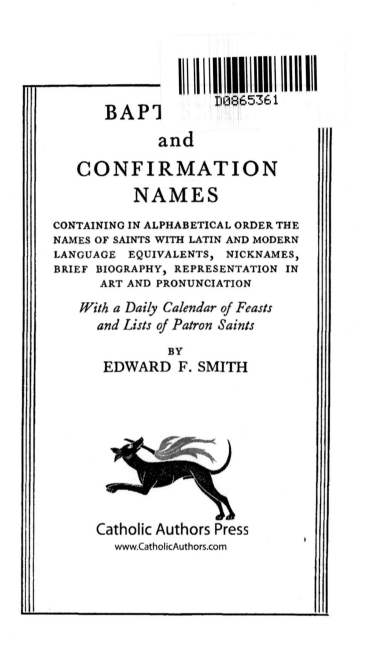

BAPTISMAL
and
CONFIRMATION
NAMES

CONTAINING IN ALPHABETICAL ORDER THE
NAMES OF SAINTS WITH LATIN AND MODERN
LANGUAGE EQUIVALENTS, NICKNAMES,
BRIEF BIOGRAPHY, REPRESENTATION IN
ART AND PRONUNCIATION

*With a Daily Calendar of Feasts
and Lists of Patron Saints*

BY
EDWARD F. SMITH

Catholic Authors Press
www.CatholicAuthors.com

Nihil Obstat

ARTHUR J. SCANLAN, S.T.D.
Censor Librorum

Imprimatur

PATRICK CARDINAL HAYES
Archbishop of New York

NEW YORK, April 2, 1935

First published 1935
Reprinted 2007 Catholic Authors Press

ISBN: 978-0-9782985-8-6

Catholic Authors Press

www.CatholicAuthors.org

DEDICATED

LOVING REMEMBRANCE

TO

MY MOTHER

Mary Theresa Smith

BIBLIOGRAPHY

Aigrain, L'Abbé R., *Ecclesia* (Paris: Bloud et Gay, 1927)

Arthur, W., *Etymological Dictionary of Family and Christian Names*

Beleze, G., *Dictionnaire de Noms de Baptême* (Paris: L. Hachette & Cie)

Benedictines of Ramsgate, *The Book of Saints* (London: A. & C. Black, Ltd., 1921)

Butler, Rev. A., *Lives of the Saints* (New York: P. J. Kenedy & Sons)

Catholic Encyclopedia

Century Cyclopedia of Names

Charnock, R. S., *Praenomina* (London: Trübner)

Dawson, L. H. *Nicknames and Pseudonyms* (New York: E. P. Dutton & Co.)

Drake, M. & W., *Saints and Their emblems* (London: T. Werner Laurie, Ltd., 1916)

Frey, A. R., *Dictionary of Sobriquets and Nicknames* (New York: Houghton Mifflin Co.)

Grussi, A. M., *Chats on Christian Names* (Boston: The Stratford Company, 1925)

Hoffmann, Rev. A., *Liturgical Dictionary* (Collegeville: The Liturgical Press, 1928)

Holweck, Rt. Rev. F. G., *A Biographical Dictionary of the Saints* (St. Louis: B. Herder Book Co., 1924)

Latham, E., *Dictionary of Names, Nicknames and Surnames* (New York: E. P. Dutton & Co., 1904)

Lippincott's Pronouncing Dictionary of Biography and Mythology.

Long, H. A., *Personal and Family Names* (London: Hamilton Adams & Co.)

Longhead, F. H., *Dictionary of Given Names* (Glendale, Calif.: Arthur H. Clark Co., 1934)

Mackey, M. S. & M. G., *The Pronunciation of Ten Thousand Proper Names* (New York: Dodd, Mead & Co., 1922)

Mauson, C. O. S., *International Book of Names* (New York: Thomas Y. Crowell Co., 1933)

Roman Martyrology (New York: Benziger Brothers, 1933)

Scott, E.-L., *Les Noms de Baptême* (Paris: Alexandre Houssiaux)

Scovil, E. R., *Names for Children* (Philadelphia: Henry Altemus)

Sleumer, Rev. A., *Kirchenlateinische Wörterbuch* (Limburg: Verlag von Gebrüder Steffen, 1926)

Swan, H., *Christian Names, Male and Female* (New York: E. P. Dutton & Co., 1905)

Weekley, *The Romance of Names* (New York: E. P. Dutton & Co., 1914)

Weidenhan, Rev. J. L., *Baptismal Names* (Emittsburg: St. Mary's Press)

vi

PREFACE

It is the desire of the Church that at Baptism and at Confirmation her children receive the names of Saints. The Code of Canon Laws states: "Pastors should take especial care that a Christian name be given to all whom they baptize. If they cannot do this, they shall add to the name given by the parents the name of some Saint and enter both in the Baptismal Record" (Canon 761). The reason for this is that the child may have a particular patron in Heaven to watch over him as well as an ideal model for his imitation. This compilation is therefore offered that the laity may be provided with a convenient source of selection, and also that the Clergy may have at hand the Latin nomenclature for use with the Ritual.

Each name is followed by the Latin form (with accent and genitive case), the feast day, a brief biography, the signification of the name, its pronunciation and, for the more common ones, the representation of the Saint in art. There are likewise given with their pronunciations the modern language equivalents, derivatives, variants, and nicknames; these latter, however, not for imitation, but as a key to the basic name.

In the second part of the book will be found a list of patrons of countries, also one of professions, etc., and those invoked in sickness and difficulties. This is followed by a list in calendar form of the names of the Saints according to the day of their feast.

ABBREVIATIONS

Ab. Abbot or Abbess
Ap., App. Apostle or Apostles
Ar. Arabian
Aram. Aramaic
Archb. Archbishop
A. S. Anglo-Saxon
B., BB. Bishop or Bishops
Bav. Bavarian
Bl. Blessed
Boh. Bohemian
Bulg. Bulgarian
C.,CC. Confessor or Confessors
Celt. Celtic
Cent. Century
D. Doctor
Dan. Danish
Dea. Deacon
der. derivative
dim. diminutive
d. u. date unknown
Du. Dutch
Emp. Emperor
Eng. English
fam. familiar form
Fr. French
Ger. German
Gr. Greek
Heb. Hebrew
Her. Hermit
Hung. Hungarian
indecl. indeclinable

Ir. Irish
It. Italian
Lat. Latin
Lith. Lithuanian
M., MM. Martyr or Martyrs
Mat. Matron
Nor. Norwegian
P., PP. Pope or Popes
Pat. Patriarch
Pen. Penitent
Per. Persian
Pol. Polish
Port. Portuguese
Pr. Priest
Pron. Pronunciation
Proph. Prophet
Q. Queen
R. M. Roman Martyrology
Rus. Russian
Sc. Scotch
Sig. Signification
Slav. Slavic
Sp. Spanish
St. Saint
Sw. Swedish
Syr. Syrian
Teut. Teutonic
V., VV. Virgin or Virgins
var. variant
Wid. Widow

KEY TO PRONUNCIATION

ā	as in	fade		ō	as in	note
a̧	"	all		ŏ	"	not
ă	"	far		ȯ	"	or
ȧ	"	comma		o͞o	"	hood
ă	"	at		ō͞o	"	moon
ĕ	"	she		ou or ŏw	"	now
ĕ	"	met				
ē	"	her		ū	"	cute
				ŭ	"	up
ī	"	bite		ū	"	rule
ĭ	"	hit		ṅ	"	nasal

A

Aarão (ä-rŏwṅ′), Port. Aaron.

AARON (*indecl.*) Jul. 1. R. M.
First Jewish high-priest, appointed by God, and brother of Moses. *Sig.* Heb. high mountain. *Pron.* â′rŏn.
(ä′rŏn), Lat.

Abdenago (ăb-dĕn′a-gō), same as Azarias

ABDIAS (*indecl.*), Nov. 19. R. M.
Minor prophet. *Sig.* Heb. servant of God. *Pron.* ăb-dē′ăs.
(äb-dē′äs), Lat.

ABDON (*indecl.*), M. Jul. 30. R. M.
3 Cent. Persian noble martyred with St. Sennen. He visited prisons and buried the bodies of martyrs. *Sig.* Heb. servile. *Pron.* ăb′dŏn.
(äb′dŏn), Lat.

Abe (āb), dim. Abraham or Abram

ABEL (*indecl.* or Abélus, i). Dec. 28.
Second son of Adam, slain by his brother Cain. Regarded as first martyr. His sacrifice is mentioned in sacrifice of Mass. Type of Christ and invoked for the dying. *Sig.* Heb. breath. *Pron.* ā′bĕl.
(ä′bĕl), Lat.

Abele (ä-bā′lä), It. Abel

Abelus (ä-bā′lŭs), Lat. Abel

Abie (ā′bĭ), dim. Abraham or Abram.

ABRAHAM (*indecl.*—gen. Ábrahæ; or Abrahámus, i), Pat. Oct. 9. R. M.
Greatest patriarch of Old Testament, father of the Hebrew nation, specially favored by God and buried

by angels. *Sig.* Heb. father of a multitude. *Pron.*
ā'brȧ-hăm. Patron of hotel-keepers.
(ä-brä-än'), Fr.
(ä'brä-häm), Lat., Ger.
Abrahamo (ä-brä-ä'mō), It. Abraham
Abrahamus (ä-brä-hä'mŭs), Lat. Abraham
Abrahan (ä-brä-än'), Sp. Abraham.
Abrahão (ä-brä-ŏwn'), Port. Abraham
Abram (*indecl.* or Abrámus, i), name of Abraham
before it was changed by God. *Sig.* Heb. father of a
height. *Pron.* ā'brăm.
(ä'bräm), Lat.
(ä-bräm'), Sp.
(ä-brăn'), Fr.
Abramo (ä-brä'mō), It. Abram.
Abramus (ä-brä'mŭs), Lat. Abram.
Absalom (ăb'sȧ-lŏm), var. Absolon.
Absolom (ăb'sŏ-lŏm), var. Absolon.

ABSOLON (*indecl.*), M. Early Church. Mar. 2. *Sig.*
Heb. father of peace. *Pron.* ăb'sŏ-lŏn.

ABUNDANTIA (Abundántia, æ), V. Jan. 19.
9 Cent. Spoleto. *Sig.* Lat. plenty. *Pron.* ă-bŭn-dänt'sĭä
(ä-bŭn-dänt'sē-ä), Lat.

ABUNDANTIUS (Abundántius, ii), Dea., M. Sept. 16.
R. M.
4 Cent. Rome. *Sig.* Lat. plenty. *Pron.* ă-bŭn-dänt'
sĭ-ŭs.
(ä-bŭn-dänt'sē-ŭs), Lat.

ABUNDIUS (Abúndius, ii), Pr., M. Sept. 16. R. M.
3 Cent. Rome. *Pron.* ă-bŭn'dĭ-us.
(ä-bŭn'dē-ŭs), Lat.

Aby (ā′bĭ), dim. Abraham, Abram.

Accurse (ä-kürs′), Fr. Accursius

ACCURSIUS (Accúrsius, ii), M. Jan. 16. R. M.
13 Cent. Franciscan slain by Moors. In art shown
with sword in breast. *Pron.* ă-kûr′shē-ŭs.
(ä-kōōr′sē-ŭs), Lat.

ACHARD (Aicárdus, i), Ab. Sept. 15. R. M.
7 Cent. Benedictine at Jumièges. Model of prayer and
austerity. *Pron.* ä-shär′.
(ä-shär′), Fr.
Achill (ä-kēl′), Ger. Achilles
Achille (ä-shēl′), Fr. Achilles
(ä-kē′lä), It.

ACHILLES (Achílles, is), B. C. May 15
4 Cent. Larissa, Greece. *Pron.* ă-kĭl′ēz
(ä-kē′läz), Lat.

ACHILLEUS (Achílleus, i), Dea., M. Ap. 23. R. M.
3 Cent. One of apostles of Vienne. In art shown with
church in hand. *Pron.* ă-kĭl′ē-ŭs
(ä-kē′lä-ŭs), Lat.
Also 1 Cent. M. with St. Nereus. May 12
Achim (ä′kēm), Rus. Joachim

ADA (Áda, æ), Ab. May 4
7 Cent. Benedictine. *Sig.* Teut. happy. *Pron.* ā′dă.
Also used for Edith.
(ä′dä), Lat.
Adalard (ä-dä-lär′), Fr. Adalhard

ADALBERT (Adalber′tus, i), B. M. Ap. 23. R. M.
10 Cent. Prague. Apostle of Prussians and Slavs,
patron of Poland and Bohemia. In art with chains

at feet, or having lance with club at bottom. *Sig.*
Teut. nobly bright. *Pron.* ă'dăl-bērt.
(ä-däl-bâr'), Fr.
(ä'däl-bĕrt), Ger.
Adalberto (ä-däl-bĕr'tō), Sp. Adalbert
Adalbertus (ä-däl-bâr'tŭs), Lat. Adalbert

ADALHARD (Adalhárdus, i), Ab. Jan. 2
29 Cent. Corbie. Relative and adviser of Charlemagne. In art shown giving alms. *Sig.* Teut.
nobly stern. *Pron.* ăd'ăl-härd.
Adalhardt (ăd'ăl-härt), var. of Adalhard
Adalhardus (ä-däl-här'dŭs), Lat. Adalhard
Adaline (ă'dà-lĭn), var. of Adeline

ADALRIC (Adalrícus, i), M. May 21.
29 Cent. Boy tortured to death by Norsemen. *Sig.*
Teut. noble king. *Pron.* ă'dăl-rĭk.
Adalricus (ä-däl-rē'kŭs), Lat. Adalric
Adalrik (ă'däl-rēk), Ger. Ulric

ADAM (*indecl.* or Adámus, i), Ab. May 16.
13 Cent. Benedictine. Patron invoked against epilepsy. Also abbreviated form of Adamnan. *Sig.*
Heb. earth-man. *Pron.* ă'dăm.
(ä-däṅ'), Fr.
(ä'däm), Lat., Ger., Dan.

ADAMNAN (Adamnánus, i), Ab. Sept. 23.
8 Cent. Iona. Writer of life of St. Columba. Also
called Adam. *Sig.* little Adam. *Pron.* ă'dăm-năn.
Adamnanus (ä-däm-nä'nŭs), Lat. Adamnan
Adamo (ä-dä'mō), It. Adam
Adamus (ä-dä'mŭs), Lat. Adam
Adan (ä-dän'), Sp. Adam

Adão (ä-dŏwn'), Port. Adam
Adaucte (ä-dōkt'), Fr. Adauctus

ADAUCTUS (Adau'ctus, i), M. Aug. 30. R. M.
4 Cent. *Sig.* added to, bestowed on unknown saint
martyred with St. Felix. *Pron.* ă-dŏwk'tŭs.
(ä-dŏwk'tŭs), Lat.
Addie, Addy (ăd'ē), dims. Adelaide, Audrey
Ade (ād), Ada, Edith, Adam

ADELA (Adéla, æ), Wid. Nov. 23
11 Cent. Belgium. Wife of Count Baldwin of Flanders.
After his death she became a Benedictine. Also
used for Adelaide. *Sig.* Teut. noble cheer. *Pron.*
ă'dĕ-là.
(ä-dā'lä), Lat., Sp.
Adelaida (ä-dä-lä'ē-dä), It. Sp. Adelaide

ADELAIDE (Adelháidis, is), Wid., Emp., Dec. 16
10 Cent. Wife of Otto I, peacemaker of Europe. "She
never forgot a kindness, nor ever remembered an
injury." In art with church in hand. *Sig.* Ger. of
noble birth. *Pron.* ă'dĕ-lād.
Adélaïde (ä-dā-lä-ēd'), Fr. Adelaide
Adelard (ä-dā-lär') Fr. Adalhard

ADELBERT (Adelbértus, i), C. June 25
8 Cent. Disciple of Sts. Egbert and Willibrord in
Holland. Also var. Adalbert. *Sig.* Teut, nobly
bright. *Pron.* ă'dĕl-bērt.
Adelberta (ă-dĕl-bēr'tà), fem. of Adelbert
Adelbertus (ä-dĕl-bâr'tŭs), Lat. Adelbert
Adelbrecht (ä'dĕl-brĕkt), Ger. Ethelbert or Adalbert

Adèle (ä-dĕl′), Fr. Adela, Adelaide
(ä-dä′lĕ), Ger.

ADELGUND (Aldegun′dis, is), V. Ab. Jan. 30
7 Cent. Maubeuge. Invoked against cancer. *Sig.*
Teut. noble war. *Pron.* ă′dĕl-gŭnd
Adelhaidis (ä-dĕl-hä′ĭ-dĭs), Lat. Adelaide
Adelhard (ă′dĕl-härd), var. of Adalhard
Adelheid (ä′dĕl-hīt), Ger. Adelaide
Adelhelm (ă′dĕl-hĕlm), var. of Aldhelm
Adelia (ă-dēl′yà), var. of Adeline
Adelicia (ă-dĕ-lē′shà), var. of Adelaide
Adelina (ă-dĕ-lē′nä), Lat., It. Adeline
(ă-dĕ-lī′nà), Eng. var.
Adeline (ă′dĕ-līn), var. of Adelaide
(äd′-lēn′), Fr.
(ä-dä-lē′nē), Ger.
Adelphe (ä-dĕlf′), Fr. Adelphus

ADELPHUS (Adélphus, i), B. C. Aug. 29. R. M.
5 Cent. Metz. *Sig.* Gr. brotherly. *Pron.* ă-dĕlf′ŭs
(ä-dĕl′fŭs), Lat.
Adelric (ă′dĕl-rĭk), var. of Adalric

ADELTRUDE (Adeltru′dis, is), V. Ab. Feb. 25.
7 Cent. Maubeuge. Daughter of Sts. Madegar and
Waltrude. In art shown holding pot of wax in
flames. *Sig.* Teut. noble maid. *Pron.* ă′dĕl-trūd
Adeltrudis (ä-dĕl-trōō′dis), Lat. Adeltrude
Adeodat (ä-dä-ō-dä′), Fr. Adeodatus

ADEODATUS (Adeoda′tus, i), P. C. Nov. 8. R. M.
7 Cent. Also called Deusdedit. First Pope to use
leaden seals on Decrees, whence the name "Bull."
Sig. Lat. God-given. *Pron.* ā-dē-ŏd′ à-tŭs
(ä-dä-ō-dä′tŭs), Lat.

Adhelm (ăd′hĕlm), var. of Aldhelm
Adhemar (ăd′ā-mär), var. of Aimard
Adilred (ăd′ĭl-rĕd), var. of Aelred

ADO (Ăḋo, ónis), B. C. Dec. 16. R. M.
9 Cent. Nobleman, scholar, Bishop of Vienne. Composer of a Martyrology. In art shown studying Scriptures. *Sig.* Teut. noble. *Pron.* ă′dō.
(ä′dō), Lat.
Adolf (ä′dŏlf), Du., Dan., Ger., Sw. Adolph
Adolfo (ä-dōl′fō), It., Sp. Adolph

ADOLPH (Adólphus, i), B. C. Feb. 11.
13 Cent. Osnabruck. Friend of poor. *Sig.* Teut. noble wolf or hero. *Pron.* ä′dŏlf or á-dŏlf′.
(ä′dŏlf), Ger.
Adolphe (ä-dōlf′), Fr. Adolph
Adolpho (ä-dōl′fō), Port. Adolph
Adolphus (ä-dōl′fŭs), Lat. Adolph
(á-dŏl′fŭs), Eng.

ADRIA (Ádria, æ), M. Dec. 2. R. M.
3 Cent. Rome. *Sig.* Lat. black. *Pron.* ä′drĕ-á.
(ä′drĕ-ä), Lat.
Adriaan (ä′drē-än), Du. Adrian

ADRIAN III (Hadriánus, i), P. C. Jul. 8. R. M.
9 Cent. Reconciler of Eastern Churches. Also called Hadrian. *Sig.* Lat. black. *Pron.* ä′drē-ăn.
(ä-drē-än′) Sp.
Also M. at Nicomedia under Diocletian, Sept. 8.
Adriana (ä-drē-ăn′á),fem. Adrian
Adriano (ä-drē-ä′nō), It., Port., Sp. Adrian
Adrião (ä-drē-ŏwṅ′), Port-Adrian
Adrien (ä-drē-ăṅ′), Fr. Adrian
Adrienne (ä-drē-ĕn′), Fr. Adriana

Aedan (ā'dăn), var. of Aidan
Aedannus (ā-dä'nŭs), Lat. Aidan
Aegidius (ā-jē'dē-ŭs), Lat. Giles

AELRED (Aelrédus, i), C. Ab. Mar. 2.
12 Cent. Rievaulx, Yorkshire. *Pron.* āl'rĕd.
Aelredus (āl-rā'dŭs), Lat. Aelred

AEMILIAN (Aemiliánus, i), M. Apr. 29.
3 Cent. Soldier martyred in Africa. *Pron.* ā-mĭ'lĭ-ăn.

AEMILIANA (Aemiliána, æ), V. M. Jan. 5. R. M.
6 Cent. Aunt of St. Gregory the Great, martyred at
Rome. *Pron.* ā-mĭ-lĕ-ăn'à.
(ā-mē-lē-ä'nä), Lat.
Aemilianus (ā-mē-lē-ä'nŭs), Lat. Aemilian
Aemilius (ā-mē'lē-ŭs'), Lat. Emil.

AENGUS (Áengus), B. C. Mar. 11.
9 Cent. Ireland, called the "Culdee." Compiler of a
Martyrology. Bishop of Clonenagh. Also called
Angus. *Sig.* Celt, noble youth. *Pron.* ān'gŭs.
Aenne (ĕn'nĕ), Ger. cor. of Anne
Afonso, Affonso (äf-fōn'sō), Port. Alphonsus

AFRA (Áfra, æ), M. Aug. 5
4 C. Augsburg. Patron of penitents. In art shown
surrounded by flames. *Pron.* ăf'rà
Also 2 Cent. M. at Brescia. May 24. R. M.
(ä'frä), Lat.

AGABIUS (Agábius, ii), B. C. Aug. 4. R. M.
3 Cent. Verona. Noted for love of poor. *Pron.* à-gā'-
bĭŭs.
(ä-gä'bē-ŭs), Lat.
Agapit (ä-gä-pē'), Fr. Agapitus

Agapito (ä-gä-pē'tō), Sp. Agapitus

AGAPITUS (Agapítus, i), M. Aug. 18, R. M.
  3 Cent. Noble youth 15 years old beheaded at Pal-
    estrina. *Sig.* Gr. loved. *Pron.* ă-gà-pē'tŭs.
  (ä-gä-pē'tŭs), Lat.
  Also Deacon, M., 3 Cent. Aug. 6.

Agata (ä'gä-tä), It., Port., Sp. Agatha
  (ä-gä'tä), Sw.

AGATHA (Ágatha, æ), V. M. Feb. 5. R. M.
  3 Cent. Palermo. Woman of great beauty and wealth
    mutilated and burnt with coals. Mentioned in
    Litany of Saints and Canon of Mass. In art shown
    holding pincers or instruments of torture or with
    severed breasts on platter. *Sig.* Gr. good, kind.
  Pron. ăg'à-thà
  (ä'gä-thä), Lat.
  (ä'gä-tä), Port.
Agathe (ä-gät'), Fr. Agatha
  (ä-gä'tĕ), Dan., Ger.

AGATHO (Ágatho, ónis), P. C. Jan. 10. R. M.
  7 Cent. Palermo, of which he is patron. Wonder-
    worker renowned for virtue, miracles and learning.
    In art shown embracing a leper. *Sig.* Gr. good, kind.
  Pron. ă'gà-thō.
  (ä'gä-thō), Lat.
Agathon (ä'gä-thŏn), Ger. Agatho
  (ä-gä-tŏń'), Fr.
Agato (ä'gä-tō), It. Agatho
Agericus (ä-jä-rē'kŭs), Lat. Alger
Aggæus (ä-gä'ŭs), Lat. Aggeus.

AGGEUS (Aggæ'us, i), Proph. July. 4. R. M.
  6 Cent. B. C. Minor Prophet. *Sig.* Heb. of feast.
  Pron. ă-gē'ŭs
Aggie, Aggy (ă'gē), dim. for Agnes, Agatha

AGILBERT (Aglibértus, i), M. June 24. R. M.
  3 Cent. Christolio. *Sig.* Teut. formidably bright.
  Pron. ă'jĭl-bērt.

AGILBERTA (Agliber'ta, æ), V. Ab. Aug. 10.
  7 Cent. Jouarre. *Sig.* Teut. formidably bright. *Pron.*
  ă-jĭl-bĕr'tâ.
Agliberta (ä-glē-bâr'tä), Lat. Agilberta
Aglibertus (ä-glē-bâr'tŭs), Lat. Agilbert

AGNELLUS (Agnéllus, i), C. (Bl.), Mar. 13.
  13 Cent. Pisa. Founder of English Franciscan
  Province, received habit from St. Francis. *Sig.*
  Gr. pure, sacred. *Pron.* ăg-nĕl'ŭs.

  (ä-nyā'lŭs), Lat.
  Also 7 Cent. Naples. C. Dec. 14.

AGNES (Ágnes, étis), V. M. Jan. 21 and 28. R. M.
  3 Cent. Girl 13 years of age. She was cast into flames
  which she extinguished by prayer and was then
  slain. Named in Canon of Mass. In art shown with
  lamb and sword. *Sig.* Gr. pure, sacred. *Pron.*
  ăg'nĕs.
  (ä'nyĕs), Lat.

AGNES OF ASSISI (Bl.), Ab. Nov. 16
  13 Cent. Sister of St. Clare. In art shown holding
  lamb.

AGNES OF MONTEPULCIANO, V. Apr. 20. R. M.
  14 Cent. Dominican prioress. In art shown with
  lamb, lily and book.

Agnès (än-yĕs'), Fr. Agnes
Agnese (än-yā'sä), It. Agnes
Agnete (äg-nä'tĕ), Dan. Agnes
Agnola (ä-nyō'lä), It. dim. Angelina
Agostina (ä-gō-stē'nä), It. Augustina
Agostinho (ä-gōs-tēn'yō), Port. Augustine
Agostino (ä-gō-stē'nō), It. Augustine
Agricol (ä-grē-kōl'), Fr. Agricola
AGRICOLA (Agrícola, æ), B. C. Mar. 17. R. M.
    6 Cent. Chalons-sur-Seine. Sig. Lat. farmer. Pron.
    ă-grĭk'ō-là.
    (ä-grē'kō-lä), Lat.
Agustin (ä-hōōs'tēn), Sp. Augustine.
Ahrend (ä'rĕnt), Ger. Arnold
Aicardus (ä-ē-kär'dŭs), Lat. Achard
Aichard (ā-shär'), Fr. Achard
Aichardus (ä-ē-kär'dŭs), var. Lat. Achard

AIDAN (Aedánnus, i), B. C. Aug. 31. R. M.
    7 Cent. Irish monk of Lindisfarne who introduced
    Christianity into Northumbria. In art shown with
    torch in hand or stag nearby. Sig. Celt. fire. Pron.
    ā'dăn.
Aileen (ālēn'), Ir. Helen
Ailred (āl'rĕd), var. of Aelred

AIMARD, C. Oct. 5
    10 Cent. Abbot of Cluny. Pron. ā'märd or ā-mär'
Aimé (ā-mä'), Fr. Amator
Aimée (ā-mä'), Fr. Amata
Aimerich (ī'mĕ-rĭk), Ger. Emeric
Al (ăl), dim. Albert, Alfred
Alacoque (ä-lä-kōk'), see St. Margaret Mary
Alain (ä-lăṅ'), Fr. Allan

Alan (ă'lăn), var. of Allan, also Hilary
Alano (ä-lä'nō), It., Sp. Allan
Alard (ä-lär'), Fr. Adalard

ALARIC (Alarícus, ī), C. Sept. 29.
  Sig. Teut, noble ruler, all rich. *Pron.* ă'lä-rĭk.
  (ä-lä-rēk'), Fr. Alaric
Alarich (ä'lä-rĭk), Dan., Ger. Alaric
Alarico (ä-lä-rē'kō), It., Sp. Alaric
Alaricus (ä-lä-rē'kŭs), Lat. Alaric
Albain (äl-băn'), Fr. Alban

ALBAN (Albánus, i), M. June 21. R. M.
  4 Cent. First Martyr of Britain. In art shown with
  palm, cross and sword, or with fountain. *Sig.* Lat.
  white. *Pron.* äl'băn.
Albano (äl-bä'nō), It. Alban
Albanus (äl-bä'nŭs), Lat. Alban

ALBERIC (Alberícus, i), B. C. Mar. 4
  8 Cent. Benedictine, Utrecht. Also used for Aubrey.
  Sig. Teut, elf-king. *Pron.* äl'bĕ-rĭk
  (äl-bä-rēk'), Fr.
Alberich (äl'bĕ-rĭk), Du., Ger., Alberic
Alberico (äl-bä-rē'kō), It. Alberic
Albericus (äl-bä-rē'kŭs), Lat. Alberic
Alberik (äl'bĕ-rĭk), Dan. Alberic

ALBERT the GREAT (Albértus, i), B. C. D., Nov. 15.
  13 Cent. Ratisbonne. Known as Albertus Magnus,
  a Dominican, most learned man of his time,
  called "Doctor Universalis," teacher of St. Thomas
  Aquinas. Taught with renown at Cologne and
  Paris. Canonized and declared a Doctor of the
  Church by Pope Pius XI. In art shown as

Dominican with mitre and open book. *Sig.* Teut.
nobly bright, illustrious. *Pron.* ăl'bĕrt.
(äl-bâr'), Fr.
(äl'bĕrt), Ger.
Also 12 Cent. B. M., Liége, Cardinal, Nov. 21. R. M.

ALBERTA (Albérta, æ), V. M. Mar. 11
3 Cent. Agen. Sister of St. Faith. *Sig.* Teut. nobly
bright, illustrious. *Pron.* ăl-bĕr'tȧ.
(äl-bâr'tä), Lat.
Albertina (ăl-bĕr-tē'nȧ), dim. Alberta
Albertine (äl-bĕr-tēn'), Fr. Albertina
Albertino (äl-bĕr-tē'nō), It. Albertinus

ALBERTINUS (Albertínus, i), C. Sept. 3.
13 Cent. Montone. Benedictine. Invoked against
hernia. *Sig.* Teut. nobly bright, illustrious. *Pron.*
ăl-bĕr-tē'nŭs.
(äl-bâr-tē'nŭs), Lat.
Alberto (äl-bĕr'tō), It., Sp. Albert
Albertus (äl-bâr'tŭs), Lat. Albert
Albin (äl-băṅ'), Fr. Albinus

ALBINA (Albína, æ), V. M. Dec. 16. R. M.
3 Cent. Campania. *Sig.* Lat. white. *Pron.* ăl-bī'nȧ.
(äl-bē'nä), Lat.
Albino (äl-bē'no), It. Albinus

ALBINUS (Albínus, i), B. C. Sept. 15. R. M.
4 Cent. Lyons. *Sig.* Lat. white. *Pron.* ăl-bī'nŭs.
(äl-bē'nŭs), Lat.
Albrecht (äl'brĕkt), Dan., Ger., Albert
Albret (äl-brā'), Fr. Albert
Alcantara (ăl-kăn'tȧ-rȧ), *see* St. Peter.
Alcibiad (äl-sē-bē-äd'), Fr. Alcibiades

ALCIBIADES (Alcibíades, is), M. June 2
   2 Cent. One of 48 Martyrs of Lyons. *Sig.* Gr. generous and violent. *Pron.* ăl-sĭ-bī′ȧ-dēz.
   (äl-chē-bē′ä-dāz), Lat.

ALCUIN (Alcuínus, i), (Bl.), C. Ab., May 19
   9 Cent. Founder of Palace School of Charlemagne,
   philosopher, theologian, writer, and one of most
   learned men of his time. *Sig.* Teut. hall friend.
   Pron. ăl′kū-ĭn
Alcuino (äl-kōō-ē′nō), It. Alcuin.
Alcuinus (äl-kōō-ē′nŭs), Lat. Alcuin
Aldebert (ăl′dĕ-bĕrt), var. of Adalbert
Aldegonde (äl-dā-gônd′), Fr. Adelgund
Aldegundis (äl-dā-gŭn′dĭs), Lat. Adelgund
Aldelmus (äl-dĕl′mŭs), Lat. Aldhelm
Alderic (ăl′dĕ-rĭk), var. of Aldric
Aldetrude (äl-dā-trüd′), Fr. Adeltrude

ALDHELM (Aldélmus, i), B. C. May 25. R. M.
   8 Cent. Benedictine, Bishop of Sherborne. In art
   shown receiving deed from St. Wulstan. *Sig.* Teut.
   noble helmet. *Pron.* ăld′hĕlm.
Aldobrando (äl-dō-brän′dō), It. Hildebrand (St.
   Gregory VII)

ALDRIC (Aldrícus, i), B. C. Jan. 7.
   9 Cent. Bishop of Le Mans, confessor to Louis the
   Pious. *Pron.* äl′drĭk.
   (äl-drēk′), Fr.
Aldricus (äl-drē′kŭs), Lat. Aldric
Aleander (ä-lä-än′dĕr), Sp. Alexander
Aleck (ă′lĕk), dim. Alexander, Alexis
Alejandra (ä-lä-hän′drä), Sp. Alexandra
Alejandrina (ä-lä-hän-drē′nä), Sp. dim. Alexandra

Alejandro (ä-lä-hän′drō), Sp. Alexander

Alejo (ä-lä′hō), Sp. Alexis

ALENA (Aléna, æ), V. M. June 18
7 Cent. Brabant, converted by St. Amand. Invoked
against toothache. *Pron.* ă-lē′nà.
(ä-lä′nä), Lat.

ALEPH (Aléphus, i), M. Mar. 6.
(d. u.) Martyred with St. Anthimus. *Pron.* ä′lĕf.
Alephus (ä-lä′fŭs), Lat. Aleph
Alessandra (ä-lĕs-sän′drä), It. Alexandra
Alessandro (ä-lĕs-sän′drō), It. Alexander
Alessio (ä-lĕs′sē-ō), It. Alexis

ALETH (Alíthius, ii), B. C. Jul. 11
5 Cent. Cahors. Husband of St. Rufina, after whose
death he became a bishop. *Pron.* ä′lĕth.

ALETHIUS (Aléthius, ii), M. July 8.
(d. u.) Nice. *Pron.* ă-lē′thĭ-ŭs.
(ä-lä′thē-ŭs), Lat.
Alewijn (ä-lĕ-wīn′), Du. Alvin
Alex (ă′lĕks), dim. Alexander, Alexis

ALEXANDER (Alexánder, dri), P. M. May 3. R. M.
2 Cent. Martyred with Sts. Eventius and Theodulus,
whom he baptized in prison. Named in Canon of
Mass. In art shown pierced all over with nails.
Sig. Gr. helper of men. *Pron.* ăl-ĕgs-ăn′dĕr.
(ä-lĕk-sän′dĕr), Lat.

ALEXANDRA (Alexándra, æ), M. May 18. R. M.
4 Cent. Burned to death in Asia Minor. *Sig.* Gr.
helper of men. *Pron.* ăl-ĕgs-ăn′drà.
(ä-lĕk-sän′drä), Lat.

Alexandre (ä-lĕk-säṅ'dr), Fr. Alexander
  (ä-lĕk-sän'drä), Port.
Alexandrina (ăl-ĕgs-ăn-drī'nå), dim. Alexandra
Alexandrine (ä-lĕk-sän-drēn'), Fr. Alexandrina
Alexandro (ä-lä-hän'drō), Sp. Alexander
Alèxe (ä-lĕks'), Fr. Alexis
Alexei (ä-lĕk-sä'ē), Rus. Alexis

ALEXIA (Aléxia, æ), V. June 29
  (ä-lĕk'sē-ä), Lat. *Sig.* Gr. helper. *Pron.* ă-lĕk'sĭ-å.

ALEXIS (Aléxius, ii), C. Jul. 17. R. M.
  5 Cent. Wealthy Roman, gave up riches and left
  home. Years later he returned and, unknown to all,
  lived in poverty in his father's house. Patron of
  Alexian Brothers', pilgrims and belt-makers. In
  art with ladder in arms. *Sig.* Gr. helper. *Pron.*
  ă-lĕk'sĭs.
  (ä-lĕk-sē'), Fr.

ALEXIS FALCONIERI, C. Feb. 17. R. M.
  13 Cent. Florence. One of seven Holy Founders of
  Servite Order. Died at age of 110 years. *Pron.*
  fäl-kō-nē-ä'rē.
Alexius (ä-lĕk'sē-ŭs), Lat. Alexis
Alf (ălf), dim. Alfred
Alfeo (äl-fä'ō), It., Sp. Alpheus
Alfons (äl'fŏns), Dan., Ger., Alphonsus
Alfonso (äl-fŏn'sō), It., Sp., also Eng. var. Alphonsus
Alfonsus (äl-fŏn'sŭs), Lat. var. Alphonsus

ALFRED (Alfrédus, i) (Bl.), B. C. Aug. 15
  9 Cent. Hildesheim. *Sig.* Teut. good counselor. *Pron.*
  ăl'frĕd
  (äl'frāt), Ger., Dan.
  (äl-fräd'), Fr., Port.

ALFREDA (Alfréda, æ), V. May 20
9 Cent. Daughter of King of Mercia. *Sig.* Teut. good
counselor. *Pron.* ăl-frē'dà.
(äl-frā'dä), Lat.
Alfredo (äl-frā'dō), It., Sp., Port. Alfred
Alfredus (äl-frā'dŭs), Lat. Alfred
Alfried (äl'frēd), Ger. Alfred

ALGER (Agerícus, i), Ab. Apr. 11
7 Cent. St. Martin's, Tours. *Pron.* ăl'jĕr.
Alice (ă'lĭs), var. of Adelaide
(ä-lēs'), Fr.
(ä-lē'sē), Ger.
Alicia (ă-lē'sĭ-à), var. of Alice
(ä-lē'thē-ä), Sp.
(ä-lē'chē-ä), Lat., It.
Alick (ă'lĭk), dim. Alexander
Aline (ä-lēn'), var. of Alena, Adelaide
Alisa (ä-lē'sä), It. Alice
Alithius (ä-lĭ'thē-us), Lat. Aleth
Alix (ă'lĭks), cor. Adelaide

ALLAN (Alánus, i), C. Jan. 13.
(d. u.) Wales. Also called Elian, Hilary. *Sig.* Celt.
harmony. *Pron.* ăl'lăn.
Also 6 Cent. Cornish noble, C. Jan. 12
Allen (ăl'lĕn), var. of Allan
Allie, Ally (ăl'lĭ), dim. Alice, Adelaide
Alma (ăl'mà), used for Blessed Virgin. *Sig.* loving,
sweet
Almeric (ăl'mĕ-rĭk), var. of Emeric
Almerik (äl'mĕ-rĭk), Du., Dan. Emeric

ALODIA (Alódia, æ), V. M. Oct. 22. R. M.
9 Cent. Put to death by Moors in Spain. *Pron.*
ă-lō′dĭá
(ä-lō′dē-ä), Lat.
Alois (äl-wä′), Fr. Aloysius
Aloisia (ä-lō-ē′sē-ä), It., Lat. Aloysia
Aloisio (ä-lō-ē′sē-ō), It. Aloysius
Aloisius (ä-lō-ē′sē-ŭs), Lat. var. Aloysius
Alonso, Alonzo (a-lŏn′zō), Alphonsus
(ä-lōn′sō, ä-lōn′thō), Sp.
Aloys (äl-wä′), Fr. Aloysius
Aloyse (äl-wäs′), Fr. Aloysia

ALOYSIA (Aloy′sia, æ), V. M. Sept. 12.
Japan. *Sig.* Teut. famous war. *Pron.* ăl-ō-ĭs′ĭ-á.
(ä-lō-ē′sē-ä), Lat.

ALOYSIUS (Aloy′sius, ii), Gonzaga, C. June 21. R. M.
16 Cent. Spain. At age of nine made vow of perpetual virginity; at seventeen renounced princely
dignity and entered Society of Jesus. Died at
twenty-three while caring for sick in epidemic.
Model of innocence, piety and penance, patron of
youth and students, invoked against sore eyes and
epidemics. In art shown with surplice, lily and
crucifix. *Sig.* Teut. famous war. *Pron.* ăl-ō-ĭsh′ŭs.
(ä-lō-ē′sē-ŭs), Lat.
Alphæus (äl-fā′ŭs), Lat. Alpheus
Alphée (äl-fā′), Fr. Alpheus
Alphége (äl-fäjh′), Fr. Elphege

ALPHEUS (Alphæ′us, i), M. Nov. 17. R. M.
3 Cent. Martyred with St. Zacchaeus. *Sig.* Heb. ex-
change. *Pron.* ăl′fē-ŭs or ăl-fē′ŭs

ALPHIUS (Álphius, ii), M. May 10. R. M.
3 Cent. Sicily. *Pron.* ăl'fĭ-ŭs
Alphons (äl-fŏns'), Dan., Ger. Alphonsus
Alphonsa (ăl-fŏn'sà), fem. Alphonsus
Alphonse (äl-fŏns'), Fr. Alphonsus
Alphonso (ăl-fŏn'sō), var. Alphonsus

ALPHONSUS MARY DE LIGUORI (Alph'onsus, i),
B. C. D. Aug. 2. R. M.
17 Cent. Born at Naples, lawyer, moralist, theological and ascetical writer, and great Doctor of devotion to Mary and prayer. Founder of Congregation of Most Holy Redeemer (Redemptorists). In art shown at prayer with monstrance, or writing before crucifix. *Sig.* Teut. eager for battle. *Pron.* ăl-fŏn'sŭs.
(äl-fŏn'sŭs), Lat.

ALPHONSUS RODRIGUEZ, C. Oct. 31. R. M.
17 Cent. Wealthy Spanish merchant who became a Jesuit lay-brother at Majorca. Noted for his patience and humility.

ALTMANN (Altmánnus, i), B. C. Aug. 8
11 Cent. Passau. Supporter of Pope Gregory VII. *Pron.* ält'măn.
Altmannus (ält-mä'nŭs), Lat. Altmann
Aluin (ä-lü-ăń'), Fr. Alvin
Aluino (ä-lōō-ē'nō), Sp., It., Alvin
Aluinus (ä-lōō-ē'nŭs), Lat. Alvin
Aluredus (ä-lōō-rä'dŭs), Lat. var. Alfred

ALVIN (Aluínus, i), B. C. Dec. 27, Oct. 3.
11 Cent. Leon. Also called Alvitus. *Sig.* Teut. beloved by all. *Pron.* ăl'vĭn.
Alvino (äl-vē'nō), It. Alvin

Alwin (ăl'wĭn), var. Alvin
  (äl'vēn), Ger.
Alwis (ăl'wĭs), dim. Aloysius
Amabel (ă'mȧ-bĕl), var. Amabilis
Amabella (ă-mȧ-bĕī'ȧ), dim. Amabel
Amadæus (ä-mä-dā'ŭs), Lat. Amadeus
Amadée (ä-mä-dā'), Fr. Amadeus
Amadeo (ä-mä-dā'ō), It., Sp. Amadeus

AMADEUS (Amadæ'us, i), B. C. Jan. 28
  12 Cent. Cistercian. *Sig.* Lat. love God. *Pron.*
  ăm-ȧ-dē'ŭs.
Amalberge (ä-mäl-bârzh'), Fr. Amalburga

AMALBURGA (Amelbérga, æ), V. Jul. 10
  8 Cent. Benedictine, Flanders. In art shown with
  picture of Crucifixion. *Pron.* ä'mäl-bērg-ȧ.
Amalia (ä-mä'lē-ä), Ger., Du. Amalburga

AMAND (Amándus, i), B. C. Feb. 6. R. M.
  7 Cent. Maestricht. Missioner in Flanders, Brabant
  and Holland. Patron of Flanders. In art shown
  with church in hand. *Sig.* worthy of love. *Pron.*
  ä'mănd.
  (ä-män'), Fr.
Amanda (ȧ-män'dȧ), Amabilis or fem. Amand
Amandine (ä-män-dēn'), Fr. Amanda
Amandus (ä-män'dŭs), Lat. Amand

AMATA (Amáta, æ) (Bl.), V. June 10
  13 Cent. Bologna. Also called Amy. *Sig.* Lat. loved.
  Pron. ă-mä'tȧ.
  (ä-mä'tä), Lat., It.

AMATOR (Amátor, óris), B. C. May 1. R. M.
5 Cent. Auxerre, husband of St. Martha. *Pron.*
ă-mä′tôr.
(ä-mä′tōr), Lat.

AMATUS (Amátus, i), B. C. Sept. 13. R. M.
7 Cent. Sens. *Sig.* Lat. loved. *Pron.* ă-mä′tŭs.
(ä-mä′tŭs), Lat.
Ambrogio (äm-brō′jō), It. Ambrose
Ambroise (ŏn-brwäz′), Fr. Ambrose
Ambros (äm′brōs), Ger. Ambrose

AMBROSE (Ambrósius, ii), B. C. D. Dec. 7 and Apr. 4.
R. M.
4 Cent. Treves. Bishop of Milan, one of four great
Western Doctors, champion against Arianism;
converted and baptized St. Augustine; orator,
hymn-writer, and once a Roman prefect. In art
shown with angel of St. Matthew, scourge or bee-
hive. Patron of wax-chandlers. *Sig.* Lat. divine,
immortal. *Pron.* ăm′brōz.
Ambrosia (ăm-brō′zhà), fem. Ambrose
Ambrosio (äm-brō′sē-ō), Sp., Ambrose
(än-brō′zē-ō), Port.
Ambrosius (äm-brō′zē-ŭs), Lat., Ger., Du. Ambrose
Amé (ä-mä′), Fr. Amator
Amédée (ä-mā-dā′), Fr. Amadeus
Amedeo (ä-mā-dā′ō), It. Amadeus
Amedeus (ă-mē-dē′ŭs), var. Amadeus
Amelberga (ä-mĕl-bâr′gä), Lat. Amalburga
Amelia (à-mēl′yà), var. Amalburga
(ä-mä′lē-ä), It., Sp., Port.
Amélie (ä-mä-lē′), Fr. Amalburga
Amerigo (ä-mä-rē′gō), It. Emeric

AMOS (*indecl.*), Proph. Mar. 31. R. M.
> 8 B. C. One of minor prophets of Old Testament, martyred in Palestine. *Sig.* Heb. strong, courageous. *Pron.* ā'mŭs.
> (ä-mōs'), Fr.

Amy (ā'mĭ), dim. Amata, Amabilis
Ana (ä'nä), Sp. Anne
Anaclet (ä-nä-clā'), Fr. Anacletus
Anacleto (ä-nä-clā'tō), It. Anacletus

ANACLETUS (Anaclétus, i), P. M. July. 13. R. M.
> 2 Cent. Mentioned in Canon of Mass. Ordained by St. Peter. *Pron.* ă-nȧ-klē'tŭs.
> (ä-nä-klā'tŭs), Lat.

ANANIAS (Ananías, æ), Dec. 16. R. M.
> Noble youth of Old Testament, friend of Prophet Daniel, cast into fiery furnace by Nabuchodonosor and saved by an angel. Also called Sidrach. *Sig.* Heb. grace of the Lord. *Pron.* ăn-ăn-ī'ȧs.
> (ä-nä-nē'äs), Lat.
> Also Jan. 25. Converted Jew to whom God sent St. Paul for instruction.

Ananie (ä-nä-nē'), Fr. Ananias
Anastagio (ä-nä-stä'jō), It. Anastasius
Anastase (ä-nä-stäz'), Fr. Anastasius

ANASTASIA (Anastásia, æ), M. Dec. 25. R. M.
> 4 Cent. Noble widow burnt alive for the Faith. Mentioned in Canon of Mass. In art shown burning at stake. *Sig.* Gr. who will rise again. *Pron.* ăn-ă-stä'shĭ-ȧ.
> (ä-nä-stä'sē-ä), Lat.

Anastasie (ä-nä-stä-sē'), Fr. Anastasia
Anastasio (ä-nä-stä'sē-ō), It. Anastasius

ANASTASIUS (Anastásius, ii), P. C. Dec. 19.
5 Cent. Champion against Arianism. *Sig.* Gr. who
will rise again. *Pron.* ăn-ă-stā'shĭ-ŭs.
(ä-nä-stä'sē-ŭs), Lat.
Also 7 Cent., Persian monk, M. Jan. 22.

ANATOLE (Anatólius, ii), B. C. Jul. 3. R. M.
3 Cent. Laodicea. *Sig.* Gr. Eastern. *Pron.* ăn'à-tŏl.
(ä-nä-tŏl'), Fr.

ANATOLIA (Anatólia, æ), V. M. Jul. 9. R. M.
3 Cent. Thora. In art shown with torches and
serpents. *Sig.* Gr. Eastern. *Pron.* ă-nà-tō'lĭ-à.
Anatolio (ä-nä-tō'lē-ō), It. Anatole
Anatolius (ä-nä-tō'lē-ŭs), Lat. Anatole
Ancas (än'käs), Lith. John
Anders (än'dērs), Du., Sw. Andrew
André (än-drä'), Fr., Port. Andrew
Andrea (än-drä'ä), It. Andrew
Andreas (än-drä'äs), Lat., Dan., Ger. Andrew
Andres (än-drĕs'), Sp. Andrew

ANDREW (Andréas, æ), Ap. Nov. 30. R. M.
First Apostle called by Christ, brother of St. Peter,
crucified on X-shaped cross named after him.
Mentioned twice in Canon of Mass. Patron of
Scotland and Russia. In art shown with cross
saltire. *Sig.* Gr., strong, manly. *Pron.* ăn'drü.

ANDREW AVELLINO, C., Pr. Nov. 10. R. M.
16 Cent. Naples, a Theatine, friend of St. Charles.
In art shown with angels, singing the Office. *Pron.*
ä-vĕl-lē'nō.

ANDREW CORSINI, B. C. Feb. 4. R. M.

14 Cent. Fiesole, a Carmelite. Model of penance and humility. In art shown with wolf and lamb. *Pron.* kôr-sē'nĕ.

Andries (än-drēs'), Du. Andrew
Andrieu (äṅ-drē-ŭh'), Fr. Andrew

ANDRONICUS (Andrónicus, i), C. Oct. 9. R. M.

Patron of silversmiths. *Sig.* Gr. conqueror of men. *Pron.* ăn-drō-nī'kŭs. (än-drō'nē-kŭs), Lat.

Andy (ăn'dĭ), dim. Andrew
Ange (äṅjh), Fr. Angelus

ANGELA OF FOLIGNO (Ángela, æ) (Bl.) , Wid. Pen. Jan. 4.

14 Cent. Franciscan Tertiary, wrote book of revelations and visions. In art shown holding chained devil. *Sig.* Gr. angel. *Pron.* ăn'jĕ-là. (än'jā-lä), Lat.

ANGELA MERICI, V. May 31. R. M.

16 Cent. Foundress of Ursuline Nuns at Brescia for the education of young girls. In art shown with angels ascending ladder. *Pron.* mĕ-rē'chē.

Angèle (äṅ-zhāl'), Fr. Angela

ANGELICA (Angélica, æ), V. Mar. 24.

Sig. Gr. angel-like. *Pron.* ăn-jĕl'ĭ-kà. (än-jā'lē-kä), Lat., It. (än-gä'lē-kä), Ger.

ANGELINA (Angelína, æ), V. M. Oct. 21.

(d. u.) *Sig.* Gr. angel. *Pron.* ăn-jĕ-lī'nà. (än-jā-lē'nä), Lat. (än-gä-lē'nä), Ger.

ANGELINA OF CORBARA (Bl.), Mat., Jul. 21.
14 Cent. Franciscan.

ANGELINA OF SPOLETO (Bl.), V., June 29.
15 Cent. Franciscan renowned for miracles.
Angeline (än-zhā-lēn'), Fr. Angelina
Angélique (än-zhā-lēk'), Fr. Angelica
Angelo (än'jā-lō), It. Angelus

ANGELUS (Ángelus, i), Pr. M. Oct. 13
13 Cent. Friar Minor martyred by Moors.
Sig. Gr. angel. Pron. ăn'jĕ-lŭs.
(än'jā-lŭs), Lat.
Angiola (än-jō'lä), It. dim. Angelina
Angus (ăng'gŭs), see Aengus.

ANIANUS (Aniánus, i), B. C. Dec. 7
4 Cent. Chartres. Pron. ă-nĭ-ä'nŭs.
(ä-nē-ä'nŭs), Lat.
Anicet (ä-nē-sā'), Fr. Anicetus
Aniceto (ä-nē-chā'tō), It. Anicetus

ANICETUS (Anicétus, i), P. M. Apr. 17. R. M.
2 Cent. Syrian. Sig. Gr. unconquered. Pron. ă-nĭ-
sē'tŭs.
(ä-nē-chā'tŭs), Lat.

ANICIA (Anícia, æ), M. May 11.   Pron. ă-nĭ'sĭ-á
(ä-nē'chē-ä), Lat.
Anisia (ă-nĭ'sĭ-á), var. of Anysia
Anita (ä-nē'tä), Sp. dim. Anne
Ann (ăn), Anna (ăn'nà), var. of Anne
Anna (än'nä), Lat., It., Ger. Anne
Annabel, Annabelle (ăn'nà-bĕl), dim. Anne

ANNE (Ánna, æ), July 26. R. M.
Mother of Blessed Virgin, wife of St. Joachim. In art
shown teaching the child Mary. *Sig.* Heb. grace.
Pron. ăn
(än), Fr.
Annetta (ăn-nĕt'tà), dim. Anne
Annette (ä-nĕt'), Fr. dim. Anne
Annie (ăn'nĭ), dim. Anne
Annot (ăn'nŏt), Sc. Anne
Annunciata (ä-nŭn-chē-ä'tä), It. Blessed Virgin (feast
of Annunication.)
Annunziata (ä-nün-tsē-ä'tä), It. Blessed Virgin (feast
of Annunciation.)

ANSBERT (Ansbértus, i), B. C. Feb. 9. R. M.
7 Cent. Rouen., Chancellor of K. Clothaire III. In-
voked against fever. *Pron.* ăns'bērt.
(äns-bâr'), Fr.
Ansbertus (äns-bâr'tŭs), Lat. Ansbert
Anscar, Anschar (äns'kär), var. of Oscar
Anschair (äṅ-shär'), Fr. Oscar
Anscharius (äns-kä'rē-ŭs), Lat. Oscar
Ansgar (äns'gär), var. Oscar
Ansel (ăn'sĕl), var. of Anselm

ANSELM (Ansélmus, i), B. C. D. Apr. 21. R. M.
11 Cent. Archb. of Canterbury, noted scholar, phi-
losopher, theologian and champion of the rights of
the Church. In art holding model of ship or with
Papal bull. *Sig.* Teut. divine helmet. *Pron.* ăn'sĕlm.
(än'sĕlm), Ger.
Anselma (ăn-sĕl'mà), fem. Anselm
Anselme (äṅ-sĕlm'), Fr. Anselm
Anselmo (än-sĕl'mō), It., Port., Sp. Anselm
Anselmus (än-sĕl'mŭs), Lat. Anselm

Ansgar (ăns'gär), var. of Oscar
Ansgarius (äns-gä're-ŭs), Lat. var. Oscar
Anshelm (äns'hĕlm), Ger. Anselm
Anthime (äṅ-tēm'), Fr. Anthimus

ANTHIMUS (Ânthimus, i), Pr. M. May 11. R. M.
4 Cent. Thrown into Tiber River, rescued by an
angel, and afterwards beheaded. *Pron.* ăn'thĭ-mŭs.
(än'thē-mŭs), Lat.
Antimo (än'tē-mō), It. Anthimus
Anthon (ăn'thŏn), var. of Antony [of Antony
Anthony (ăn'tō-nĭ—commonly pron. ăn'thō-nĭ), var.
Antoine (äṅ-twän'), Fr. Antony
Antoinette (ăṅ-twȧ-nĕt' or ăn-tō-nĕt'), dim. of Antonia.
Anton (än'tōn), Ger. Antony

ANTONIA (Antónia, æ), V. M. May 4. R. M.
3 Cent. Byzantium. Burned at stake. *Sig.* It. in-
estimable. *Pron.* ăn-tō'nĭ-ȧ.
(än-tō'nē-ä), Lat.
Antonie (äṅ-tō-nē'), Fr. Antonia
(än-tō'nē-ĕ), Ger.
Antonietta (än-tō-nyĕt'tä), It. Antoinette, Antonia
Antoniette (än-tō-nyĕt'tē), Ger. Antoinette, Antonia
Antonin (äṅ-tō-naṅ'), Fr. Antoninus

ANTONINA (Antonína, æ), V. M. Mar. 1. R. M.
3 Cent. Portugal. Drowned in cask. *Sig.* Lat. little
Antonia. *Pron.* ăn-tō-nĭ'nȧ.
(än-tō-nē'nä), Lat., It., Sp.

ANTONINE (Antonínus, i), B. C. May 10. R. M.
14 Cent. Dominican, Archb. of Florence, noted for
humility, and charity toward poor, learned writer.
Sig. Lat. little Antony. *Pron.* ăn'tō-nĭn.
(äṅ-tō-nēn'), Fr. for Antonina.

Antonino (än-tō-nē′nō), It., Sp. Antonine
Antoninus (än-tō-nē′nŭs), Lat. Antonine
Antonio (än-tō′nē-ō), It., Port., Sp. Antony
Antonita (än-tō-nē′tä), Sp. dim. Antonia
Antonito (än-tō-nē′tō), Sp. dim. Antony
Antonius (än-tō′nē-ŭs), Lat., Ger. Antony

ANTONY THE GREAT (Anto′nius, ii), Ab., C. Jan. 17. R. M.
    4 Cent. Father of monasticism in Egypt. Patron of herdsmen. In art shown with staff, bell and pig. *Sig.* Lat., priceless, praiseworthy. *Pron.* ăn′tō-nǐ.

ANTONY DANIEL, M. Sept. 26.
    17 Cent. Slain by Indians near Ontario, Canada. Member of Society of Jesus. Canonized in 1930 by Pope Pius XI.

ANTONY MARY ZACCARIA, C. Jul. 5. R. M.
    16 Cent. Cremona. Founder of Barnabites. Canonized by Pope Leo XIII.

ANTONY OF PADUA, C. June 13. R. M.
    13 Cent. Lisbon. Disciple of St. Francis of Assisi, miracle-worker. In art shown with Infant Jesus, who stands on open book.
Anusia (ă-nū′sǐ-à), Gr. Anysia.

ANYSIA (Any′sia, æ), M. Dec. 30. R. M.
    4 Cent. Thessalonica. *Sig.* Gr. complete. *Pron.* ă-nē′sǐ-à.
    (ä-nē′sē-ä), Lat.
Apollin (ä-pō-lăṅ′), Fr. Apollonius
Apollinaire (ä-pŏl-lē-nâr′), Fr. Apollinaris

APOLLINARIS (Apollina'ris, is), B. M. Jul. 23. R. M.
1 Cent. Disciple of St. Peter, sent by him as bishop
to Ravenna. Tortured by pagans and put to death
Sig. Lat. of Apollo. *Pron.* ă-pŏl-lĭ-nā'rĭs.
(ä-pŏl-lē-nä'rĭs), Lat.

Apolline (ä-pō-lēn'), Fr. Apollonia

APOLLONIA (Apollo'nia, æ), V. M. Feb. 9. R. M.
3 Cent. Alexandria. Her teeth were broken and then
drawn out. Invoked against toothache. In art
shown holding pincers. *Sig.* Gr. of Apollo. *Pron.*
ă-pŏ-lō'nĭ-ȧ.
(ä-pŏl-lō'nē-ä), Lat.

Apollonie (ä-pōl-lō-nē'), Fr. Apollonia

Apostles:
  Simon Peter
  Andrew
  James the Greater
  John the Evangelist
  Philip
  James the Less
  Thomas
  Bartholomew
  Matthew
  Matthias (who took the place of Judas).
  Paul (though not of the Twelve, is reckoned an
    Apostle).
  Barnabas (though not of the Twelve, is called an
    Apostle).
  Thaddeus or Jude
  Simon Zelotes

APULEIUS (Apuléius, i), M. Oct. 7. R. M.
1 Cent. Rome. Martyred with St. Marcellus. *Pron.*
ă-pŭ-lē'ŭs. (ä-pōō-lā'ĭ-ŭs), Lat.

Aquiles (ä-kē′lĕs), Sp. Achilles
Aquin (ä-kăṅ′), Fr. Aquinas, St. Thomas
Aquinas (ă-kwī′năs), see St. Thomas
Araldo (ä-räl′dō), It. Harold
Arcade (är-käd′), Fr. Arcadius
Arcadio (är-kä′dē-ō), It. Arcadius

ARCADIUS (Arcádius, ii), M. Jan. 12. R. M. 4 Cent. Caesarea. In art shown with lighted taper, club and sword. Pron. är-kā′dĭ-ŭs. (är-kä′dē-ŭs), Lat.

Archambaud, Archambault (är-shŏṅ-bō′), Fr. Archibald

ARCHANGELO (Archan′gelus, i) (Bl.), C. Apr. 16. 16 Cent. Bologna, Canon Regular of St. Augustine. Sig. Lat. archangel. Pron. ärk-ăn′jĕ-lō.

Archangelus (ärk-än′jā-lŭs), Lat. Archangel, Archangelo.
Archibald (är′chē-bạld), var. Erkonwald. Pron. är′chē-bạld.
Archibaldo (är-chē-bäl′dō), Sp. Archibald
Archibaldus (är-chē-bäl′dŭs), Lat. Archibald
Archie (är′chĭ), dim. Archibald
Archimbald (är′kĭm-bält), Ger. Archibald
Archy (är′chĭ), dim. Archibald
Arcibaldo (är-chē-bäl′dō), It. Archibald
Arègle (ä-räg″l), Fr. Agricola
Arent (ä′rĕnt), Dan. Arnold
Ariadna (ă-rē-äd′nä), Lat. Ariadne.
ARIADNE (Ariádna, æ), V. M. Sept. 17. R. M. (d.u.) Phrygia. Pron. ă-rĭ-äd′nē.

ARILDA (Arílda, æ), V. M. Oct. 30.
(d. u.) Gloucestershire. *Pron.* á-rĭl′dá.
(ä-rēl′dä), Lat.
Aristide (ä-rĭs-tēd′), Fr. Aristides.

ARISTIDES (Aristídes, is), C. Aug. 31. R. M.
2 Cent. Athens. Writer and philosopher. *Sig.* Gr.
son of the best. *Pron.* ăr-ĭs-tī′dēz.
(ä-rĭs-tē′dāz), Lat.
Armand (är-mŏñ′), Fr. Herman
Armando (är-män′dō), It. Herman
Armant (är-mŏñ′), Fr. Herman
Armyn (är′mĭn), var. Herman
Arnaldo (är-näl′dō), Sp. Arnold
Arnaud, Arnauld, Arnaut (är-nō′), Fr. Arnold

ARNOLD (Arnóldus, i), C. Jul. 18.
9 Cent. Musician at court of Charlemagne. Patron
of musicians. In art shown with fish which has ring
in mouth. *Sig.* Teut. strong as an eagle. *Pron.*
är′nŭld.
(är′nōlt), Ger.
Arnoldine (är-nōl-dēn′), fem. Arnold
Arnoldo (är-nōl′dō), It. Arnold
Arnoldus (är-nōl′dŭs), Lat. Arnold
Arnoud (är-nōō′), Fr. Arnulph
Arnoul (är-nōōl′), Fr. Arnulph, Arnold
Arnoulf (är-nŭlf′), Fr. Arnulph
Arnulf (är′nŭlf), var. Arnulph

ARNULPH (Arnúlphus, i), B. C. Jul. 18. R. M.
7 Cent. Missionary to Franks, Bishop of Metz. *Sig.*
Teut. eagle wolf. *Pron.* är′nŭlf.
Arnulphus (är-nŭl′fŭs), Lat. Arnulph

Aroldo (ä-rōl'dō), It. Harold
Aron (ä-rŏn'), Sp. Aaron
Aronne (ä-rŏn'ä), It. Aaron
Arsène (är-sän'), Fr. Arsenius
Arsenio (är-sä'nē-ō), It. Arsenius

ARSENIUS (Arsénius, ii), Dea. C. Jul. 19. R. M.
     5 Cent. Wealthy Roman noble. *Pron.* är-sē'nĬ-ŭs.
     (är-sä'nē-ŭs), Lat.

ARTEMAS (Ártemas, æ), M. Jan. 25
     (d. u.) Puteoli. Boy stabbed to death by pagan boys.
     Sig. Gr. gift of Diana. *Pron.* är'tē-mǎs.
     (är'tä-mäs), Lat.
Artème (är-täm'), Fr. Artemas

ARTEMIA (Artémia, æ), Wid. Feb. 25.
     Rome. Teacher of St. Constantia. *Sig.* Gr. gift of
     Diana. *Pron.* är-tē'mĬ-à.
     (är-tä'mē-ä), Lat.

ASAPH (Ásaphus, i), B. C. May 1. R. M.
     6 Cent. Wales. *Sig.* Heb. collector. *Pron.* ā'sǎf.

Asaphus (ä'sä-fŭs), Lat. Asaph

ASICUS (Ásicus, i), B. C. Apr. 27
     5 Cent. Disciple of St. Patrick, B. of Elphin. Skillful
     metal-worker. *Pron.* ǎ'sĬ-kŭs.
     (ä'sē-kŭs), Lat.
Assunta (äs-sŭn'tà), Blessed Virgin, Assumption.
Asta (äs'tä), Ger. dim. Augusta
Atanagio (ä-tä-nä'jō), It. Athanasius
Atanasia (ä-tä-nä'sē-ä), It., Sp. Athanasia
Atanasio (ä-tä-nä'sē-ō), Sp. Athanasius
Athanase (ä-tä-näz'), Fr. Athanasius

ATHANASIA (Athanásia, æ), Wid. Aug. 14. R. M.
9 Cent. Greece. Built Abbey of Timia. In art shown
with star on breast. *Sig.* Gr. immortal. *Pron.*
ăth-à-nā'shà.
(ä-thä-nä'sē-à), Lat.

ATHANASIUS THE GREAT (Athanásius, ii), B.C.D.
May 2. R. M.
4 Cent. One of the four great Doctors of the East,
Patriarch of Alexandria, opponent of the Arians
and defender of the Blessed Trinity. Exiled four
times from see. In art shown as Greek archbishop
with book in hand. *Sig.* Gr. immortal. *Pron.*
ăth-à-nā'shŭs.
(ä-thä-nä'sē-ŭs), Lat.

ATTRACTA (Attrácta, æ), V. Aug. 11.
5 Cent. Ireland. Renowned for charity to poor and
hospitality to homeless. Founded monastery at
Sligo and at Roscommon. *Pron.* ă-trăk'tà.
(ä-träk'tä), Lat.
Atty (ăt'tǐ), dim. Attracta
Aubain (ō-băṅ'), Fr. Alban

AUBERT (Authbértus, i), B. C. Dec. 13. R. M.
7 Cent. Bishop of Cambrai and Arras. Adviser of
King Dagobert. *Pron.* ō-bâr'.
(ō-bâr'), Fr., also for Albert.
Aubin (ō-băṅ'), Fr. Albinus
Aubrey (ạ'brǐ), var. of Alberic
Aubri (ŏ-brē'), Fr. Alberic
Aubrie (ō-brē'), Fr. Aubrey

AUDIFAX (Aŭdifax, ĭfacis), M. Jan. 19. R. M.
   3 Cent. Son of noble Persians, Sts. Marius and
   Martha, beheaded. *Pron.* ạ'dĭ-făks.
   (ŏw'dē-fäx), Lat.

Audrey (ô'drĭ), var. of Ediltrude, Etheldreda,
   Ethelreda.

AUGUST (Augústus, i), B. C. Oct. 7. R. M.
   6 Cent. Archb. of Bourges. *Sig.* Lat. venerable.
   Pron. ạ'gŭst.
   (ŏw'gŭst), Ger., Sw., Dan.

AUGUSTA (Augústa, æ), V. M. Mar. 27.
   (d. u.). Italy. Daughter of barbarian chief. *Sig.*
   Lat. venerable. *Pron.* ạ-gŭs'tȧ.
   (ŏw-gōōs'tä), Ger., Dan.

Auguste (ō-gŭst'), Fr. August
   (ō-gŭst'ĕ), Fr. Augusta

Augustijn (ŏw'gŭs-tīn), Du. Augustine

Augustin (ạ-gŭs'tĭn), var. Augustine
   (ŏw-gŭs-tēn'), Ger.
   (ō-gŭs-tăn'), Fr.

Augustina (ạ-gŭs-tē'nȧ), fem. Augustine

AUGUSTINE (Augustínus, i), B. C. D. Aug. 28.
   R. M.
   4 Cent. Great sinner who was converted by prayers
   of his mother, St. Monica, baptized by St. Ambrose,
   and became Bishop of Hippo. One of greatest
   lights of Church and one of four great Doctors of
   West. Wrote "The City of God," "Confessions"
   and voluminous works. In art shown robed as
   bishop, with tall cross, and flaming heart in hand.
   Sig. belonging to August. *Pron.* ạ-gŭs'tĭn, ạ'gŭs-
   tĭn or ạ'gŭs-tēn.

AUGUSTINE OF CANTERBURY, B. C.   May 28
(in England May 26). R. M.
6 Cent. Benedictine Monk sent by Pope Gregory
the Great to convert England. Baptized King
Ethelbert. First Archbishop of Canterbury, and
Apostle of England. In art shown baptizing King.

Augustine (ō-güs-tēn'), Fr. Augustina
Augustino (ŏw-gōōs-tē'nō), Sp. Augustine
Augustinus (ŏw-gŭs-tē'nŭs), Lat. Augustine
Augusto (ŏw-gōōs'tō), It., Sp. August
Augustus (ŏw-gŭs'tŭs), Lat. August
Aurèle (ō-rāl'), Fr. Aurelius

AURELIA (Aurélia, æ), V. Oct. 15. R. M.
11 Cent. Princess of France. *Sig.* Lat. golden. *Pron.*
ą-rē'lĭ-ȧ or rēl'yȧ.
(ŏw-rā'lē-ä), It., Sp., Lat., Ger., Du.

AURELIAN (Aureliánus, i), B. C.   June 16. R. M.
6 Cent. Bishop of Arles. *Sig.* Lat. golden. *Pron.* ą-rēl'-
yăn.

Aureliano (ō-rā-lē-ä'nō), Sp. Aurelian
Aurelianus (ŏw-rā-lē-ä'nŭs), Lat. Aurelian
Aurélie (ō-rā-lē'), Fr. Aurelia
Aurelie (ou-rā-'lē-ē), Ger. Aurelia
Aurelien (ō-rāl-yăṅ'), Fr. Aurelian
Aurelio (ŏw-rā'lē-ō), It., Sp. Aurelius

AURELIUS (Aurélius, ii), B. M.   Nov. 12. R. M.
2 Cent. Asia. *Sig.* Lat. golden. *Pron.* ą-rē'lĭ-ŭs.
(ŏw-rā'lē-ŭs), Lat.

Austen (ąs'tĕn), var. Augustine
Austin (ąs'tĭn), var. Augustine
Authbertus (ŏwth-bâr'tŭs), Lat. Aubert

Avellino (ă-vĕl-lē′nō), **Avellinus** (ă-vĕl-lē′nŭs), *see* St. Andrew.

Avit (ä-vē′), Fr. Avitus

AVITUS (Avi′tus, i), June 17. R. M.
  6 Cent. Orleans. *Pron.* ă-vē′tŭs. ‿
  (ä-vē′tŭs), Lat.

Awdry (ô′drĭ), var. Audrey, Etheldreda

Axel (ăks′ĕl), Dan. Absolon

Ayyub (ī-yōōb′), Ar. Job

Azariah (ăz-à-rī′à), var. Azarias

AZARIAS (Azarías, æ), Dec. 16. R. M.
  6 B. C. Youth cast into fiery furnace by Nabucho-
  donosor in Babylon. Also called Abdenago. *Sig.*
  Heb. helped of the Lord. *Pron.* ăz-à-rī′ăs.

B

Bab (băb), dim. Barbara

Babette (bä-bĕt′), Fr. dim. Elizabeth, Barbara

BACCHUS (Bácchus, i), M. Oct. 7. R. M.
  3 Cent. Barbara, Roman officer. *Pron.* bă′kŭs.
  (bä′kŭs), Lat.

Baccio (bä′tchō), It. Blase

Badduino (bäd-dōō-ē′nō), It. Baldwin

BALBINA (Balbína, æ), V. Mar. 31. R. M.
  2 Cent. Rome. Daughter of St. Quirinus. *Pron.*
  băl-bī′nà.
  (bäl-bē′nä), Lat.

Balbine (bäl-bēn′), Fr. Balbina

Baldassare (bäl-däs-sä′rä), It. Balthasar

Baldie (băl′dĭ), Sc. dim. Archibald

Baldo (bäl′dō), Ger. dim. Archibald

BALDOMER (Baldomérus, i), C. Feb. 27. R. M.
7 Cent. Lyons. Patron of locksmiths. *Sig.* Teut.
princely fame. *Pron.* băl'dō-mēr.
Baldomerus (bäl-dō-mā'rŭs), Lat. Baldomer
Baldovino (bäl-dō-vē'nō), It. Baldwin
Balduin (bäl'dŏŏ-ēn), Dan., Ger. Baldwin
Balduino (bäl-dŏŏ-ē'nō), It. Baldwin
Balduinus (bäl-dŏŏ-ē'nŭs), Lat. Baldwin

BALDWIN (Balduínus, i), Ab. Jul. 15
12 Cent. Rieti. *Sig.* Teut. bold winner. *Pron.* băld'-
wĭn.
Baltasar (bäl-tä-sär'), Sp. Balthasar.

BALTHASAR, BALTHASSAR (*indecl.*), K. Jan. 11.
One of Magi consecrated by St. Thomas the Apostle.
Sig. Per. war counsel. *Pron.* bäl-tä'zär.
Balthazar (bäl-tä'zär), var. Balthasar
Baptist (băp'tĭst), *see* St. John.
(bäp'tēst), Ger.
Baptista (bäp-tēs'tä), Lat. Baptist
Baptiste (bä-tēst'), Fr. Baptist
Barat (bä-rä'), St. Madeleine Sophie

BARBARA (Bárbara, æ), V. M. Dec. 4. R. M.
3 Cent. Syria. Because of her faith her father is said
to have shut her up in a tower, where she died.
Patron of fireworks-makers, artillerymen, prisoners, founders, stone-masons, grave-diggers; invoked against lightning, fire, impenitence and sudden death. One of Fourteen Holy Helpers. In art
shown with tower in background, crown of spikes
on head or palm in hand or holding chalice with
host. *Sig.* Gr. strange, foreign. *Pron.* bär'bä-rȧ.
(bär'bä-rä), Lat.

Barbarita (bär-bä-rē'tä), Sp. dim. Barbara.
Barbe (bärb), Fr. Barbara
Barend, Barent (bä'rĕnt), Du., Ger., Bernard
Barna (bär'nä), It. dim. Barnabas
Barnaba (bär'nä-bä), It. Barnabas

BARNABAS (Bárnabas, æ), Ap. June 11. R. M.
Not one of the Twelve, but called Apostle for his
preaching. Friend and companion of St. Paul.
Stoned to death by Jews on Island of Cyprus.
In art shown with Gospel in hand. *Sig.* Heb. son
of consolation. *Pron.* bär'nà-băs.
(bär'nä-bäs), Lat., Du., Ger.
(bär-nä-bäs'), Sp.
Barnabé (bär-nä-bā'), Fr., Port. Barnabas
Barnaby (bär'nà-bǐ), var. Barnabas
Barnard (bär'närd), var. Bernard
Barney (bär'nǐ), dim. Bernard, Barnabas
Barr (bär), dim. Finbar
Barry (băr'rǐ), dim. Finbar
Bart (bärt), dim. Bartholomew
Bartel (bär'tĕl), Dan., Sw. Bartholomew
Barthel (bär'tĕl), Ger. dim. Bartholomew
Barthélemi, Barthélemy (bär-täl-mē'), Fr. Bartholomew
Barthólo (bär-tō'lō), Sp. Bartholomew
Bartholomæus (bär-thō-lō-mä'ŭs), Lat. Bartholomew
Bartholomäus (bär-tō-lō-mä'ŭs), Ger. Bartholomew
Bartholomeu (bär-tō-lō-mä'ū), Port. Bartholomew

BARTHOLOMEW (Bartholomæ'us, i), Ap. Aug. 24.
R. M.
Believed to be the Nathanael chosen by Christ.
Preached the Gospel in India, where he was mar-

tyred. In art shown with large knife. *Sig.* Heb. warlike son. *Pron.* bär-thŏl'ō-mū

Bartle (bär't'l), cont. Bartholomew

Bartlet, Bartlett (bärt'lĕt), dim. Bartholomew

Bartley (bärt'lĭ), dim. Bartholomew

Bartólo (bär-tō'lō), Sp. dim. Bartholomew

Bartolome (bär-tō-lō-mā'), Sp. Bartholomew

Bartolomée (bär-tō-lō-mā'), Fr. Bartholomew

Bartolomeo (bär-tō-lō-mā'ō), It. Bartholomew

Bartolomeu (bär-tō-lō-mā'ū), Port. Bartholomew

Bartolommeo (bär-tō-lō-mā'ō), It. Bartholomew

BARUCH (*indecl.*), Proph. Sep. 28, Nov. 15.
Companion and secretary of Prophet Jeremias. *Sig.* Heb. blessed. *Pron.* bā'rŭk.

BASIL THE GREAT (Basílius, ii), B. C. D. Jan. 1, June 14. 4 Cent. Caesarea. Lawgiver of the monastic life in the East, orator, writer against heretics, one of the greatest Greek Doctors. Brother of Sts. Gregory of Nyssa and Macrina. Bishop of Caesarea. In art shown near fire with dove on arm. *Sig.* Gr. kingly, royal. *Pron.* băz'ĭl or bā'zĭl.

Basile (bä-zēl'), Fr. Basil

Basilia (bä-zĭl'ĭ-à), fem. Basil

BASILIDES (Basílides, is), M. June 12. R. M.
4 Cent. Roman soldier. *Sig.* Gr. royal. *Pron.* bă-sĭ-lī'dēz.
(bä-sē'lē-dāz), Lat.

Basilio (bä-sē'lē-ō), It., Sp., Port. Basil

BASILISSA (Basilíssa, æ), M. Apr. 15. R. M.
1 Cent. Noblewoman said to have buried Sts. Peter and Paul. *Sig.* Gr. royal. *Pron.* bă-sĭ-lĭs'sà.
(bä-sē-lĭs'sä), Lat.

Basilius (bä-sē'lē-ŭs), Lat. Basil.

BASILLA (Basílla, æ), V. M. May 20. R. M.
3 Cent. Noble Roman maiden. *Sig.* Gr. royal. *Pron.*
bă-zíl'lȧ.
(bä-síl'lä), Lat.
Bastian (bäs-tē-än'), Ger. cont. Sebastian.

Bastiano (bäs-tē-ä'nō), It. dim. Sebastian
Bastião (bäs-tē-ŏwṅ'), Port. dim. Sebastian
Bastien (bäs-tē-ăṅ'), Fr. Sebastian
Bat (băt), cor. Bartholomew

BATHILDA (Bathíldis, is), Q. Jan. 30. R. M.
7 Cent. Wife of King Clovis II of Burgundy. Found-
ress of monasteries of Corbie and Jumièges. *Sig.*
Teut. commanding battle maid. *Pron.* bă-tíl'dȧ.
Bathilde (bä-tēld'), Fr. Bathilda
Bathildis (bä-tēl'dĭs), Lat. Bathilda
Batiste (bä-tēst'), Fr. Baptist
Battista (bät-tēs'tä), It. Baptist
Baudouin (bō-dōō-ăṅ'), Fr. Baldwin
Bautista (bŏw-tēs'tä), Sp. Baptist
Bautolomeo (bŏw-tō-lō-mä'ō), Sp. Bartholomew
Bea (bē'ȧ), dim. Beatrice

BEAN (Beánus, i), B. C. Dec. 16. R. M.
11 Cent. Scotsman, Bishop of Murtlach and later of
Aberdeen.
Beanus (bā-ä'nŭs), Lat. Bean
Beat (bā-'ä), Fr. Beatus

BEATA (Beáta, æ), V. M. Sept. 6
Spanish Saint martyred near Sens, France, under
Aurelian. *Sig.* Lat. blessed, happy. *Pron.* bē-ä'tȧ.
(bä-ä'tä), Lat.
Beatie (bē'tĭ), cont. Beatrice

BEATRICE (Beátrix, ícis), M. Jul. 29. R. M.
4 Cent. Rome. Sister of Sts. Simplicius and Faustinus. In art with cords in left hand, candle in right.
Sig. joy-bringer. *Pron.* bē'à-trĭs.
(bā-ä-trē'tchä), It.
Béatrice (bā-ä-trēs'), Fr. Beatrice
Beatrix (bā-á-trĭks), Lat., Dan., Du., Sw., Ger. Beatrice
(bē'à-trĭks), Eng. var. Beatrice
Béatrix (bā-ä-trēks'), Fr. Beatrice
Beatriz (bā-ä-trēth'), Sp. Beatrice
(bā-ä-trēs'), Port.

BEATUS (Beátus, i), C. May 9. R. M.
3 Cent. Italian who evangelized Laon, France. *Sig.*
Lat. blessed, happy. *Pron.* bē-ä'tŭs.
Beda (bā'dä), Lat. Bede

BEDE (Béda, æ), the Venerable, C. D. May 27. R. M.
7 Cent. Benedictine priest, "the brightest ornament
of the English nation," Father of English history.
Sig. Teut. prayer. *Pron.* bēd.
Bède (bād), Fr. Bede

BEGGA (Bégga, æ), Mat. Dec. 17. R. M.
7 Cent. Sister of St. Gertrude of Nivelle and grand-
mother of Charles Martel. Foundress of Audenne
Monastery. *Sig.* Teut. prayer. *Pron.* bĕg'gà.
Bela, Bella (bā'lä), **Belle** (bĕl), Sp. cont. Isabella
Belica (bā-lē'kä), Sp. dim. Isabel
Belita (bā-lē'tä), Sp. dim. Elizabeth
Bellarmine (bĕl'lär-mĭn), *see* St. Robert
Belshazzar (bĕl-shăz'zär), var. Balthasar
Beltran (bĕl-trän'), Sp. Bertram
Ben (bĕn), dim. Benjamin, Benedict

Benedetta (bā-nä-dĕt'tä), It. Benedicta
Benedetto (bā-nä-dĕt'tō), It. Benedict

BENEDICT (Benedíctus, i), Ab. Mar. 21. R. M.
5 Cent. Patriarch of Monks. Retired at 14 to Subiaco,
and became founder of Western Monasticism.
Brother of St. Scholastica. In art shown with book
having serpent resting on it, and raven at feet.
Sig. Lat. blessed. *Pron.* bĕn'ĕ-dĭkt.

BENEDICT BISCOP, Ab. Jan. 12. R. M.
7 Cent. Northumbrian noble, founder of Monastery
of Jarrow.

BENEDICT JOSEPH LABRE, C. Apr. 16. R. M.
18 Cent. Born Amettes, France, lived in solitude,
visiting shrines of Europe and begging his food.

BENEDICT THE MOOR, C. Apr. 4. R. M.
16 Cent. Negro, born near Messina, Italy, became
Franciscan Brother.
Bénédict (bā-nä-dĭkt'), Fr. Benedict

BENEDICTA (Benedícta, æ), V. M. June 29. R. M.
3 Cent. Sens. Sister of St. Sanctian. *Sig.* Lat. blessed.
Pron. bĕn-ĕ-dĭk'tä.
(bā-nä-dĭk'tä), Lat.
(bā-nä-dē'tä), Port.
Bénédicte (bā-nä-dĭkt'), Fr. Benedicta.
Benedicto (bā-nä-dĭk'tō), Sp. Benedict
(bā-nä-dē'tō), Port.
Benedictus (bā-nä-dĭk'tŭs), Lat. Benedict
Benedikt (bĕn'ā-dēkt), Ger., Slav., Benedict
Benedikta (bā-nä-dēk'tä), Ger. Benedicta
Benet (bĕn'ĕt), dim. Benedict
Bénézet (bā-nä-zā'), Fr. var. Benedict

Bengt (bĕngt), Sw. Benedict
Beniamino (bĕn-yä-mē′nō), It. Benjamin
Bénigne (bä-nēn′yĕ), Fr. Benignus

BENIGNUS (Benígnus, i), B. M. June 28. R. M.
  6 Cent. Probably Bishop of Chartres, retired to
  Utrecht. *Sig.* Lat. gentle. *Pron.* bĕ-nĭg′nŭs.
  (bä-nē′nyŭs), Lat.
Benita (bä-nē′tä), Sp. Benedicta
Benito (bä-nē′tō), Sp., It., Benedict

BENJAMIN (*indecl.*) 4th Sun. of Advent.
  Youngest son of Patriarch Jacob. *Sig.* Heb. son of
  the right hand. *Pron.* bĕn′jà-mĭn.
  (bĕn′yä-mēn), Dan., Ger.
  (bŏṅ-zhä-măṅ′), Fr.
  5 Cent. Also Deacon, M. Mar. 31. R. M.
Benjy (bĕn′jĭ), cont. Benjamin
Bennet, Bennett (bĕn′nĕt), dim. Benedict
Bennie (bĕn′nē), dim. Benedict, Benjamin

BENNO (Bénno, ónis), B. C. June 16. R. M.
  11 Cent. Ab. of Hildesheim, B. of Meissen. Supporter
  of Church against Henry IV. Apostle of Slavs.
  Also called Benedict. *Sig.* Teut. firm bear. *Pron.*
  bĕn′nō.
  (bĕn′nō), Lat.
Benny (bĕn′nĭ), dim. Benedict, Benjamin
Benôit (bä-nwä′), Fr. Benedict
Benôite (bä-nwät′), Fr. Benedicta
Bento (bĕn′tō), Port. Benedict
Benvenute (bŏṅ-vä-nüt′), Fr. Benvenutus

BENVENUTUS (Benvenútus, i), B. C. Mar. 22. R. M.
13 Cent. Franciscan, B. of Osimo. He lay down to die
before high altar. *Sig.* It. welcome. *Pron.* bĕn-
vä-noō'tŭs.
(bĕn-vä-noō'tŭs), Lat.

Beppo (bĕp'pō), It. fam. Joseph
Berchmans (bĕrk'mänz), *see* St. John
Berchtold (bērk'tōld), var. Berthold
Berdrand (bĕr'dränt), Ger. Bertram
Berend (bä'rĕnt), Ger. Bernard

BERENICE (Bereníce, es), V. M. Oct. 4
4 Cent. Daughter of St. Domnina, with whom she
was martyred in Syria. Also called Veronica. *Sig.*
Gr. bringing victory. *Pron.* bērĕ-nī'sē.
(bä-rä-nē'chä), Lat.
Bérénice (bä-rä-nēs'), Fr. Berenice
Berenike (bĕ-rĕ-nē'kä), Gr. Berenice
Bernabe (bĕr-nä-bä'), Sp. Barnabas

BERNADETTE SOUBIROUS (Bernárda, æ), V.
Apr. 16
Born in 1844, at 14 she beheld the Blessed Virgin at
Lourdes, who ordered her to have the Miraculous
Medal struck. She became a Sister of Charity at
Nevers, died in 1879 and was canonized Dec. 8,
1933. *Sig.* Teut. bold as a bear. *Pron.* bĕr-nä-dĕt'
soō-bē-roō'.

Bernal (bär-näl'), Sp. Bernard

BERNARD (Bernárdus, i), Ab. C. D. Aug. 20. R. M.
12 Cent. Called the "Mellifluous Doctor." Second
founder of the Cistercians, Ab. of Clairvaux,

hymn-writer, writer of mystical theology and considered the last of the Fathers. Strongly devoted to the Blessed Virgin. Patron of wax-chandlers. In art shown with three mitres at feet with beehive, also with angel holding crozier. *Sig.* Ger. bold as a bear. *Pron.* bĕr'närd. (bār-när'), Fr.

Bernarda (bâr-när'dä), Lat. Bernadette (bĕr-när'dà), Eng. fem. Bernard

Bernardin (bār-när-dăṅ'), Fr. Bernardine

BERNARDINE OF SIENNA (Bernardínus, i), C. May 20. R. M.

15 Cent. Franciscan, ascetic writer devoted to Holy Name of Jesus and Blessed Virgin. In art shown with I. H. S. on breast, mitre at feet, or with Infant Jesus in his arms. *Sig.* Teut. bold as a bear. *Pron.* bĕr'när-dĭn. (bâr-när-dēn'), Fr.

Bernardino (bêr-när-dē'nō), It., Sp., Bernardine

Bernardinus (bâr-när-dē'nŭs), Lat. Bernardine

Bernardo (bâr-när'dō), It., Sp. Bernard

Bernardus (bâr-när'dŭs), Lat. Bernard

Bernhard (bĕrn'härt), Dan., Ger., Sw. Bernard

Bernhardina (bĕrn-här-dē'nä), Ger. fem. Bernardine

Bernhardinus (bĕrn-här-dē'nŭs), Ger. Bernardine

Bernice (bĕr-nĭ'sē), var. Berenice

Bernie (bĕr'nĭ), dim. Bernard

Bert (bĕrt), dim. Herbert, Bertram, Bertha, Albert

Berta (bâr'tä), It., Sp. Bertha

Berte (bârt), Fr. Bertha

Bertel (bĕr'tĕl), Dan., Ger., Nor. Bartholomew

BERTHA (Bértha, æ), Wid., Ab. Jul. 4
  8 Cent. France. *Sig.* Ger. bright, beautiful. *Pron.*
  bĕr'thà.
  (bĕr'tä), Du., Ger.
  (bâr'tä), Lat.
Berthe (bârt), Fr. Bertha

BERTHOLD (Berthóldus, i), C. Mar. 29
  12 Cent. First General of Carmelites. *Sig.* Teut.
  bright, firm. *Pron.* bēr'tōld.
  (bâr-tōl'), Fr.
Bertholdus (bâr-tōl'dŭs), Lat. Berthold
Bertie (bĕr'tĭ), dim. Herbert, Bertram, Bertha, Albert
Bertilia (bâr-tē'lē-ä), Lat. Bertille
Bertilla (bĕr-tĭl'là), var. Bertille

BERTILLE (Bertília, æ), V. Jan. 3.
  7 Cent. Belgian recluse. *Sig.* Teut. bright battle
  maid. *Pron.* bĕr-tēl'.
  Also 12 C. Nov. 5. Abbess of Jouarre.

BERTIN (Bertínus, i), Ab. Sept. 5. R. M.
  7 Cent. Benedictine of Luxeuil. *Sig.* Teut. bright
  friend. *Pron.* bĕr-tăṅ'.
  (bâr-tăṅ'), Fr.
Bertinus (bâr-tē'nŭs), Lat. Bertin

BERTRAM (Bertrámus, i), B. C. Jul. 3.
  7 Cent. Bishop of Le Mans. *Sig.* Ger. bright raven.
  Pron. bĕr'trăm.
  (bĕr'träm), Ger.
Bertramus (bâr-trä'mŭs), Lat. Bertram

Bertrand (bĕr'trănd), var. Bertram. *See also* St.
  Louis.
  (bâr-trăṅ'), Fr.

Bertrando (bâr-trän'dō), It. Bertram
Bertrão (bĕr-trŏwn'), Port. Bertram.
Berty (bĕr'tĭ), dim. Herbert, Bertram, Bertha, Albert
Bess (bĕs), dim. Elizabeth
Bessie, Bessy (bĕs'sĭ), dims. Elizabeth
Bet (bĕt), dim. Elizabeth
Betsey, Betsy (bĕt'sĭ), dims. Elizabeth
Beth (bĕth), dim. Elizabeth
Bettino (bĕt-tē'nō), It. dim. Benedict
Betty (bĕt'tĭ), dim. Elizabeth
Beuve (bĕv), Fr. Bova
Biagio (bē-ä'jō), It. Blase
Bianca (bē-än'kä), It. Blanche
Biasio (bē-ä'sē-ō), It. Blase

BIBIANA (Bibiána, æ), V. M. Dec. 2. R. M.
    4 Cent. Rome. Daughter of Sts. Flavian and
    Daphrose, sister of St. Demetria, all martyrs. Also
    called Vivian. In art shown bound to pillar. *Sig.*
    Lat. lively. *Pron.* bĭb-ĭ-ä'nà.
    (bē-bē-ä'nä), Lat.
Bibiane (bē-bē-än'), Fr. Bibiana
Bice (bē'chä), It. dim. Beatrice
Biddy (bĭd'dĭ), dim. Bridget
Bill (bĭl), dim. William
Billiart (bē-yär'), Bl. Julie
Billie, Billy (bĭl'lĭ), dims. William
Birgitta (bēr-jē'tä), Lat. Bridget
Birgitte (bēr-gĭt'tĕ), Dan. Bridget

BIRINUS (Birínus, i), B. C. Dec. 3. R. M.
    7 Cent. Missionary of Wessex. *Pron.* bĭ-rī'nŭs.
    (bē-rē'nŭs), Lat.

Blaanus (blä'ä-nŭs), Lat. Blane
Blaas (bläs), Du. Blase
Blain (blān), var. of Blane
Blaise (blāz), Eng. and Fr. Blase
Blanca (blän'kä), Du., Dan., Ger., Lat., Sp. Blanche

BLANCH (Blánca, æ), V. M. Jul. 5
    5 Cent. Also called Gwen. *Sig.* Teut. white. *Pron.*
    blănch.
    Also (Bl.) Queen of France, mother of St. Louis,
    Nov. 30.
Blanche (blănch), var. of Blanch
    (blänsh), Fr.

BLANDA (Blánda, æ), M. May 10. R. M.
    3 Cent. Rome. Wife of St. Felix, with whom she was
    martyred. *Sig.* Lat. flatterer. *Pron.* blăn'dä.
    (blän'dä), Lat.

BLANDINA (Blandína, æ), V. M. June 2. R. M.
    2 Cent. One of Martyrs of Lyons, a young girl who
    was beheaded. *Sig.* Lat. mild. *Pron.* blăn-dĭ'nä.
    (blän-dē'nä), Lat.
Blandine (blän-dēn'), Fr. Blandina

BLANE (Bláanus, i), B. C. Aug. 10
    7 Cent. Scotsman, Bishop of Kingarth. *Pron.* blān.
Blanka (bläng'kä), Ger., Sw. Blanch
Blas (bläs), Sp. Blase

BLASE (Blásius, ii), B. M. Feb. 3. R. M.
    4 Cent. Bishop of Sebaste. Saved boy choking to
    death from fish bone, hence throats are blessed on
    his feast. Patron of wool-combers and invoked
    against diseases of throat. *Sig.* Lat. babbler.
    Pron. blāz.

Blasius (blä′sē-ŭs), Lat. Blase
Bob (bŏb), dim. Robert
Bobbie (bŏb′bĭ), dim. Robert
Bona (bō′nà), var. Bova
   (bō′nä), Ger., It., Lat., Sp. Bova
Bonaventura (bō-nä-vĕn-tōō′rä), It., Lat. Bonaven-
   ture.

BONAVENTURE (Bonaventúra, æ), B. C. D. Jul. 14.
   R. M.
   13 Cent. Tuscany. Of Order of Friars Minor of which
   he is the second founder; one of greatest lights of
   Church; called "Seraphic Doctor." Wrote "Mas-
   ter of Sentences," commentaries on Sacred Scrip-
   ture, ascetical and mystical works; friend of St.
   Thomas Aquinas, Cardinal and Bishop of Albano.
   In art as bishop, with cardinal's hat nearby. *Sig*.
   Lat. good luck. *Pron*. bŏn-à-vĕn′tūr.
   (bō-nä-vŏn-tür′), Fr.
Bonet (bō-nä′), Fr. Bonitus

BONIFACE (Bonifátius, ii), B. M. June 5. R. M.
   8 Cent. Devonshire. Apostle of Germany, anointed
   Pepin as King of France. Archbishop of Mainz,
   martyred by pagans in Friesland. Also called
   Winifrid, his baptismal name. In art shown with
   axe at foot of oak or pierced by a sword. *Sig*. Lat.
   well-doer. *Pron*. bŏn′ĭ-făs.
   (bō-nē-fäs′), Fr.
   Also 3 Cent. Martyr at Tarsus, May 14.
Bonifacio (bō-nē-fä′chō), It. Boniface
   (bō-nē-fä′thē-ō), Sp.
   (bō-nē-fä′sē-ō), Port.
Bonifacius (bō-nē-fä′chē-ŭs), Du., Ger., Lat. Boniface
Bonifatius (bō-nē-fät′sē-ŭs), Lat. Boniface

Bonifazio (bō-nē-fät′sē-ō), It. Boniface

BONITUS (Bonítus, i), B. C. Jan. 15. R. M.
 8 Cent. Clermont. *Sig.* Lat. goodly. *Pron.* bō-nē′tŭs.
 (bō-nē′tŭs), Lat.
Bonne (bŏn), Fr. Bona
Bonny (bŏn′nĭ), dim. Bonaventure

BONOSA (Bonósa, æ), V. M. Jul. 15. R. M.
 3 Cent. Porto Romano. Invoked against smallpox.
 Pron. bō-nō′sȧ.
 (bō-nō′sä), Lat.
Bont (bŏṅ), Fr. Bonitus
Bopp (bŏp), Sw. fam. James
Boppi (bŏp′pē), Sw. fam. Joseph
Borgia (bôr′jä), *see* St. Francis.
Boris (bô′rĭs), used in East for Romanus.
Borromeo (bŏr-rō-mā′ō), *see* St. Charles.
Bortolo (bōr′tō-lō), It. Bartholomew
Botolph (bō′tŏlf), var. Botulph

BOTULPH (Botúlphus, i), Ab. June 17
 7 Cent. Icanhoe, Lincolnshire. Brother of St. Adulph.
 Boston is a contraction of St. Botulph's Town.
 Sig. Teut. commanding wolf. *Pron.* bō′tŭlf.
Botulphus (bō-tŭl′fŭs), Lat. Botulph
Boudewijn (bŏw′dĕ-wīn), Du. Baldwin

BOVA (Bóva, æ), V. M. Apr. 24. R. M.
 7 Cent. Daughter of King Sigibert of Austrasia.
 Also called Bona. *Pron.* bō′vȧ.
 (bō′vä), Lat.
Brébeuf (brā-bēf′), *see* St. John.

BRENDAN (Brendánus, i), Ab. May 16. R. M.
 6 Cent. Born in Kerry, founded many monasteries

including Clonfert. Said to have reached the shores
of North America. Patron of sailors. *Sig.* Celt.
sword. *Pron.* brĕn'dăn.

Brendanus (brĕn-dä'nŭs), Lat. Brendan.

Briccius (brĭk'chē-ŭs), Lat. var. of Brice

BRICE (Bríctius, ii), B. C. Nov. 13. R. M.
5 Cent. Archbishop of Tours, disciple of St. Martin.
Also called Britius, Briccius, Brixius. *Pron.* brĭs.
(brēs), Fr.

Brictius (brĭkt'sē-ŭs), Lat. Brice

Bride (brīd), var. of Bridget

BRIDGET OF KILDARE (Brígida, æ), V. Feb. 1.
R. M.
6 Cent. She asked God to disfigure her face to guard
her virginity, and it recovered its beauty when she
entered the religious life. She was a friend of St.
Patrick and was present at his death. She is known
as the "Mary of Ireland" and is its second patron.
Also patron of dairymen. In art shown holding
cross with flame over her head or holding lamp.
Sig. Celt. strength. *Pron.* brĭj'ĕt.

BRIDGET OF SWEDEN, Wid. Oct. 8
14 Cent. A princess who, after death of her husband,
became a Cistercian and founded Order of the
Most Holy Savior (Bridgettines). Patron of pilgrims. In art shown with staff and holding heart
surmounted by cross.

Bridgid (brĭj'ĭd), var. of Bridget

Brieuc (brē-ŭc'), Fr. Brioc

Brigid (brĭj'ĭd), var. of Bridget

Brigida (brē'jē-dä), Lat., It. Bridget
(brē'hē-dä), Sp.

Brigit (brĭj'ĭt), var. of Bridget
Brigita (brē'jē-tä), It. Bridget
Brigitta (brē-gēt'tä), Ger. Bridget
(brē-hĭt'tä), Du.
Brigitte (brē-zhēt'), Fr. Bridget

BRIOC (Brĭocus, i), B. C. May 1
5 Cent. Wales. Founded monastery of Saint-Brieuc.
Invoked against insanity. *Pron.* brē'ŏk.
Briocus (brē'ō-kŭs), Lat. Brioc.
Britius (brĭ'sĭ-ŭs), var. of Brice.

BRONISLAVA (Bronisláva, æ), (Bl.) V. Aug. 30.
13 Cent. Cracow. Relative of St. Hyacinth. Invoked
against pestilence or cholera. *Sig.* Slav. weapon
glory. *Pron.* brō-nĭs-lä'vä.
(brō-nĭs-lä'vä), Lat.

BRUNO (Brúno, ónis), C. Oct. 6. R. M.
11 Cent. Cologne. Founder of Carthusian Order,
vowed to solitude, prayer and manual labor. In
art shown with crucifix intertwined with leaves
and flowers, with star on breast or globe under
feet. *Sig.* Ger. brown. *Pron.* brü'nō.
(brü-nō'), Fr.
Brush (brŭsh), fam. Ambrose
Buenaventura (bwä-nä-vĕn-tōō'rä), Sp. Bonaventure

BURCHARD (Burchárdus, i), B. C. Oct. 14. R. M.
8 Cent. A wealthy Englishman, Bishop of Wurzburg.
Pron. bŏŏr'kärt.
(bür-shär'), Fr.
Burchardus (bōōr-kär'dŭs), Lat. Burchard
Burga (bēr'gà), dim. Walburga
Burkhart (bērk'härt), var. of Burchard

C

Cäcilia (tsä-tsē'lē-ä), Ger. Cecilia
Caddie (kăd'dĭ), dim. Caroline

CADOC (Cadocus, i), B. M. Jan. 23.
    6 Cent. Son of Welsh chieftain, founder of Llancarvan Monastery. Invoked against scrofula and deafness. *Sig.* Celt. defense. *Pron.* kă'dŏk.
Cadocus (kä-dō-kŭs), Lat. Cadoc
Caecilia (chä-chē'lē-ä), Lat. Cecilia
Caecilius (chä-chē'lē-ŭs), Lat. Cecil

CAESARIA (Caesária, æ), V. Jan. 12.
    6 Cent. Sister of St. Caesarius of Arles, abbess at Arles. *Pron.* sē-zä'rĭ-á.
    (chä-sä'rē-ä), Lat.

CAESARIUS (Caesárius, ii), B. C. Aug. 27. R. M.
    6 Cent. Archbishop of Arles, light of the Church. *Pron.* sē-zä'rĭ-ŭs.
    (chä-sä'rē-ŭs), Lat.
Caio (kä'yō), It. Caius

CAIUS (Cáius, ii), P. M. Apr. 22. R. M.
    3 Cent. Though not actually martyred, suffered much for Faith. *Sig.* Lat. parents' joy. *Pron.* kā'ŭs.
    Also 1 Cent., B. C., disciple of St. Barnabas, Sept. 27.
    (kä'yŭs), Lat.

CAJETAN (Cajetánus, i), C. Aug. 7. R. M.
    16 Cent. Thienna. Founder of Clerks Regular (Theatines), devoted to rigorous poverty. *Sig.* Lat. rejoiced in. *Pron.* kăj'ĕ-tăn.
    (kä-zhä-täṅ'), Fr.

Cajetano (kä-yä-tä'nō), It. Cajetan
Cajetanus (kä-yä-tä'nŭs), Lat. Cajetan
  (kăj-ĕ-tā'nŭs), Eng. var.
Calasanctius (kä-lä-sänk'sē-ŭs), *see* St. Joseph.
Calixte (kä-lēkst'), Fr. Callistus

CALLISTA (Callísta, æ), V. M. Apr. 25.
  (d. u.), Syracuse, together with brother, St. Evodius.
  Sig. Lat. of the chalice. *Pron.* kă-lĭs'tá.
  (kä-lĭs'tä), Lat.
Calliste (kä-lēst'), Fr. Callistus

CALLISTUS I (Callístus, i), P. M. Oct. 14. R. M.
  3 Cent. Established Ember Days. *Sig.* Lat. of the
  chalice. *Pron.* kă-lĭs'tŭs.
  (kä-lĭs'tŭs), Lat.
Callixtus (kă-lĭx'tŭs), var. of Callistus

CALOCERUS (Calocérus, i), B. C. Feb. 11. R. M.
  2 Cent. Ravenna. *Pron.* kăl-ō-sēr'ŭs.
  (kä-lō-chä'rŭs), Lat.
Calogerus (kä-lō-jē'rŭs), var. of Calocerus
Camila (kä-mē'lä), Sp. Camilla

CAMILLA (Camílla, æ), V. Jul. 27.
  14 or 15 Cent. *Sig.* Lat. attendant at sacrifice. *Pron.*
  kă-mĭl'lá.
  (kä-mēl'lä), Lat., It.
Camille (kä-mēl' or kä-mē'yĕ), Fr. Camilla, Camillus
Camillo (kä-mēl'lō), It. Camillus
  (kä-mēl'yō), Sp.

CAMILLUS De LELLIS (Camíllus, i), C. Jul. 14 and
  18 R. M.
  17 Cent. Abruzzi. Founder of Congregation of Clerks
  Regular Ministering to the Sick. Patron of hos-

pitals and the sick. Named in Litany of the Dying. *Sig.* Lat. attendant at sacrifice. *Pron.* kă-mĭl'lŭs.
(kä-mēl'lĭs), Lat.
Camilo (kä-mē'lō), Sp. Camillus.
Campion (kămp'ĭ-ŏn), *see* Edmund (Bl.)

CANDIDA (Cándida, æ), Mat. Sept. 4. R. M.
1 Cent. Naples. Woman cured by St. Peter. *Sig.* Lat. white. *Pron.* kăn'dĭ-dà.
(kän'dē-dä), Lat.
Candide (kän-dēd'), Fr. Candidus

CANDIDUS (Cándidus, i), M. Feb. 2. R. M.
3 Cent. Rome, with St. Fortunatus and others. *Sig.* Lat. white. *Pron.* kăn'dĭ-dŭs.
(kän'dē-dŭs), Lat.
Candres (kän'dr'), Fr. Candidus

CANICE (Cánicus, i), Ab. C. Oct. 11. R. M.
6 Cent. Preached throughout Ireland and Scotland. Patron of Kilkenny. Also called Kenneth, Kenny. *Pron.* kă'nĭs.
Canicus (kä'nē-kŭs), Lat. Canice
Canisius (kă-nē'sē-ŭs), *see* St. Peter
Cantius (kăn'sĭ-ŭs), *see* St. John Kenty.
Canut (kä-nü'), Fr. Canute

CANUTE IV (Canútus, i), K. M. Jan. 19. R. M.
11 Cent. Denmark. Father of Charles the Good. *Sig.* Teut. hill. *Pron.* kà-nūt'
Canutus (kä-nōō'tŭs), Lat. Canute
Capistran (kăp'ĭs-trăn), *see* St. John.
Capistrano (kä-pĭs-trä'nō), *see* St. John.

CARINA (Carína, æ), M. Nov. 7. R. M.
  At Ancyra. *Sig.* Lat. keel. *Pron.* kă-rī′nȧ.
  (kä-rē′nä), Lat.
Caritas (kä′rē-täs), Lat. Charity
Carl (kärl), Du., Ger. Charles
Carlo (kär′lō), It. Charles
Carlos (kär′lōs), Sp., Port. Charles
Carlota (kär-lō′tä), Sp., Port. Charlotte
Carlotta (kär-lŏt′tä), It. Charlotte
Carmel (kär′mĕl), Mary (Our Lady of Mt. Carmel)
Carmela (kär-mĕl′ȧ), var. Carmel
Carmelita (kär-mĕ-lē′tä), dim. Carmela
Carmine (kär′mĭn), var. Carmel
Carolina (kă-rō-lē′nä), Du., It., Port., Sp. Caroline
Caroline (kăr′ō-lĭn), fem. Charles
  (kä-rō-lē′nĕ), Du., Dan., Ger. Caroline
  (kä-rō-lēn′), Fr.
Carolo (kä′rō-lō), It. Charles
Carolus (kä′rō-lŭs), Lat. Charles
Carrie (kăr′rĭ), dim. Caroline

CARTHAGE (Carthágus, i), the Younger, B.C. May 14
  7 Cent. Lismore. *Pron.* kär′thȧj.
  Also the Elder, B. C. Westmeath, 6 Cent. Mar. 5.
Carthagus (kär-thä′gŭs), Lat. Carthage
Casey (kā′sĭ), dim. Catherine

CASILDA (Casílda, æ), V. Apr. 9
  11 Cent. Toledo, Spain. *Pron.* kă-sĭl′dȧ.
  (kä-sĭl′dä), Lat.

CASIMIR (Casimírus, i), K. C. Mar. 4. R. M.
  15 Cent. Poland, devoted to Passion and Holy
  Eucharist. *Sig.* Slav. show forth peace. *Pron.*
  kă′zĭ-mēr.

Casimira (kăs-ĭ-mē′rà), fem. Casimir
Casimiro (kä-sē-mē′rō), Sp. Casimir
Casimirus (kä-sē-mē′rŭs), Lat. Casimir
Caspar (kăs′pĕr), var. of Gaspar
   (käs′pĕr), Ger.
Casparo (käs-pä′rō), It. Casper
Casper (kăs′pĕr), var. of Caspar

CASSIA (Cássia, æ) M. Jul. 20. R. M.
   (d. u.) Martyred with Sts. Sabinus and others. *See
   also* St. Rita of Cassia. *Pron.* kă′shà.
   (käs′sē-ä), Lat.

CASSIAN (Cassiánus, i), M. Aug. 13. R. M.
   3 Cent. School-teacher pierced to death by pagan
   pupils at Imola. *Pron.* kăsh′ĭ-ăn.
   Also Bishop of Autun, 4 Cent. Aug. 5. R. M.
Cassianus (kä-sē-ä′nŭs), Lat. Cassian
Cassie (kăs′sĭ), dim. Cassia
Cassien (kä-sē-ăṅ′), Fr. Cassian
CASTOR (Cástor, óris), C. Feb. 13.
   4 Cent. Coblentz. *Pron.* kăs′tŏr.
   (käs′tōr), Lat.

CATALDUS (Catáldus, i), B. C. May 10.
   7 Cent. Taranto. *Pron.* kă-täl′dŭs.
   (kä-täl′dŭs), Lat.
Catalina (kä-tä-lē′nä), Sp. Catherine
Caterina (kä-tä-rē′nä), It. Catherine
Cathaldus (kä-täl′dŭs), Lat. var. of Cataldus
Catharina (kä-thä-rē′nä), Du., Lat., Port. Catherine
   (kăth-à-rī′nà), Eng. var. of Catherine
Catharine (kä-tä-rē′nĕ), Dan. Catherine
   (kăth′à-rĭn), Eng. var. of Catherine

CATHERINE OF ALEXANDRIA (Catharína, æ), V. M. Nov. 25. R. M.
4. Cent. Confounded pagan philosophers with her learning and eloquence. One of the Fourteen Holy Helpers. In art shown with spiked wheel. Patron of jurists, philosophers, students, millers, wagonmakers, teachers, etc. *Sig.* Gr. pure. *Pron.* kăth'ĕr-ĭn.
(kä-trēn), Fr.

CATHERINE OF BOLOGNA, V. Mar. 9. R. M.
15 Cent. Poor Clare, ascetical writer, author of "Revelations on Seven Spiritual Weapons." Patron of painters. In art carrying Infant Jesus, or holding brush and painting of Crucifixion.

CATHERINE OF GENOA, Wid. Sept. 15. R. M.
16 Cent. Of family of Flisca (Fieschi) Adorna, ascetical writer. Converted her husband to a good life and devoted herself to poor and sick. Called "Apostle of Purgatory."

CATHERINE LABOURÈ, (Bl.), V. Nov. 28.
1830, Paris. Sister of Charity to whom Blessed Virgin revealed the Miraculous Medal. Beatified, 1933.

CATHERINE RICCI, Feb. 2. R. M.
16 Cent. Entered convent of 3rd Order of St. Dominic at 14, noted for austerity and penance. In art with crown of thorns. *Pron.* rēt'chē.

CATHERINE OF SIENNA, V. Apr. 30. R. M.
14 Cent. Marvel of penance and humility, ascetical writer who labored for peace of Europe. Dominican tertiary blessed with Stigmata. Invoked against headache and pestilence. In art with crucifix upon a heart, or espoused to Infant Jesus.

CATHERINE OF SWEDEN, V. Mar. 24. R. M.

14 Cent. Daughter of St. Bridget of Sweden, ascetical writer, Abbess of Wadstena. In art as abbess holding lily.

Catty (kăt'tĭ), cor. of Martha

Cayetano (kä-yä-tä'nō), Sp. Cajetan

Ceadda (chä-ä'dä), Lat. Chad

CECIL (Caecĭlius, ii), Pr. C. June 3

3 Cent. Teacher of St. Cyprian. *Sig.* dim-sighted. *Pron.* sē'sĭl or sĕs'ĭl.

Cecile (sä-sēl'), Fr. Cecil, Cecilia.

CECILIA (Caecĭlia, æ), V. M. Nov. 22. R. M.

2 Cent. Rome. Married involuntarily to pagan Valerius, she converted him and both were martyred. She was struck three blows with an axe and died three days later. Patron of musicians, singers, organ-builders, poets. In art shown with small organ on arm. Also called Cicely. *Sig.* Lat. blind. *Pron.* sĕ-sĭl'ĭ-à.

(chä-chē'lē-ä), It.

(thä-thē'lē-ä), Sp.

Cecilie (sĕ'sĭ-lĭ), var. of Cecilia

Cecilio (chä-chē'lē-ō), It. Cecil

Cecily (sĕs'ĭ-lĭ), var. of Cecilia

Cedd (kĕd), **Cedda** (kĕd'à), var. of Chad

CELESTA (Celésta, æ), M. Apr. 16.

Sig. Gr. heavenly. *Pron.* sē-lĕs'tà.

(chä-lĕs'tä), Lat.

Celeste (sä-lĕst), Fr. Celesta

Célestin (sä-läs-tăn'), Fr. Celestine

CELESTINE (Cœlestínus, i), P. C. Apr. 6

5 Cent. Condemned heresy of Nestorius; sent

St. Patrick to Ireland. *Sig.* Lat. heavenly. *Pron.*
sĕl'ĕs-tĭn.
Celestino (chā-lās-tē'nō), It. Celestine
Celia (sēl'yȧ), dim. Cecilia
Célie (sā-lē'), Fr. Celia.

CELINE (Celínia, æ), V. Oct. 21
　6 Cent. Mother of St. Remi. *Sig.* Lat. heavenly.
　　Pron. sĕ-lēn'.
Céline (sā-lēn'), Fr. Celine
Célinie (sā-lē-nē'), Fr. Celine
Cella (sĕl'lȧ), cont. Marcella
Celse (sāls) Fr. Celsus.

CELSUS (Célsus, i), M. Jul. 28. R. M.
　1 Cent. Disciple of St. Nazarius and martyred with
　　him at Milan. *Pron.* sĕl'sŭs.
　(chĕl'sŭs), Lat.
　Also 12 Cent. Archbishop of Armagh, Apr. 6.
Cenzi (sĕn'zĭ), dim. Crescentia
Cephas (sē'fȧs), var. of Peter. *Sig.* Aram. a rock.
Césaire (sā-zâr'), Fr. Caesarius
Césarie (sā-zä-rē'), Fr. Caesaria

CESLAS (Cesláüs, i), C. Jul. 16.
　13 Cent. Received habit from St. Dominic, became
　　spiritual director of St. Hedwig. Apostle of
　　Silesia. *Sig.* Slav. honor glory. *Pron.* sĕs'lȧs.
Ceslaus (chās-lä'ŭs), Lat. Ceslas
Chabanel (shä-bä-nāl'), *see* St. Noël.

CHAD (Ceádda, æ), B. C. Mar. 2. R. M.
　7 Cent. Lichfield. *Sig.* Celt. defence. *Pron.* chăd.
Chantal (shän-täl'), *see* St. Jane Frances.
Charitas (kä'rē-täs), var. Caritas.

CHARITY (Cáritas, átis), M. Aug. 1. R. M.
2 Cent. Daughter of St. Sophia, martyred at 9 years of age. *Sig.* Gr. love. *Pron.* chă'rĭ-tĭ.

CHARLES BORROMEO (Cárolus, i), B. C. Nov. 4. R. M.
16 Cent. Archbishop of Milan, Cardinal, devoted to reform of clergy and to plague-stricken. In art shown as cardinal administering Communion to plague-stricken. *Sig.* Teut. strong. *Pron.* chärlz bŏr-rō-mä'ō.
(shärl), Fr.

CHARLES GARNIER, M. Sept. 26.
One of American Martyrs put to death by Indians near Ontario, Canada, in 1649. Canonized in 1930. *Pron.* gär-nyä'.

Charley, Charlie (chär'lĭ), dim. Charles

Charlotta (shär-lŏt'tä), Du., Sw. Charlotte

Charlotte (shär'lŏt), var. of Caroline
(shär-lŏt'tĕ), Dan.
(shär-lŏt'), Fr.

Cherubino (kä-rōō-bē'nō), It. Cherubinus

CHERUBINUS (Cherubínus, i) (Bl.), C. Dec. 17.
15 Cent. Augustinian. Avigliana. *Pron.* chĕr-ü-bī'nŭs (chä-rōō-bē'nŭs), Lat.

Chetry (chĕ'trĭ), cor. Charity

Chiara (kē-ä'rä), It. Clare

Chim (kĭm), dim. Joachim

Cholly (chŏl'lĭ), dim. Charles

Chréstien, Chrétien (krä-tē-äṅ'), Fr. Christian

Chrétienne (krä-tē-ĕn'), Fr. Christiana

Chris (krĭs), dim. Christian, Christopher

Chrisostomos (krĭs-sŏs'tō-mŏs), Ger. Chrysostom.
See St. John.

Chrissie, Chrissy (krĭs'sĭ), dim. Christina

CHRISTIAN (Christiánus, i), B. C. June 12
12 Cent. Brother of St. Malachy, Bishop of Chlogher.
Sig. Lat. believer in Christ. Pron. krĭs'chăn.
(krēs'tē-än), Ger., Dan.

CHRISTIANA (Christiána, æ), M. Apr. 16
3 Cent. Corinth. Tortured and thrown into sea.
Also fem. Christian. Sig. Lat. believer in Christ.
Pron. krĭs-tĭ-ăn'á.
(krēs-tē-ä'nä), Ger., Lat.

Christiano (krēs-tē-ä'nō), It., Port., Sp. Christian
Christianus (krĭs-tē-ä'nŭs), Lat. Christian
Christie (krĭs'tĭ), dim. Christian, Christopher

CHRISTINA (Christína, æ), V. M. Jul. 24. R. M.
4 Cent. Noblewoman of Bolsena who destroyed
idols of her father. Patron of millers, archers,
mariners. In art shown with millstone. Sig. Gr.
believer in Christ. Pron. krĭs-tē'ná.
Christine (krēs-tēn'), Fr. Christina
(krĭs-tēn'), Eng.
(krēs-tē'nĕ), Ger.
Christoffer (krĭs'tŏf-fĕr), Dan. Christopher
Christoph (krēs'tŏf), Ger. Christopher
Christophe (krēs-tŏf'), Fr. Christopher

CHRISTOPHER (Christóphorus, i), M. Jul. 25. R. M.
3 Cent. Asia Minor. Supposed to have carried
Christ-Child across stream on his shoulders. So
represented in art. One of Fourteen Holy Helpers.
Patron of travelers, automobilists, invoked against

hail, thunderstorms and sudden death. *Sig.*
Gr. Christ-bearer. *Pron.* krĭs'tō-fẽr.
Christophorus (krĭs-tō'fō-rŭs), Lat., Ger. Christopher
Christovão (krēs-tō-vŏwṅ), Port. Christopher
Christy (krĭs'tĭ), dim. Christian, Christopher

CHRODEGANG (Chrodegángus, i), B. C. Mar. 6.
8 Cent. Counselor of Charles Martel. 1 B. of Metz.
Sig. Teut. famed progress. *Pron.* krō'dĕ-găng.
Chrodegangus (krō-dā-gän'gŭs), Lat. Chrodegang
Chrysanthe (krē-sänt'), Fr. Chrysanthus

CHRYSANTHUS (Chrysánthus, i), M. Oct. 25. R. M.
3 Cent. Buried alive with St. Darius at Rome. *Sig.*
Gr. gold flower. *Pron.* krĭ-săn'thŭs.
(krē-sän'thŭs), Lat.
Chrysogone (krē-sō-gōn'), Fr. Chrysogonus

CHRYSOGONUS (Chrysógonus, i), Pr. M. Nov. 24.
R. M.
4 Cent. Rome. Spiritual director of St. Anastasia.
Mentioned in Canon of Mass. *Sig.* Gr. born with
gold. *Pron.* krĭ-sŏg'ŏ-nŭs.
(krē-sō'gō-nŭs), Lat.
Chrysole (krē-sōl'), Fr. Chrysolius

CHRYSOLIUS (Chrysólius, ii), B. M. Feb. 7.
4 Cent. An Armenian who labored in Gaul. *Sig.*
Gr. golden. *Pron.* krĭ-sō'lĭ-ŭs.
(krē-sō'lē-ŭs), Lat.
Chrysostom (krĭs'ŏs-tŏm), *see* St. John.
Chrysostôme (krē-sō-stōm'), Fr. Chrysostom
Cicely (sĭs'ē-lĭ), var. of Cecilia
Cilinia (sĭ-lĭn'ĭ-à), var. of Celine
(chē-lē'nē-ä), Lat.

Cilly (sĭl'lĭ), dim. Cecilia
Cipriano (chē-prē-ä'nō), It. Cyprian
  (thē-prē-ä'nō), Sp.
Ciriaco (chē-rē'ä-kō), It. Cyriacus
  (thē-rē'ä-kō), Sp.
Cirilo (thē-rē'lō), Sp. Cyril
Cirillo (chē-rēl'lō), It. Cyril
Ciro (chē'rō), It. Cyrus
  (thē'rō), Sp.
Cis (sĭs), dim. Cecilia
Cissy (sĭs'sĭ), dim. Cecilia

CLAIR (Clárus, i), M. Nov. 4. R. M.
  7 Cent. English priest, nobleman, who lived as hermit near Cherbourg. Invoked against sore eyes. *Sig.* Lat. illustrious. *Pron.* klâr.
Clair (klâr), Fr. Clair
Claire (klâr), Fr. Clare
Clara (klă'rà), var. of Clare
  (klä'rä), Lat.

CLARE OF ASSISI (Clára, æ), V. Aug. 12. R. M.
  13 Cent. Founded Poor Clares with St. Francis of Assisi. By carrying the monstrance she preserved her convent from attack by the Saracens. In art shown holding monstrance. Invoked against sore eyes. *Sig.* Lat. illustrious. *Pron.* klâr.

CLARE OF THE CROSS, V. Aug. 17 R. M.
  14 Cent. Augustinian Nun, of Montefalco, devoted to the Passion, consecrated to God from her youth. After death a crucifix was found engraved on her heart.

CLARENCE (Claréntius, ii), B. C. Apr. 26. R. M.
  7 Cent. Vienne. *Sig.* Lat. illustrious. *Pron.* klăr'ĕns.

Clarentius (klä-rĕnt′sē-ŭs), Lat. Clarence
Claribel (klă′rĭ-bĕl), dim. Clare
Clarice (klăr′ĭs), der. of Clare
   (klä-rēs′), Fr.
Clarissa (klă-rĭs′sa), der. of Clare
Clarisse (klä-rēs′), Fr. Clarissa
Clarus (klä′rŭs), Lat. Clair
Clas (kläs), Du. Nicholas

CLAUDE (Cláudius, ii), B. C. June 6. R. M.
   7 Cent. Besançon. *Sig.* Lat. lame. *Pron.* kląd.
   (klōd), Fr.

CLAUDE DE LA COLUMBIÈRE, Feb. 15 (Bl.)
   17 Cent. Jesuit, spiritual director of St. Margaret
   Mary. *Pron.* kō-lŭm-byâr′

CLAUDIA (Cláudia, æ), Wid. Aug. 7.
   1 Cent. Wife of Roman Senator Pudens, both converted by St. Peter. *Sig.* Lat. lame. *Pron.* klą′dĭ-à.
   (klŏw′dē-ä), Lat., Ger., It., Sp.

CLAUDIAN (Claudiánus, i), M. Feb. 26. R. M.
   3 Cent. Perge. *Pron.* klą′dĭ-ăn.
Claudianus (klŏw-dē-ä′nŭs), Lat. Claudian
Claudie (klō-dē′), Fr. Claudia
Claudien (klō-dē-ăṅ′), Fr. Claudian
Claudina (klą-dē′nà), var. of Claudia
Claudine (klō-dēn′), Fr. dim. Claudia
Claudio (klŏw′dē-ō), It., Sp. Claude
Claudius (klŏw′dē-ŭs), Lat. Claude
   (klą′dĭ-ŭs), Eng. var.
Claus (kläs), Du. Nicholas
Claver (klä′vĕr), *see* St. Peter
Clem (klĕm), dim. Clement
Clèmence (klä-moṅs) Fr. Clementia

Clemens (klā'mĕnz), Du., Ger., Lat. Clement

CLEMENT I (Clémens, éntis), P. M. Nov. 23. R. M.
1 Cent. Disciple of St. Peter, first of Apostolic
Fathers. Named in Canon of Mass. In art shown
with anchor. *Sig.* Lat. mild. *Pron.* klĕm'ĕnt.

CLEMENT MARY HOFBAUER, C. Mar. 15. R. M.
19 Cent. Redemptorist, glory of the clergy, Apostle
of Vienna, spread his Order in Poland, Germany
and Switzerland.

Clément (klā-mäṅ'), Fr. Clement

Clemente (klā-mĕn'tā), It., Sp. Clement

Clementia (klĕ-mĕn'shȧ), fem. Clement

Clementina (klĕm-ĕn-tē'na), var. of Clementia

Clementine (klĕm'ĕn-tēn or tĭn), var. of Clementia

Clemento (klā-mĕn'tō), It. Clement

CLEOPHAS (Cléophas, æ), M. Sept. 25. R. M.
One of the disciples who met Our Lord on the road
to Emmaus. He was put to death by Jews at the
same place. *Sig.* Gr. great glory. *Pron.* klē'ō-fȧs.
(klā'ō-fäs), Lat.

Cléophas (klā-ō-fä'), Fr. Cleophas

Clet (klā), *see* John Francis (Bl.)

CLETUS (Clétus, i), P. M. Apr. 26. R. M.
1 Cent. Third Pope. He divided Rome into parishes.
Named in Canon of Mass. *Pron.* klē'tŭs.
(klā'tŭs), Lat.

Clodoald (klō'dō-ȧld), var. of Cloud

Clodoaldus (klō-dō-äl'dŭs), Lat. Cloud

Clodoveo (klō-dō-vā'ō), Sp. var. Louis

CLOTILDA (Clotíldis, is), Q. June 3. R. M.
    6 Cent. Queen of France. *Sig.* Teut. famous battle
    maid. *Pron.* klō-tĭl'dȧ.
Clotilde (klō-tēld'), Fr. Clotilda
Clotildis (klō-tĭl'dĭs), Lat. Clotilda

CLOUD (Clodoáldus, i), Pr. C. Sept. 7. R. M.
    6 Cent. Grandson of St. Clotilda, son of King
    Clodomir of Orleans. Patron of nail-makers. In
    art holding nails in hand. *Pron.* klōō or klŏwd.
    (klōō), Fr.
Cnut (knōōt), var. Canute
Cœlestinus (chä-lĕs-tē'nŭs), Lat. Celestine
Coemgenus (kō-ĕmjä'nŭs), Lat. Kevin
Cola (kō'lä), It. cont. Nicholas
Coleta (kō-lä'tä), Lat. Colette
Coletta (kō-lĕt'tä), It. Colette

COLETTE (Coléta, æ), V. Mar. 6. R. M.
    15 Cent. Reformer of Poor Clares at Corbie, devoted
    to the Passion. Helped to end Great Schism of
    West.
    (kō-lĕt'), Fr.
Colin (kō-lăṅ'), Fr. Nicholas
    (kō'lĭn), Eng.

COLMAN (Colmánus, i), B. C. Nov. 24.
    6 Cent. Poet and musician led to piety by Sts.
    Brendan and Ita. Bishop of Cloyne. *Pron.* kŏl'-
    măn.
    Also 6 Cent., Bishop of Dromore, June 7.
Colmanus (kōl-mä'nŭs), Lat. Colman

COLUMBA (Colúmba, æ), Ab. June 9. R. M.
    6 Cent. Founder of many monasteries, notably

Iona. Bishop of Donegal, Apostle of Caledonia. *Sig.* Lat. dove. *Pron.* kŏ-lŭm′bà. (kō-lŭm′bä), Lat.

COLUMBAN (Columbánus, i), Ab. C. Nov. 21. R. M.
7 Cent. Born in Leinster, Abbot of Luxeuil, which he founded, also of Bobbio. Invoked against inundations and insanity. *Sig.* Lat. dove. *Pron.* kŏ-lŭm′băn.
Columbanus (kō-lŭm-bä′nŭs), Lat. Columban (kŏl-ŭm-bā′nus), Eng. var.
Columbino (kō-lŭm-bē′nō), It. Columbinus

COLUMBINUS (Columbínus, i), C. Aug. 12.
8 Cent. Monk at Lerins. *Sig.* Lat. dove. *Pron.* kŏl-ŭm-bī′nŭs.
(kō-lŭm-bē′nŭs), Lat.
Columbkill (kŏl′ŭm-kĭl), var. Columba.
Côme (kōm), Fr. Cosmas

COMGALL (Comgállus, i), Ab. May 10.
6 Cent. Ab. and founder of Bangor. *Pron.* kŏm′găl
Comgallus (kōm-gäl′lŭs), Lat. Comgall
Comgan (kŏm′găn), var. of Congan
Comganus (kōm-gä′nŭs), Lat. Congan

CONAN (Conánus, i), B. C. Jan. 26.
7 Cent. Sodor, Ireland. *Sig.* Celt. wisdom. *Pron.* kō′năn.
Conanus (kō-nä′nŭs), Lat. Conan.
Concepcion (kōn-thäp-thē-ōn′), Sp. Conception, in honor of Bl. Virgin
Conception (kŏn-sĕp′shŏn), in honor of Immaculate Conception, Dec. 8.

CONCESSA (Concéssa, æ), M. Apr. 8. R. M.
(d. u.) Carthage.   *Pron.* kŏn-sĕs'á.
(kŏn-chä'sä), Lat.
Concetta (kōn-chät'tä), It.   Conception
Condé (kōṅ-dā'), Fr.   Condedus

CONDEDUS (Conde'dus, i), Oct. 21.
7 Cent. English hermit who lived at Fontenelle.
(kŏn-dā'dŭs), Lat.

CONGAN (Congánus, i), Ab. Oct. 13.
8 Cent. Brother of St. Kentigern, Scotland. *Pron.*
kŏn'găn.

CONLETH (Conléthus, i), B. C. May 13
5 Cent. First Bishop of Kildare, director of St.
Bridget. *Pron.* kŏn'lĕth.
Conlethus (kōn-lā'thŭs), Lat. Conleth
Connie (kŏn'nĭ), dim. Conrad, Cornelius, Constance

CONRAD (Conrádus, i), B. C. Nov. 26. R. M.
10 Cent. Constance. *Sig.* Ger. bold in counsel, reso-
lute. *Pron.* kŏn'răd.
(kōn'rät), Ger.
Conrade (kôṅ-räd'ĕ), Fr. Conrad
Conradin (kōn-rä-dăṅ'), Fr. var. Conrad
Conrado (kōn-rä'dō), It., Sp. Conrad
Conradus (kŏn-rä'dŭs), Lat. Conrad

CONSTANCE (Constántia, æ), V. Jan. 28.
4 Cent. Daughter of Constantine the Great. *Sig.*
Lat. firm. *Pron.* kŏn'stăns.
Also V. M., companion of St. Ursula, 5 Cent. June 18.
(kōn-stäns'), Fr.
Constancia (kōn-stän'thē-ä), Sp. Constance.
Constancio (kōn-stän'thē-ō), Sp. Constant

CONSTANT (Constántius, ii), B. C. Sept. 1. R. M.
6 Cent. Aquino. *Sig.* Lat. firm. *Pron.* kŏn′stănt.
Also 2 Cent. Bishop of Perugia, M. Jan. 29. R. M.
Constantia (kŏn-stänt′sē-ä), Lat. Constance
Constantin (kŏn-stän-tăn′), Fr. Constantine
(kōn-stän-tēn′), Ger.

CONSTANTINE (Constantínus, i), M. Mar. 11. R. M.
6 Cent. Cornish prince, founder of monastery at
Carthage. *Sig.* Lat. firm. *Pron.* kŏn′stăn-tīn.
Also 2 Cent. Bishop of Perugia, M. Apr. 12. R. M.

Constantino (kōn-stän-tē′nō), It., Sp., Port. Constan-
tine
Constantinus (kŏn-stän-tē′nŭs), Lat. Constantine
Constantius (kŏn-stänt′sē-ŭs), Lat. Constant
Constanz (kōn′stänts), Ger. Constant
Constanza (kōn-stän′zä), Ger. Constance
(kōn-stän′thä), Sp.
Constanzia (kōn-stan′tsē-ä), Ger. Constance
Consuelo (kŏn-swä′lō), Sp. Blessed Virgin Mary,
Our Lady of Consolation
Cora (kô′rȧ), dim. Cordelia

CORDELIA (Córdula, æ), V. M. Oct. 22. R. M.
5 Cent. Companion of St. Ursula. *Sig.* Lat. warm-
hearted. *Pron.* kôr-dēl′yȧ.
(kôr-dä′lē-ä), Ger., Lat.
Cordelie (kôr-dä-lē′), Fr. Cordelia
Cordula (kōr′dōō-lä), Lat. Cordelia
Corneille (kôr-nāl′ or kôr-nä′yĕ), Fr. Cornelius

CORNELIA (Cornélia, æ), M. Mar. 31. R. M.
Early Church, Africa. *Sig.* Lat. horn. *Pron.* kôr-
nēl′yȧ.
(kōr-nä′lē-ä), It., Ger., Lat.

Cornélie (kôr-nā-lē′), Fr. Cornelia
Cornelio (kōr-nā′lē-ō), Du., It., Port., Sp. **Cornelius**
Cornelis (kōr-nā′lĭs), Du. Cornelius

CORNELIUS (Cornélius, ii), P. M. Sept. 16. R. M.
3 Cent. Condemned Novatians. Named in Canon
of Mass. *Sig.* Lat. horn. *Pron.* kôr-nēl′yŭs.
(kōr-nā′lē-ŭs), Lat., Ger.
Also a centurion baptized by St. Peter, and who became Bishop of Caesarea. Feb. 2. R. M.
Corney (kôr′nĭ), Ir. cont. Cornelius

CORONA (Coróna, æ), M. May 14. R. M.
2 Cent. Syrian martyred with husband, St. Victor.
Invoked in financial matters and games of chance.
Sig. Lat. crown. *Pron.* kô-rō′nà.
(kō-rō′nä), Lat.
Corradino (kōr-rä-dē′nō), It. dim. **Conrad**
Corrado (kōr-rä′dō), It. Conrad
Corsini (kôr-sē′nĭ), *see* St. Andrew
Cosimo (kō′sē-mō), It. Cosmas

COSMAS (Cósmas, æ), M. Sept. 27. R. M.
4 Cent. With brother, St. Damian, both Arab
physicians, beheaded in Cilicia under Diocletian.
Treated poor free of charge. Patrons of druggists,
physicians, bakers, dentists; invoked against
hernia and pestilence. Named in Canon of Mass.
In art shown in red robes amd round cap of doctor.
Pron. kŏz′màs.
(kŏs′mäs), Lat.

Cosme (kō′m), Fr. **Cosmos**
(kōs′mä), Sp.
Cosmo (kōs′mō), It. Cosmas
Costante (kō-stän′tä), It. Constant

Costantino (kō-stän-tē′nō), It. Constantine
Costanza (kō-stän′zä), It. Constance
  (kō-stän′thä), Sp.
Costanzo (kō-stän′zō), It. Constant
Cottolengo (kŏt-tō-lĕng′ō), *see* St. Joseph
Crépin (krä-păṅ′), Fr. Crispin
Crépinien (krä-pē-nē-ăṅ′), Fr. Crispinian
Crescence (krä-säṅs′), Fr. Crescent
Crescens (krä′shĕnz), Lat. Crescent

CRESCENT (Créscens, éntis), B. M. June 27. R. M.
  1 Cent. First Bishop of Mayence. *Sig.* Lat. growing.
  Pron. krĕ′sĕnt.
  Also disciple sent by St. Paul to preach in Galatia.
  Dec. 29.
  (krä-soṅ′), Fr.

CRESCENTIA (Crescéntia, æ), V. M. June 15. R. M.
  4 Cent. Tutor of St. Vitus, martyred with St. Modestus. *Sig.* Lat. growing. *Pron.* krĕ-sĕn′shà.
  (krä-shĕnt′sē-ä), Lat.

CRESCENTIAN (Crescentiánus, i), M. Nov. 24. R. M.
  4 Cent. Rome. *Sig.* Lat. growing. *Pron.* krĕ-sĕn′shăn.
Crescentianus (krä′shĕnt-sē-ä′nŭs), Lat. Crescentian
Crescentina (krĕ-sĕn-tē′nà), dim. Crescentia

CRESCENTINUS (Crescentínus, i), M. June 1
  3 Cent. Roman soldier who retired near Città di
  Castello as a hermit. Invoked against headache.
  Sig. Lat. growing. *Pron.* krĕ-sĕn-tī′nŭs.
  (krä-shĕn-tē′nŭs), Lat.

CRESCENTIUS (Crescéntius, ii), M. Sept. 14. R. M.
  4 Cent. Rome. Boy 11 years old beheaded for Faith.

Son of St. Enthymius. *Sig.* Lat. growing. *Pron.*
krĕ-sĕn'shŭs.

(krā-shĕnt'sē-ŭs), Lat.

Crisostomo (krē-sŏs'tō-mō), It., Sp. Chrysostom.

CRISPIN (Crispínus, i), M. Oct. 25. R. M.
   3 Cent. Shoemaker beheaded at Soissons with St.
   Crispinian. Patron of shoemakers, cobblers, har-
   ness-makers, tanners. In art shown with strips of
   leather in hands, or with awl. *Sig.* Lat. curly-
   headed. *Pron.* krĭs'pĭn.
   (krēs-păṅ'), Fr.

CRISPINA (Crispína, æ), V. M. Dec. 5. R. M.
   4 Cent. Africa. *Sig.* Lat. curly-headed. *Pron.* krĭs-
   pī'na.
   (krĭs-pē'nä), Lat.

CRISPINIAN (Crispiniánus, i), M. Oct. 25.
   3 Cent. Shoemaker beheaded at Soissons with St.
   Crispin. Patron of his trade. *Sig.* Lat. curly-
   headed. *Pron.* krĭs-pĭn'ĭ-ăn.

Crispinianus (krĭs-pĭ-nē-ä'nŭs), Lat. Crispinian
Crispino (krēs-pē'nō), It. Crispin
Crispinus (krĭs-pē'nŭs), Lat. Crispin.
Crispo (krēs'pō), It., Sp. Crispus

CRISPUS (Críspus, i), M. Oct. 4. R. M.
   1 Cent. Ruler of synagogue at Corinth baptized by
   St. Paul. *Pron.* krĭs'pŭs.
   (krēs'pŭs), Lat., Ger.

Cristiano (krē-stē-ä'nō), It., Port., Sp. Christian
Cristina (krēs-tē'nä), Sp., It. Christina
Cristinha (krēs-tēn'yä), Port. Christina
Cristobal (krēs-tō-bäl'), Sp. Christopher

Cristoforo (krēs-tō'fō-rō), It. Christopher
Cristoval (krēs-tō-väl'), Sp. Christopher

CUMGAR (Cumgárus, i), Ab. Nov. 2
  6 Cent. Son of Prince of Devon and founder of several monasteries. *Pron.* kŭm'gär.
Cumgarus (kŭm-gä'rŭs), Lat. Cumgar.
Cunegonda (kōō-nä-gōn'dä), It. Cunegunda
Cunégonde (kü-nĕ-gōnd'), Fr. Cunegunda

CUNEGUNDA (Cunegúndis, is), Emp. Mar. 3. R. M.
  11 Cent. Wife of St. Henry, Emperor of Germany. *Sig.* Teut. bold war. *Pron.* kŭ-nĕ-gŭn'dȧ.
Cunegundis (kōō-nä-gōōn'dĭs), Lat. Cunegunda
Curado (kōō-rä'dō), It. Conrad
Curé of Ars, *see* St. John Baptist Vianney

CUTHBERT (Cuthbértus, i), B. C. Mar. 20. R. M.
  7 Cent. Bishop of Lindisfarne and Durham. Wonderworker of Britain. Patron of sailors. *Sig.* A. S. noted splendor. *Pron.* kŭth'bĕrt.

CUTHBERT MAYNE (Bl.), M. Nov. 29.
  16 Cent. A converted Protestant minister. Protomartyr of English seminaries on Continent. Hanged at Cornwall.
Cuthberta (kŭth-bĕrt'ȧ), fem. Cuthbert
Cuthbertus (kŭth-bâr'tŭs), Lat. Cuthbert
Cy (sī), Cyrus
Cypriaan (sē'prē-än), Du. Cyprian

CYPRIAN (Cypriánus, i), M. Sept. 26. R. M.
  4 Cent. Converted by St. Justina and martyred with her at Nicomedia. *Sig.* Gr. of Cyprus. *Pron.* sĭp'rĭ-ăn.
  (sē-prē-äṅ'), Fr.

(tsē'prē-än), Ger.
Also 3 Cent. B. M. Sept. 16.
Carthage, apologist, writer, philosopher, named in
Canon of Mass. Invoked against pestilence.

Cypriana (sĕp-rĭ-ăn'à), fem. Cyprian
Cypriano (sē-prē-ä'nō), Port. Cyprian
Cyprianus (chē-prē-ä'nŭs), Lat. Cyprian
Cyprien (sē-prē-ăṅ'), Fr. Cyprian

CYR (Quíricus, i), M. June 16. R. M.
4 Cent. Asia Minor. Boy 3 years old martyred with
mother, St. Julitta. Also called Dominic. *Pron.*
sēr.

CYRA (Cy'ra, æ), Aug. 3. R. M.
5 Cent. Syria. Recluse devoted to severe penance
with St. Mariana. Also called Dominica. *Pron.*
sē'rà.
(chē-rä), Lat.

CYRIAC (Cyríacus, i), Dea. M. Aug. 8. R. M.
4 Cent. Rome. One of the Fourteen Holy Helpers.
Sig. Gr. lordly. *Pron.* sē'rĭ-ăk.
(chē-rē'ä-kŭs), Lat.

CYRIACA (Cyríaca, æ), Wid. M. Aug. 21.
Rome. Also var. Dominica. *Sig.* Gr. lordly. *Pron.*
sĭ-rē'ă-kà.
(chē-rē'ä-kä), Lat.
Cyriaque (sē-rē-äk'), Fr. Cyriac

CYRIL (Cyríllus, i), B. C. Jul. 7. R. M.
9 Cent. Greece. Brother of St. Methodius, with
whom he preached to Slavs of Dalmatia, Poland
and Hungary. Slav alphabet attributed to him.
Sig. Gr. lordly. *Pron.* sĭr'ĭl.

CYRIL OF ALEXANDRIA, B. C. D. Feb. 9. R. M.
4 Cent. Egyptian who wrote commentaries on Scriptures. Champion against Nestorius. Bishop of Gortyna. Champion of Divine Maternity of Blessed Virgin.

CYRIL OF JERUSALEM, B. C. D. Mar. 18. R. M.
4 Cent. Great writer, upheld Divinity of Christ against Arians.
Cyrill (tsē'rēl), Ger. Cyril.

CYRILLA (Cyrílla, æ), M. Jul. 5. R. M.
4 Cent. Aged Christian widow of Cyrene, Africa, who refused to burn incense to idols. *Sig.* Gr. lordly. *Pron.* sĭ-rĭl'á.
(chē-rēl'lä), Lat.
Cyrille (sē-rēl'or sē-rē'y'), Fr. **Cyril**
Cyrillo (sē-rēl'lō), Port. Cyril
Cyrillus (chē-rēl'lŭs), Lat. Cyril

CYRINUS (Cyrínus, i), M. June 12. R. M.
4 Cent. Roman soldier. *Pron.* sĭ-rī'nŭs.
(chē-rē'nŭs), Lat.

CYRUS (Cy'rus, i), M. Jan. 31. R. M.
4 Cent. Egyptian physician. *Sig.* Per. sun. *Pron.* sī'rŭs.
(chē'rŭs), Lat.

D

Dafrosa (dä-frō'sä), Lat. Dafrose

DAFROSE (Dafrósa, æ), M. Jan. 4. R. M.
4 Cent. Mother of Sts. Bibiana and Demetria, and wife of St. Flavian. *Pron.* dă'frōz.

DAGOBERT (Dagobértus, i), K. M. Dec. 23.
7 Cent. K. of Austrasia, patron of Stenay. *Sig.* Teut.
bright as day. *Pron.* dă'gō-bĕrt.
(dä-gō-bâr'), Fr.
Dagobertus (dä-gō-bâr'tŭs), Lat. Dagobert
Daisy (dā'zĭ), Margaret
Damascene (dă'mȧ-sēn), *see* St. John
Damase (dä-mäs'), Fr. Damasus

DAMASUS (Dámasus, i), P. C. Dec. 11. R. M.
4 Cent. Patron of St. Jerome, defined Canon of
Sacred Scriptures. *Pron.* dăm'ȧ-sŭs.
(dä'mä-sŭs), Lat.

DAMIAN (Damiánus, i), M. Sep. 27. R. M.
3 Cent. Arabian physician who with Cosmas, his
brother, treated poor without pay. Named in
Canon of Mass. In art shown with red robe and
round cap of doctor. *Sig.* Gr. taming. *Pron.*
dā'mĭ-ăn.
Damiano (dä-mē-ä'nō), It. Damian
Damianus (dä-mē-ä'nŭs), Lat. Damian
Damien (dä-myăṅ'), Fr. Damian.
Dan (dăn), dim. Daniel

DANIEL (Dániel, élis), Proph. Jul. 21. R. M.
One of four great prophets. Of tribe of Juda, taken
captive to Babylon. Also called Balthassar.
Relics at Venice. *Sig.* Heb. divine judge. *Pron.*
dăn'yĕl.
(dä'nē-āl), Ger., Lat.
(dä-nē-āl'), Fr., Sp.
Daniela (dăn-yĕl'ȧ), fem. Daniel
Daniele, Danielle (dä-nē-ä'lä), It. Daniel
Danny (dăn'nĭ), dim. Daniel
Darby (där'bĭ), Ir. Jeremiah

DARIA (Daría, æ), M. Oct. 25. R. M.
   3 Cent. Rome. Martyred with St. Chrysanthus.
   Sig. Per. preserver. *Pron.* dà-rī′à.
   (dä-rē′ä), Lat.
Darie (dä-rē′), Fr. Darius
Dario (dä′rē-ō), It. Darius

DARIUS (Daríus, ii), M. Dec. 19. R. M.
   3 Cent. with Sts. Zosimus, Paulus and Secundus.
   Sig. Per. preserver. *Pron.* dà-rī′ŭs.
   (dä-rē′ŭs), Lat.
Dave (dāv), dim. David
Davey (dā′vǐ), dim. David

DAVID (*indecl.* or Dávid, ĭdis), K. Proph. Dec. 29.
   R. M. Ancestor of Our Lord, author of psalms.
   King of Israel. Patron of poets and musicians,
   Sig. Heb. beloved. *Pron.* dā′vĭd.
   Also B. C. Mar. 1. 6 Cent. Archb. Menevia.
   Patron of Wales. In art, preaching on hill with
   dove on shoulders.
   (dä′vĕt), Du., Dan., Ger.
   (dä-vēd′), Fr.
Davida, (dā′vĭd-à), fem. David
Davide, Davidde (dä′vē-dä), It. David
Davie, Davy (dā′vǐ), dim. David

DECLAN (Declánus, i), B. C. Jul. 24.
   6 Cent. 1st. B. of Ardmore, disciple of St. Colman.
   Pron. dĕk′lăn.
Declanus (dä-klä′nŭs), Lat. Declan.
Delia (dēl′yà), dim. Cordelia. Also used for Bridget.
Delphin (dăl-făn′), Fr. Delphinus

DELPHINA (Delphína, æ), V. Dec. 9.
13 Cent. Franciscan. Wife of Charles II of Naples.
Both took vow of virginity. *Sig.* Gr. of Delphi.
Pron. dĕl-fī'nȧ.
(dĕl-fē'nä), Lat.
Delphine (dāl-fēn'), Fr. Delphina

DELPHINUS (Delphínus, i), B. C. Dec. 24. R. M.
4 Cent. Bordeaux. *Sig.* Gr. of Delphi. *Pron.* dĕl-fī'nŭs.
(dĕl-fē'nŭs), Lat.

DEMETRIA (Demétria, æ), V. M. June 21. R. M.
4 Cent. Rome. Sister of St. Bibiana, daughter of
Sts. Flavian and Dafrose. *Pron.* dĕ-mē'trĭȧ.
(dā-mä'trē-ä), Lat.
Demetrio (dā-mä'trē-ō), It., Port. Demetrius

DEMETRIUS (Demétrius, ii), M. Oct. 8. R. M.
4 Cent. Saloniki. Proconsul. *Pron.* dĕ-mē'trĭ-ŭs.
(dā-mä'trē-ŭs), Ger., Lat.
Démétrius (dā-mä-trē-üs'), Fr. Demetrius

DENIS (Diony'sius, ii), B. M. Oct. 9. R. M.
First B. of Paris, martyred with Sts. Rusticus and
Eleutherius on Montmartre in 1 or 3 Cent. Dis-
ciple of St. Paul. Invoked against headache and
rabies. In art carrying his head in his hands. *Pron.*
dĕn'ĭs.
(dĕ-nē'), Fr.
Denise (dā-nēs'), Fr. Dionysia
Dennis (dĕn'ĭs), var. of Denis
Denys (dĕ-nē'), Fr. Denis
Déodat (dā-ō-dä'), Fr. Deodatus
Deodato (dā-ō-dä'tō), It. Deodatus

DEODATUS (Deodátus, i), B. C. June 20
   7 Cent. Nevers. *Sig.* Lat. given to God. *Pron.*
   dē-ō-dā′tŭs.
   (dā-ō-dä′tŭs), Lat.

DERMOT (Diarmáda, æ), Ab. C. Jan. 10.
   6 Cent. Inis Clothrann, Longford. Also Irish for
   Jeremiah. Also called Diarmaid. *Sig.* Celt. free-
   man. *Pron.* dûr′mŏt.
Derrick (dĕr′rĭk), cor. of Theodoric.
De Sales (dē sälz), *see* St. Francis
Desiderio (dā-sē-dā′rē-ō), It. Desiderius

DESIDERIUS (Desidérius, ii), B. M. May 23. R. M.
   5 Cent. Langres. Also Didier, Dizier. *Sig.* Lat.
   beloved. *Pron.* dĕz-ĭ-dē′rĭ-ŭs.
   Also an Archdeacon of Bourges, May 8.
   (dā-sē-dā′rē-ŭs), Lat.
Désiré (dā-zē-rā′), Fr. Desiderius
Deusdedit (dā-ŭs′dĕ-dĭt), var. of Adeodatus
Di (dĭ), dim. of Diana

DIANA (Diána, æ), (Bl.), V. June 10.
   13 Cent. Dominican nun at Bologna. *Pron.* dĭ-
   ăn′á.
   (dē-ä′nä), Ger., It., Lat., Sp.
Diane (dē-än′), Fr. Diana
Diarmada (dē-är-mä′dä), Lat. Dermot.
Diarmaid (dûr′màd), Ir. Dermot
Diaz (dē′äth), Sp. Didacus
Dick (dĭk), dim. Richard
Dickie, Dicky (dĭk′ē), dim. Richard
Didace (dē-däs′), Fr. Didacus

DIDACUS (Dídacus, i), C. Nov. 13. R. M.
15 Cent. Franciscan lay brother devoted to Blessed
Sacrament and to Our Lady. *Pron.* dĭd′à-kŭs.
(dē′dä-kŭs), Lat.

Didier (dē-dyâr), Fr. Desiderius
Didyme (dē-dēm′), Fr. Didymus
Didymus (dĭd′ĭ-mŭs), *see* St. Thomas, Apostle
Dié (dē-ā′), Fr. Deodatus
Diederick (dē′dĕr-ĭk), Du. Theodoric
Diego (dē-ā′gō), Sp. James, Didacus
Diègue (dē-āg′), Fr. Didacus
Dietbold (dēt′bōlt), Ger. Theobald
Dietrich (dē′trĭk), Ger. Theodoric
Dietz (dētz), Ger. cor. Theodoric
Dieudonné (dē-ŭ-dō-nā′), Fr. Deodatus

DIGNA (Dígna, æ), V. M. Sep. 22. R. M.
3 Cent. Rome. *Sig.* Lat. worthy. *Pron.* dĭg′nà.
(dē′nyä), Lat.

Diogo (dē-ō′gō), Port. James

DIOMEDE (Diomédes, is), M. Aug. 16. R. M
4 Cent. Tarsus. Physician, zealous converter, treated
poor free. *Pron.* dĭ′ō-mēd.

Diomède (dē-ō-mād′), Fr. Diomede
(dē-ō-mā′dä), It.

Diomedes (dē-ō-mā′dāz), Lat. Diomede
(dĭ-ō-mē′dēz), Eng. var.

DION (*indecl.* or Díon, ónis), M. Jul. 6. R. M.
3 Cent. martyred at Rome with St. Lucy. Also dim.
of Dionysius. *Pron.* dĭ′ŏn.
(dē′ŏn), Lat.

DIONA (Dióna, æ), M. Mar. 14. *Pron.* dĭ-ō′nà.
(dē-ō′nä), Lat.

Dionicio (dē-ō-nē'thē-ō), Sp. Denis
Dionigi (dē-ō-nē'jē), It. Denis
Dionigio (dē-ō-nē'jō), It. Denis
Dionisia (dē-ō-nē'sē-ä), Sp. Dionysia
Dionisio (dē-ō-nē̱'sē-ō), It., Sp. Denis
Dionys (dē-ō-nēs'), Ger. Denis

DIONYSIA (Diony'sia, æ), M. Dec. 6. R. M.
  5 Cent. Burned at stake with her child at Carthage.
  Pron. dī-ō-nĭ'shà.
  (dē-ō-nē'sē-ä), Lat.
Dionysio (dē-ō-nē'sē-ō), Port., Sp. Denis

DIONYSIUS (Diony'sius, ii), B. C. Apr. 8. R. M.
  2 Cent. Corinth. *Pron.* dī-ō-nĭsh'ĭ-ŭs.
  (dē-ō-nē'sē-ŭs), Lat., Ger. Denis
Dirck (dĕrk), Du. Theodoric

DISMAS (Dísmas, æ), C. Mar. 25.
  The good thief. Patron of those condemned to death
  and of the dying. *Pron.* dĭz'màs.
Dizier (dē-zyâr'), Fr. Desiderius
Dmitri (dmē'trē), Rus. Demetrius
Dob (dŏb), dim. Robert
Dobbin (dŏb'bĭn), dim. Robert

DOCTORS OF THE CHURCH

John Chrysostom	Cyril of Jerusalem
Basil	John Damascene
Gregory Nazianzen	Ephrem
Athanasius	Leo I, the Great
Ambrose	Peter Chrysologus
Augustine	Isidore
Gregory the Great	Peter Damian
Jerome	Anselm
Cyril of Alexandria	Bernard

Bonaventure	Venerable Bede
Thomas Aquinas	John of the Cross
Hilary	Peter Canisius
Alphonsus Liguori	Robert Bellarmine
Francis de Sales	

Albert the Great (Albertus Magnus)

Dodo (dō'dō), cont. Dorothy

Dol, Doll (dŏl), **Dollie, Dolly** (dŏl'lĭ), cont. Dorothy

Dolores (dō-lō'rĕs), Blessed Virgin Mary, Our Lady of Sorrows

Dolph (dŏlf), dim. Adolph

Dolphus (dŏl'fŭs), dim. Adolphus

Domenica (dō-mä'nē-kä), It. Dominica

Domenico (dō-mä'nē-kō), It. Dominic

Domingo (dō-mēng'gō), Sp. Dominic

Domingos (dō-mēng'gōs), Port. Dominic

DOMINIC (Domínicus, i), C. Aug. 4. R. M.
12 Cent. Of noble family of Guzman, in Castille, champion against Manichaean and Albigensian heresies. Founder of Friars Preachers (Dominicans), and of Dominican nuns, and propagator of devotion to the Holy Rosary. *Sig.* Lat. belonging to the Lord. *Pron.* dŏm'ĭ-nĭk.

DOMINICA (Domínica, æ), V. M. Jul. 6. R. M.
4 Cent. Nicomedia. Condemned to wild beasts and uninjured by them, then beheaded. *Sig.* Lat. belonging to the Lord. *Pron.* dŏ-mĭn'ĭ-kȧ.
(dō-mē'nē-kä), Lat.

Dominicus (dō-mē'nē-kŭs), Lat. Dominic

Dominique (dō-mē-nēk'), Fr. Dominic

DOMITIAN (Domitiánus, i), B. C. Aug. 9. R. M.
4 Cent. Third Bishop of Chalons, zealous in converting the heathen. *Pron.* dō-mĭsh'ĭ-ăn.

Domitianus (dō-mēt-sē-ä'nŭs), Lat. Domitian
Domitien (dō-mē-sē-ăṅ'), Fr. Domitian

DOMITILLA (Domitílla, æ), V. M. May 12
1 Cent. Niece of Emperors Domitian and Titus.
Pron. dŏm-ĭ-tĭl'là.
(dō-mē-tĭl'lä), Lat.
Domitille (dō-mē-tēl'lĕ), Fr. Domitilla

DOMNA (Dómna, æ), V. M. Dec. 28. R. M.
5 Cent. Irish Saint, lived as hermit near Glastonbury, Eng. *Pron.* dŏm'nà.
(dŏm'nä), Lat.

DONALD (Donáldus, i), C. Jul. 15.
8 Cent. Ogilvy, Scotland. Led life of religious with
nine daughters. Also called Donewald. *Sig.* Celt.
proud chief. *Pron.* dŏn'ăld.
Donaldus (dō-näl'dŭs), Lat. Donald
Donat (dōnä'), Fr. Donatus

DONATA (Donáta, æ), M. Dec. 31. R. M.
(d.u.) Rome. *Sig.* Lat. given. *Pron.* dō-nä'tà.
(dō-nä'tä), Lat.
Donato (dō-nä'tō), It. Donatus.

DONATUS (Donátus, i), B. M. Aug. 7. R. M.
4 Cent. Arezzo. *Sig.* Lat. given. *Pron.* dō-nä'tŭs.
(dō-nä'tŭs), Lat.
Also 9 Cent. Irishman, teacher and poet, Bishop of
Fiesole. Oct. 22.
Donewald (dŏn'ĕ-wäld), var. of Donald
Donnie, Donny (dŏn'nĭ), dim. Donald
Dora (dō'rà), dim. Dorothy, Theodora

DORCAS (Dor'cas, ădis), Wid. Oct. 25.
Woman raised to life by St. Peter at Joppe. Also
called Tabitha. *Sig.* Gr. gazelle. *Pron.* dôr'kăs.
(dōr'käs), Lat.
Dorette (dō-rĕt'), Fr. dim. Dorothy
Dorinda (dō-rĭn'dȧ), dim. Dorothy, Theodora
Doris (dō'rĭs), dim. Dorothy, Theodora
Dorotea (dō-rō-tā'ä), It., Port., Sp. Dorothy
Dorothea (dō-rō'thä-ä), Lat. Dorothy
(dō-rō-thē'ȧ), Eng. var.
(dō-rō-thä'ä), Gr.
Dorothée (dō-rō-tā'), Fr. Dorothy

DOROTHEUS (Dorótheus, i), M. June 5. R. M.
4 Cent. Priest of Tyre. *Sig.* Gr. gift of God. *Pron.*
dō-rō'thē-ŭs.
(dō-rō'thä-ŭs), Lat.

DOROTHY (Doróthea, æ), V. M. Feb. 6. R. M.
4 Cent. Young woman racked, scourged and beheaded at Cappadocia. In art with basket of fruit
and flowers. Patron of gardeners. *Sig.* Lat. gift of
God. *Pron.* dôr'ŏ-thǐ.
Dot (dŏt), dim. Dorothy
Drosis (drō'sĭs), var. Drusilla

DRUSILLA (Drusĭlla, æ), V. M. Sept. 22.
(d. u.) Antioch. *Sig.* Lat. strong. *Pron.* drū-sĭl'lȧ.
(drōō-sĭl'lä), Lat.
Drusille (drōō-zĭl'lĕ), Du., Ger. Drusilla
(drü-zēl'), Fr.
Duarte (dōō-är'tä), Port. Edward

DUBRITIUS (Dubrĭtius, ii), B. C. Nov. 14.
5 Cent. Founder of monachism in Wales. B. of

Llandaff. *Pron.* dŭ-brĭ′shĭ-ŭs.
(dōō-brēt′sē-ŭs), Lat.

DUNSTAN (Dunstánus, i), B. C. May 19. R. M.
10 Cent. First Bishop of Glastonbury, B. of Worcester and of Canterbury, adviser of King Edgar. Patron of goldsmiths, locksmiths, armorers, blacksmiths and musicians. In art seizing devil with pincers, or playing on harp. *Sig.* Teut. hill stone. *Pron.* dŭn′stăn.
Dunstanus (dŭn-stä′nŭs), Lat. Dunstan

DUTHAC (Duthacus, i), B. C. Mar. 8
11 Cent. Scotch Bishop of Ross.
Duthacus (dōō-thä-kŭs), Lat. Duthac
Dy (dī), dim. Diana
Dymphe (dănf), Fr. Dymphna

DYMPHNA (Dymp′na, æ), V. M. May 15. R. M.
6 Cent. Daughter of pagan Irish king who fled to Belgium. In art shown dragging away a demon. Patron of insane. *Pron.* dĭmf′nȧ.
Dympna (dĭmp′nä), Lat. and Eng. Dymphna.

E

Eadmundus (ā-ärd-mŭn′dŭs), Lat. var. Edmund
Eamon (ā-mŭn), Ir. Edmund
Eberardo (ā-bä-rär′dō), It. Everard
Eberhard (ā′bĕr-härt), Ger., Du. Everard
Ebert (ā′bĕrt), Ger. Everard
Eckbert (ĕk′bĕrt), Ger. Egbert
Ed (ĕd), dim. Edward, Edwin, etc.
Eddie, Eddy (ĕd′dĭ), dim. Edward, Edwin, etc.
Edelburga (ĕd′ĕl-bûr-gȧ), var. Ethelburga.
Edeline (ā-dĕ-lēn′ē), Ger. var. Adeline

EDGAR (Edgárus, i) (Bl.), K. May 24. Jul. 8.
    10 Cent. King of Anglo-Saxons, called "The Peace-
    ful." *Sig.* A. S. protector. *Pron.* ĕd'găr.
    (ĕt'gär), Ger.
Edgard (ād-gär'), Fr. Edgar
Edgardo (ĕd-gär'dō), It. Edgar
Edgaro (ĕd-gä'rō), It. var. Edgar
Edgarus (ĕd-gä'rŭs), Lat. Edgar
Edilburga (ĕ-dĭl-boōr'gà), Lat. Edelburga
Ediltrude (ĕd'ĭl-trūd), var. Etheldreda
Edita (ā'dē-tä), It. Edith

EDITH (Edítha, æ), V. Sept. 16. R. M.
    10 Cent. Nun at Wilton, daughter of K. Edgar, cared
    for sick and poor, especially lepers. *Sig.* A. S. happi-
    ness. *Pron.* ē'dĭth.
Editha (ā-dē'thä), Lat. Edith
Edmond (ād-mōn'), Fr. Edmund
    (ĕt'mŏnt), Du.
Edmondo (ĕd-mōn'dō), It., Sp. Edmund

EDMUND (Edmúndus, i), K. M. Nov. 20. R. M.
    9 Cent. King of East Angles. In art shown crowned,
    with arrow in hand. *Sig.* A. S. defender. *Pron.*
    ĕd'mŭnd.
    (ĕt'moŏnt), Ger.

EDMUND CAMPION (Bl.), M. Dec. 1.
    16 Cent. Studied at Oxford and Douai, became a
    Jesuit. Known as "Pope's Champion." Hanged
    at Tyburn under Elizabeth.

EDMUND RICH, B. C. Nov. 16. R. M.
    13 Cent. Archb. Canterbury; defender of rights of
    Church against Henry VIII; murdered by Danes.

Ẹdmunda (ĕd-mŭn'dả), fem. Edmund
Ẹdmundo (ĕd-mŏon'dō), Sp., Port. Edmund
Edmundus (ĕd-mŭn'dŭs), Lat. Edmund
Edna (ĕd'nả), var. Edwina
Edoardo (ā-dō-är'dō), It. Edward
Édouard (ā-dōo-är'), Fr. Edward
Eduard (ā'dōo-ärt), Du., Dan., Ger., Sw. Edward
Eduardo (ā-dōo-är'dō), It., Port., Sp. Edward
Eduardus (ā-dōo-är'dŭs), Lat. Edward
Eduino (ā-dōo-ē'nō), It. Edwin
Eduvigis (ā-dōo-vē'jĭs), Lat. Hedwig
Edwald (ĕd'wăld), var. Ewald

EDWARD THE CONFESSOR (Eduárdus, i), K. C.
   Oct. 13. R. M.
   11 Cent. King of England. Noted for liberality to
   poor and stainless purity. In art giving scroll to
   kneeling cleric. *Sig.* A. S. guardian. *Pron.* ĕd'wärd.
   Also the martyr, son of K. Edgar, 10 Cent. Mar. 18.
Edwarda (ĕd-wärd'ả), fem. Edward
Edwardine (ĕd-wär-dēn'), fem. Edward

EDWIN (Edwínus, i), K. M. Oct. 12.
   6 Cent. First Christian King of Northumbria, husband of St. Ethelburga. *Sig.* A. S. gainer of prop-
   erty. *Pron.* ĕd'wĭn.
   (ĕt'vĭn), Ger.
Edwina (ĕd-wē'nả), fem. Edwin
Edwinus (ĕd-wē'nŭs), Lat. Edwin
Effie (ĕf'fē), dim. Euphemia

EGBERT (Egbértus, i), C. Apr. 24. R. M.
   8 Cent. English monk, led life of prayer and penance
   at Iona. *Sig.* A. S. famous with sword. *Pron.*
   ĕg'bērt.

Egberto (ĕg-bĕr'tō), It., Port. Egbert
Egbertus (ĕg-bĕr'tŭs), Lat. Egbert
Égide (ā-zhĕd'), Fr. Giles
Egidia (ĕ-jĭd'ĭà), fem. Giles
Egidio (ā-jē'dē-ō), It. Giles
Egidius (ā-jē'dē-ŭs), Du. Ger., Lat. Giles

EGWIN (Egwínus, i), B. C. Dec. 30.
 8 Cent. Founder of Evesham Abbey, B. of Worcester. *Pron.* ĕg'wĭn.
Egwina (ĕg-wē'nà), fem. Egwin
Egwinus (ĕg-wē'nŭs), Lat. Egwin
Eileen (ī-lēn'), Ir. Helen
Eirene (ī-rēn'), var. Irene
Ekaterina (ā-kä-tä-rē'nä), Rus. Catherine
Elaine (ā-lān'), Fr. Helen
Elbert (ĕl'bērt), var. Albert
Elbertus (ĕl-bēr'tŭs), Lat. Elbert
Eldred (ĕl'drĕd), var. Aelred
Eleanor (ĕl'ē-à-nôr), var. Helen or Eleonor
Eleanora (ā-lā-ō-nō'rä), It. Eleanor

ELEAZAR (*indecl.*), M. Aug. 1
 2 B. C. One of Machabees, a chief of scribes. *Sig.* Heb. the Lord's help. *Pron.* ĕl-ē-ā'zär.

ELECTA (Elécta, æ), V. M. Aug. 1
 (d. u.) Wales. *Sig.* Lat. chosen. *Pron.* ĕ-lĕk'tà. (ā-lĕk'tä), Lat.

ELEGIUS (Elégius, ii), B. C. Dec. 1. R. M.
 7 Cent. Noyon. Counselor of Kings of Franks, skilled metal-worker and hence their patron. *Pron.* ĕ-lē'jĭ-ŭs. (ā-lā'jē-ŭs), Lat.
Elena (ā-lā'nä), It., Sp. Helen

ELEONOR (Eleonóra, æ), V. M. Aug. 16. *Sig.* Gr. light.
  Pron. ĕ'lē-ŏ-nôr.
Eleonora (ā-lā-ō-nō'rä), Lat. Eleonor
Eleonore (ā-lā-ō-nō'rĕ), Dan., Ger. Eleonor
Éléonore (ā-lā-ō-nōr'), Fr. Eleonor
Éleuthère (ā-lü-thâr'), Fr. Eleutherius

ELEUTHERIUS (Eleuthérius, ii), P. M. May 26. R. M.
  2 Cent. Condemned Montanist heretics. Sent mis-
  sioners to England. *Sig.* Gr. free. *Pron.* ĕ-lū-thē'-
  rĭ-ŭs.
  (ā-lōō-thā'rē-ŭs), Lat.
  Also 1 or 3 Cent. deacon martyred with St. Denis of
  Paris. Oct. 9.

ELFRIDA (Elfrída, æ), V. M. Dec. 8.
  9 Cent. Caestre, France. *Sig.* Teut. elf-threatener.
  Pron. ĕl-frē'dà.
  (äl-frē'dä), Lat.
Eli (ē'lĭ), dim. Elias.
Elia (ā-lē'ä), It. Elias

ELIAS (Elías, æ), Proph. Jul. 20. R. M.
  8 B. C. Taken to heaven in chariot from Mt. Carmel.
  Works related in III and IV Kings. To reappear
  and die at the end of time. Venerated by Carmel-
  ites as their founder. *Sig.* Heb. Jehovah is my
  God. *Pron.* ē-lī'ăs.
  (ā-lē'äs), Du., Ger. Lat.
Élie (ā-lē'), Fr. Elias
Eligius (ĕ-lē'jĕ-ŭs), Lat. and Eng. var. Elegius
Elijah (ē-lī'jà), var. Elias
Elinor (ĕl'ĭ-nôr), var. Helen
Elisa (ā-lē'sä), Du., Dan., Ger., It. Elizabeth
Elisabeth (ĕ-lĭz'à-bĕth), var. Elizabeth
  (ā-lē'zä-bĕt), Ger.

Élisabeth (ā-lē-zä-bĕt'), Fr. Elizabeth
Elisabetta (ā-lē-sä-bĕt'tä), It. Elizabeth
Élise (ā-lēz'), Fr. Elizabeth
Elise (ā-lē'zĕ), Ger. Elizabeth
Élisée (ā-lē-zā'), Fr. Eliseus
Eliseo (ā-lē-sā'ō), It., Sp. Eliseus

ELISEUS (Eliséus, i), Proph. June 14. R. M.
    8 B. C. Received at Samaria mantle of Elias, whom
    he succeeded. Works related in IV Kings. *Sig.*
    Heb. God is my salvation. *Pron.* ĕ-lĭ-sē'ŭs.
    (ā-lē-sā'ŭs), Lat.
Elisha (ē-lī'shá), var. Eliseus
Eliza (ĕ-lī'zá), var. Elizabeth

ELIZABETH (*indecl.* or Elizabétha, æ), Wid. Nov.
    5. R. M.
    Mother of St. John the Baptist and wife of St.
    Zachary. *Sig.* Heb. worshiper of God. *Pron.* ĕ-lĭz'-
    á-bĕth.

ELIZABETH OF HUNGARY, Wid. Nov. 19. R. M.
    13 Cent. Daughter of K. of Hungary, Duchess of
    Thuringia. Entered Third Order of St. Francis,
    of which she is patron. In art shown with lap full
    of bread and roses.

ELIZABETH OF PORTUGAL, Wid. Jul. 8. R. M.
    14 Cent. Queen of Portugal, niece of St. Elizabeth
    of Hungary. Led mortified life at court, and
    joined Third Order of St. Francis.
Élizabeth (ā-lē-zä-bĕt'), Fr. Elizabeth
Elizabetha (ā-lē-zä-bā'thä), Lat. Elizabeth
Ella (ĕl'á), dim. Helen
Ellen (ĕl'lĕn), dim. Helen

Ellick (ĕl'lĭk), dim. Alexander
Ellis (ĕl'ĭs), var. Eliseus

ELMER (Ermélius, ii), B. C. Aug. 25
    (d. u.), Mohaing, France. *Sig.* A. S. noble. *Pron.*
    ĕl'mēr.
Elmo (ĕl'mō), var. Erasmus or Peter Gonzales
Eloi (āl-wä'), Fr. Elegius
Eloïsa (ā-lō-ē'sä), It. Louise
Eloy (āl-wä'), Fr. Elegius

ELPHEGE (Elphégus, i), B. M. Apr. 19. R. M.
    11 Cent. Ab. Bath, Archb. Canterbury. *Pron.*
    ĕl'fĕ-jē.
Elphège (ĕl-fāzh'), Fr. Elphege
Elphegus (ĕl-fā'gŭs), Lat. Elphege
Elsa (ĕl'sä), Sw. Alice
Else (ĕl'sā), Dan., Ger. Alice
Elsie (ĕl'sē), dim. Adelaide, Elizabeth, Alice
Elsje (ĕls'yā), Du. Alice
Ema (ā'mä), Sp. Emma
Emanuel (ā-mä'nōō-āl), Ger. Emmanuel
Emanuele (ā-mä-nōō-ā'lā), It. Emmanuel
Emelda (ĕ-mĕl'dà), var. Imelda

EMERENTIANA (Emerentiána, æ), V. M. Jan. 23.
    R. M.
    4 Cent. Rome. Foster-sister of St. Agnes, stoned
    to death. *Sig.* Lat. deserving. *Pron.* ĕ-mĕ-rĕn-
    sĭ-ăn'à.
    (ā-mā-rĕnt-sē-ä'nä), Lat.
Emérentienne (ā-mā-rŏn-tyĕn'), Fr. Emerentiana
Émeri (ām-rē'), Fr. Emeric

EMERIC (Emerícus, i), C. Nov. 4. R. M.
11 Cent. Son of St. Stephen of Hungary, died in youth. *Sig.* A. S. powerful, rich. *Pron.* ĕm'ĕ-rĭk.
Émeric (ăm-rēk'), Fr. Emeric
Emericus (ā-mā-rē'kŭs), Lat. Emeric
Emery (ĕm'ĕ-rē), var. Emeric
Emidius (ĕ-mĭ'dĭ-ŭs), var. Emigdius

EMIGDIUS (Emyg'dius, ii), B. M. Aug. 5. R. M.
4 Cent. German B. of Ancona. *Pron.* ĕ-mĭg'dĭ-ŭs.

EMIL (Aemílius, ii), M. May 28. R. M.
(d. u.). With Sts. Felix, Priamus and Lucian. *Sig.* Gr. mild. *Pron.* ā'mēl.
Émile (ā-mēl'), Fr. Emil
Emilia (ā-mē'lē-ä), It., Port., Sp. Emily
Emiliana (ĕ-mĭl-ĭ-ăn'ä), fem. Emil
Émilie (ā-mē-lē'), Fr. Emily
Emilie (ā-mē'lē-ē), Ger. Emily
Émilien (ā-mēl-yăṅ'), Fr. Aemilian
Emilina (ĕm-ĭ-lĭn'ä), dim. Emma
Emiline (ĕm'ĭ-lĭn), dim. Emma
Emilio (ā-mē'lē-ō), It., Sp. Aemilian
Emilius (ā-mē'lē-ŭs), Lat. Emil
Emily (ĕm'ĭ-lĭ), var. Emma
Emm (ĕm), dim. Emma

EMMA (Émma, æ), Mat. June 17
11 Cent. Gurk. *Sig.* Ger. energetic, industrious. *Pron.* ĕm'mà.
(ăm-mä'), Fr.
(ā'mä), It., Lat., Ger.

EMMANUEL (Emmánuel, élis), M. Mar. 26. R. M.
(d. u.) Anatolia. With St. Quadratus. *Sig.* Heb. God with us. *Pron.* ĕm-măn'ū-ĕl. Also name applied to Christ.
(ā-mä-nü-ĕl'), Fr.
(ā-mä'nōō-āl), Lat.

Emmanuela (ĕm-mă-nū-ĕl′á), fem. Emmanuel
Emmanuele (ĕm-mä-nōō-ä′lä), It. Emmanuel
Emmelia (ĕm-mēl′yá), var. Emma
Emmeline (ĕm′ĕ-līn), var. Emma
Emmeri (äm-mä-rē′), Fr. Emeric
Emmerich (äm′mä-rĭk), Ger. Emeric
Emmerik (ĕm′mĕ-rĭk), Sw. Emeric
Emmery (ĕm′mĕ-rĭ), var. Emery
Emmie (ĕm′mĭ), dim. Emma
Emory (ĕm′ŏ-rĭ), var. Emery
Encratia (ĕn-crā′shĭ-á), var. Engratia
Encratis (ĕn-krä′tĭs), Lat. Engratia

ENDA (Éndeus, i), Ab. Mar. 21.
 5 Cent. Galway. Teacher of Sts. Brendan, Kieran,
 Finian and Kevin. *Pron.* ĕn′dá.
Endeus (ĕn′dä-ŭs), Lat. Enda
Engelbert (ĕng′gĕl-bērt), var. Englebert.
Engelbertus (än-gĕl-bēr′tŭs), Lat. Englebert
Engleberta (ĕng-g′l-bērt′á), fem. Englebert

ENGLEBERT (Engelbértus, i), B. M. Nov. 7. R. M.
 13 Cent. First B. of Cologne. *Sig.* Teut. bright angel.
 Pron. ĕn′g′l-bērt.
Engracia (ĕn-grä′thē-ä), Sp. Engratia

ENGRATIA (Encrátis, átidis), V. M. Apr. 16.
 4 Cent. Saragossa. In art shown tied to wheel or
 nailed through forehead. Also called Grace. *Sig.*
 Lat. grace. *Pron.* ĕn-grä′shĭ-á.
Engus (ĕng′gŭs), var. Angus

ENNA (Énnius, ii), B. C. Feb. 26.
 6 Cent. Clonfert. Also used for Enda. *Pron.* ĕn′ná.

Ennan (ĕn'năn), var. Adamnan
Ennius (ĕn'nē-ŭs), Lat. Enna

ENOCH (Enóchus, i), Pat. Jan. 22.
　Old Testament character, father of Methusala. For
　his piety he was "transferred" from the earth.
　Sig. Heb. consecrated. *Pron.* ē'nŏk.
Énoch (ā-nōk'), Fr. Enoch
Enochus (ā-nō'kŭs), Lat. Enoch
Enrichetta (än-rē-kĕt'tä), It. Henrietta
Enrico (ĕn-rē'kō), It. Henry
Enricus (ĕn-rē'kŭs), Lat. Henry
Enrighetta (än-rē-gät'tä), It. Henrietta
Enrique (ĕn-rē'kä), Sp., Port. Henry
Enriqueta (ĕn-rē-kä'tä), Sp. Henrietta

EPAPHRAS (Epáphras, æ), C. Jul. 19. R. M.
　1 Cent. Imprisoned with St. Paul. *Pron.* ē-păf'räs.
　(ā-päf'räs), Lat.
Ephraem (ē'frä-ĕm), var. Ephrem
Ephraim (ē'frä-ĭm), var. Ephrem.
Éphraim (ā-frä-ēm'), Fr. Ephrem

EPHREM (*indecl.*), Dea. C. D. June 18. R. M.
　4 Cent. Mesopotamia. Called "the Syrian," Father
　of the Church, poet, orator, hymn-writer, called
　the "sun of the Syrians," "Harp of the Holy
　Ghost."   Proclaimed Doctor by Benedict XV.
　Sig. Heb. very fruitful. *Pron.* ĕf'rĕm.

EPIMACHUS (Epímachus, i), M. Dec. 12, May 10.
　R. M.
　3 Cent. Alexandria. *Pron.* ĕ-pĭ'mä-kŭs.
　(ĕ-pē'mä-kŭs), Lat.
Épimaque (ä-pē-mäk'), Fr. Epimachus
Épiphane (ĕ-pē-fän'), Fr. Epiphanius

EPIPHANIUS (Epiphánius, ii), B. C. May 12. R. M.
4 Cent. Salamis, Eastern Father, linguist, writer
against heretics. *Sig.* Gr. manifestation. *Pron.*
ĕ-pĭ-fä'nĭ-ŭs.
(ĕ-pē-fä'nē-ŭs), Lat.

ERASMA (Erásma, æ), V. M. Sept. 3. R. M.
1 Cent. martyred at Aquileia with Sts. Euphemia,
Dorothy and Thecla. *Sig.* Gr. lovely. *Pron.*
ē-răz'mà.
(ā-räz'mä), Lat.
Érasme (ā-rä'sm'), Fr. Erasmus
Erasmo (ā-räs'mō), It., Sp., Port. Erasmus
Erasmos (ā-räs-mŏs'), Gr. Erasmus

ERASMUS (Erásmus, i), B. M. June 2. R. M.
4 Cent. Syria. One of Fourteen Holy Helpers, named
in Canon of Mass. Also called Elmo; patron of
sailors, women in labor, and invoked against
colic, cramps and intestinal troubles. In art shown
holding windlass. *Sig.* Gr. lovely. *Pron.* ē-răz'mŭs.
(ā-räz'mŭs), Lat., Du., Ger.
Éraste (ā-räst'), Fr. Erastus
Erastos (ā-räs-tŏs'), Gr. Erastus

ERASTUS (Erástus, i), B. M. Jul. 26. R. M.
1 Cent. Convert and companion of St. Paul. *Sig.*
Gr. lovely. *Pron.* ē-räs'tŭs.
(ā-räs'tŭs), Lat.
Erberto (ĕr-bēr'tō), It. Herbert
Erconvaldus (ĕr-kŏn-väl'dŭs), Lat. var. Erkonwald
Erconwald (ēr'kŏn-wạld), var. Erkonwald
Erconwaldus (ēr-kŏn-wäl'dŭs), Lat. Erkonwald

ERHARD (Erhárdus, i), B. C. Jan. 8. R. M.
8 Cent. Ratisbon. *Pron.* âr′härd.
Erhardus (ēr-här′dŭs), Lat. Erhard

ERIC (Eri′cus, i), K. M. May 18. R. M.
12 Cent. K. of Sweden, Apostle of Finland. *Sig.*
A. S. rich, brave. *Pron.* ĕ′rĭk.
Erica (ĕ′rĭk-à), fem. Eric
Ericus (ā-rē′kŭs), Lat. Eric
Erkenwald (ēr′kĕn-wäld), var. Erkonwald

ERKONWALD (Erconwáldus, i), B. C. Apr. 30. Nov.
14. R. M.
7 Cent. Prince of East Anglia, B. of London. Also
called Archibald. *Sig.* Teut. holy prince. *Pron.*
ēr′kŏn-wäld.
Ermano, Ermanno (ēr-mä′nō), It. Herman
Erme (ärm), Fr. Herman

ERMELINDA (Ermelíndis, is), Q. Ab. Feb. 13.
7 Cent. Ely. Daughter of K. Erconbert and St.
Sexburga, mother of St. Wereburga. *Sig.* Teut.
world serpent. *Pron.* ēr-mĕ-lĭn′dà.
Ermelindis (ēr-mä-lĭn′dĭs), Lat. Ermelinda
Ermelius (ēr-mä′lē-ŭs), Lat. Elmer

ERMIN (Ermínus, i), B. Ab. Apr. 25. R. M.
8 Cent. Laon. Ab. of Lobbes. *Sig.* Lat. lordly. *Pron.*
ĕr′mĭn.
Erminilda (ēr-mĭn-ĭl′dà), var. Ermelinda
Erminus (ēr-mē′nŭs), Lat. Ermin
Ermo (ēr′mō), It. Erasmus
Erna (ēr′nà), dim. Ernestine

ERNEST (Ernéstus, i), M. Nov. 7.
12 Cent. Missionary in Asia, martyred at Mecca.

Sig. Ger. earnest. *Pron.* ẽr'nĕst.
(ẽr-nãst'), Fr.
Ernestina (ẽr-nĕs-tẽ'nȧ), fem. Ernest
Ernestine (ẽr'nĕs-tēn), fem. Ernest
Ernesto (ẽr-nĕs'tō), It., Port. Sp. Ernest
Ernestus (ẽr-nĕs'tŭs), Lat. Ernest
Ernie (ẽr'nē), dim. Ernest, Ernestine
Ernst (ĕrnst), Du., Ger., Sw. Ernest
Errico (ĕr-rẽ'kō), It. Henry
Esaias (ā-zä'ē-äs), Du., Ger. Isaias
(ā-sī'äs), Dan.

ESDRAS (Ésdras, æ), Proph. Jul. 13. R. M.
6 B. C. Wrote several books of Old Testament. *Sig.*
Heb. help. *Pron.* ĕz'drȧs.
(ĕs-dräs'), Fr.
Esme (ĕs'mē), var. Osmund
Esperance (ā-spä-räṅs'), Fr. Hope
Esperanza (ā-spä-rän'thä), Sp. Hope
Essie (ĕs'sē), dim. Esther, Estelle
Estacio (ā-stä'sē-ō), Port. Eustace
Estéban (ĕs-tä'bän), Sp. Stephen
Estella (ĕs-tĕl'yȧ), Sp. Eustella
Ester (ĕs-tär'), Sp. Esther
(ĕs'tĕr), It.
Esterre (ĕs-tĕr'rä), It. Esther
Estevan (ĕs-tä-vän'), Sp. Stephen
Estevão (ĕs-stä-vŏwṅ'), Port. Stephen.

ESTHER (*indecl.*), Dec. 20.
Old Testament. Jewish exile in Persia chosen by K.
Assuerus to be his wife. She saved her people from
slaughter, hence Jewish feast of Purim. Also
called Hadassa. *Sig.* Per. star. *Pron.* ĕs'tĕr.
(ās-târ'), Fr.

Estienne (ā-tē-ĕn′), Fr. var. Stephen
Estie, Esty (ĕs′tē), dim. Esther, Eustella
Ethel (ĕth′ĕl), cont. Etheldreda, etc.

ETHELBERT (Ethelbértus, i), K. C. Feb. 24.
 7 Cent. First Christian Anglo-Saxon king. K. of
 Kent. Also called Albert. *Sig.* Ger. noble lord.
 Pron. ĕth′ĕl-bērt.
Ethelberta (ĕth′ĕl-bērt-à), fem. Ethelbert
Ethelbertus (ā-thĕl-bâr′tŭs), Lat. Ethelbert

ETHELBURGA (Ethelbúrga, ae or Edilbúrga, ae), V.
 Jul. 7. R. M.
 7 Cent. Daughter of King of East Angles. Ab. of
 Faremousties. Also called Edilburga. *Sig.* Teut.
 noble protection. *Pron.* ĕth′ĕl-bēr-gà.
(ā-thĕl-boōr′gä), Lat.

ETHELDREDA (Etheldréda, æ), V. June 23
 7 Cent. Ab. of Ely. Also called Ediltrude, Audrey.
 Sig. Teut. noble threatener. *Pron.* ĕth′ĕl-drĕd-à.
(ā-thĕl-drä′dä), Lat.

ETHELRED (Ethelrédus, i), K. May 4
 8 Cent. King of Mercia. Resigned and became Ab.
 of Bardney. *Sig.* Teut. noble council. *Pron.*
 ĕth′ĕl-rĕd.
Ethelreda (ĕth′ĕl-rĕd-à), var. Etheldreda
Ethelredus (ĕ-thĕl-rä′dŭs), Lat. Ethelred

ETHNA, ETHNEA, V. Jan. 11
 Daughter of K. of Ireland, converted by St. Patrick.
 She died after her first Communion.
Étienne (ā-tē-ĕn′), Fr. Stephen
Etta (ĕt′tà), cont. Henrietta
Etto (ĕt′tō), Ger. cont. Everard

Eucario (ū-kä′rē-ō), It. Eucharius
Euchaire (ŭh-shâr′), Fr. Eucharius
Euchar (oi-kär′), Ger. Eucharius
Euchario (ū-kä′rē-ō), Port., Sp. Eucharius

EUCHARIUS (Euchárius, ii), B. C. Dec. 8. R. M.
  1 Cent. Treves. *Sig.* Gr. happy hand. *Pron.* ū-kā′-
  rĭ-ŭs.
  (ū-kä′rē-ŭs), Lat.
Eucheria (ū-kĕ-rĭ-à), fem. Eucherius

EUCHERIUS (Euchérius, ii), B. C. Feb. 20. R. M.
  8 Cent. Orleans. *Sig.* Gr. happy hand. *Pron.* ū-kĕ′-
  rĭ-ŭs.
  (ū-kä′-rē-ŭs), Lat.

Eudes (ēd or ūdz), *see* St. John.
Eudocia (ū-dō′chē-ä), Lat. Eudoxia
  (ū-dō′shi-à), Eng. var.

EUDOXIA (Eudócia, æ), M. Mar. 1. R. M.
  1 Cent. Heliopolis. *Sig.* Gr. approval. *Pron.* ū-dŏks′ĭ-à
  (ū-dōk′sē-ä), Lat. var.
Eufemia (ū-fä′mē-ä), It., Sp. Euphemia
Eufrosina (ū-frō′sē-nä), Sp. Euphrosyna
Eufrosine (ū-frŏs′ĭ-nà), var. Euphrosyna
Eugen (oi-gān′), Du., Ger. Eugene

EUGENE (Eugénius, ii), B. C. Aug. 23
  7 Cent. Ab. Wicklow, B. Kerry. *Sig.* Gr. well born,
  noble. *Pron.* ū-jēn′ or ū′jēn.

EUGENE I, P. C. June 2. R. M. 7 Cent.
Eugène (ŭh-zhān′), Fr. Eugene

EUGENIA (Eugénia, æ), V. M. Dec. 25. R. M.
  3 Cent. Rome. Convert of Sts. Proclus and Hya-

cinth. *Sig.* Gr. well born, noble. *Pron.* ū-jēn'ĭ-à.
(ū-jā'nē-ä), It.
(ū-hā'nē-ä), Sp.
(oi-gā'nē-ä), Ger.
(ū-gā'nē-ä), Gr.
Eugenie (ū-jē'nē), var. Eugenia
Eugénie (ŭh-zhā-nē'), Fr. Eugenia
Eugenio (ū-jā'nē-ō), It. Eugene
(ū-hā'nē-ō), Sp.
(ū-zhā'nē-ō), Port.
Eugenios (ū-gā'nē-ŏs), Gr. Eugene
Eugenius (ū-jā'nē-ŭs), Lat. Eugene
(oi-gā'nē-ŭs), Ger.
(ū-jē'nĭ-ŭs), Eng. var.

EULALIA (Eulália, æ), V. M. Feb. 12. R. M.
4 Cent. While burning at stake, dove issued from
mouth and snow fell on her ashes. Patron of
Barcelona. Invoked against draught. *Sig.* Gr. fair
speech. *Pron.* ū-lā'lĭ-à.
(ū-lä'lē-ä), Lat.
Eulalie (ŭh-lä-lē'), Fr. Eulalia
Euloge (ŭh-lōzh'), Fr. Eulogius

EULOGIUS (Eulógius, ii), Pr. M. Mar. 11. R. M.
4 Cent. Martyred at Cordova by Mohammedans.
Sig. Gr. well-spoken. *Pron.* ū-lō'jĭ-ŭs.
(ū-lō'jē-ŭs), Lat.
Also M., 4 C. at Constantinople. Jul. 3.

EUNICE (Euníce, es), M. Oct. 28.
Slain with parents, brothers and sisters. *Sig.* **Gr.**
happy victory. *Pron.* ū'nĭs.
(ū-nē'chä), Lat.
Eunike (ū-nē'kä), Gr. Eunice

EUPHEMIA (Euphémia, æ), V. M. Sept. 16. R. M.
4 Cent. Burned at stake. Chalcedon. *Sig.* Gr. of
good report. *Pron.* ū-fē′mĭ-à.
(ū-fä′mē-ä), Lat.
(oi-fä-mē-ä), Ger.
Euphémie (ŭh-fä-mē′), Fr. Euphemia

EUPHRASIA (Euphrásia, æ), V. Mar. 13. R. M.
5 Cent. of royal family of Constantinople. Retired
to Egypt. *Sig.* Gr. mirth. *Pron.* ū-frä′zhà.
(ū-frä′zē-ä), Lat.
Euphrasie (ŭh-frä-sē′), Fr. Euphrasia

EUPHRASIUS (Euphrásius, ii), B. M. Jan. 14. R. M.
(d. u.) Africa. *Sig.* Gr. mirth. *Pron.* ū-frä′zĭ-ŭs.
(ū-frä′zē-ŭs), Lat.

EUPHROSYNA (Euphrósyna, æ), V. Jan. 1. R. M.
5 Cent. Alexandria. Egyptian Christian maiden.
Sig. Gr. mirth. Pron. ū-frŏs′ĭ-nà.
(ū-frō′sē-nä), Lat.
Eusèbe (ŭh-zäb′), Fr. Eusebius

EUSEBIA (Eusébia, æ), V. M. Oct. 29. R. M.
3 Cent. Bergamo. *Sig.* Gr. pious. *Pron.* ū-sē′bĭ-à.
(ū-sä′bē-ä), Lat.
Eusebio (ū-sä′bē-ō), It., Port., Sp. Eusebius
Eusebios (ū-sä′bē-ŏs), Gr. Eusebius

EUSEBIUS (Eusébius, ii), B. M. Aug. 1 and Dec. 16.
R. M.
4 Cent. Vercelli. Champion against Arians. *Sig.*
Gr. pious. *Pron.* ū-sē′bē-ŭs.
(ū-sä′bē-ŭs), Lat.
(oi-sä′bē-ŭs), Ger.
Also 4 Cent. Roman priest, C. Aug. 14.

EUSTACE (Eustáchius, ii), M. Sept. 20. R. M.
2. C. Roman general who refused to worship gods
and was enclosed in red-hot brazen bull with wife
and two children. *Sig.* Gr. healthy, strong. *Pron.*
ūs′tăs.
Also 7 Cent. Ab. Luxeuil. Mar. 29.
Eustache (ŭhs-täsh′), Fr. Eustace
Eustachio (ū-stä′kē-ō), It. Eustace
Eustachius (ū-stä′kē-ŭs), Lat. Eustace
Eustaquio (ū-stä′kē-ō), Sp. Eustace
Eustathe (ŭh-stät′), Fr. Eustathius

EUSTATHIUS (Eustáthius, ii), M. Jul. 28. R. M.
4 Cent. Ancyra. *Sig.* Gr. healthy. *Pron.* ū-stā-′thĭ-ŭs.
(ū-stä′thē-ŭs), Lat.
(oi-stä′tē-ŭs), Ger.
Eustazio (ū-stät′sē-ō), It. Eustace
Eustella (ū-stĕl′lå), var. Estella
Eustelle (ū-stĕl′), var. Estella
Eva (ā′vä), Lat., Du., Ger., It., Port., Sp. Eve
(ē′vå), Eng. var. Eve
Evan (ĕv′ăn), Celt. Eugene

EVANGELIST (Evangelísta, æ), (Bl.), C. Sept. 16.
(d. u.) Augustinian. Verona. *Sig.* Gr. happy mes-
senger. *Pron.* ē-văn-jĕl-ĭs′tå.
Also St. John the Evangelist.
Evangelists, the: Matthew, Mark, Luke and John,
symbolized respectively by Angel, Lion, Ox and
Eagle.
Evariste (ā-vä-rēst′), Fr. Evaristus

EVARISTUS (Evarístus, i), P. M. Oct. 26. R. M.
2 Cent. Instituted College of Cardinals. *Sig.* Gr.
best. *Pron.* ĕ-vå-rĭs′tŭs.
(ā-vä-rĭs′tŭs), Lat.

EVE (Eva, æ), V. Mar. 14.
  13 Cent. Friend of St. Juliana, with whom she urged the feast of Corpus Christi. *Sig.* Heb. life. *Pron.* ēv.
Éve (āv), Fr. Eve
Evelina (ĕv-ĕ-lī′na̍), var. Eve
Eveline (ĕv′ĕ-līn), var. Eve
Evelyn (ĕv′ĕ-lĭn), var. Eve

EVENTIUS (Evéntius, ii), M. May 3. R. M.
  2 Cent. Priest put to death with Pope St. Alexander. *Pron.* ē-vĕn′shĭ-ŭs.
  (ā-vĕnt′sē-ŭs), Lat.

EVERARD, B. June 22.
  12 Cent. Salzburg. *Sig.* strong as wild boar. *Pron.* ĕv′ĕr-ärd.
Everarda (ĕv-ĕr-ärd′a̍), fem. Everard
Everardo (ā-vā-rär′dō), It. Everard
Everhard (ĕv′ĕr-härd), var. Everard
  (ā′vĕr-härt), Du.

EVERILDA (Everíldis, is), V. Jul. 9.
  7 Cent. South of England. *Pron.* ĕv-ĕ-rĭl′da̍.
Everildis (ā-vā-rēl′dĭs), Lat. Everilda
Evrard (ā-vrä′), Fr. Everard
Évraud (ā-vrō′), Fr. Everard

EWALD (Ewáldus, i), M. Oct. 3. R. M.
  7 Cent. English missioner to Germany. *Pron.* ū′ăld.
Ewaldus (ā-wäl′dŭs), Lat. Ewald
Eymard (ā-mär′) *see* Peter Julian (Bl.)
Ezdras (ĕz′drăs), var. Esdras
Ezechia (ā-zā′kē-ä), It. Ezechias

EZECHIAS (Ezechías, æ), K. Jul. 28.
Old Testament. A pious King of Israel. *Sig.* Heb.
strength of the Lord. *Pron.* ĕz-ĕ-kī'ás.
(ā-zā-kē'äs), Lat.
Ézéchias (ā-zā-shē-äs'), Fr. Ezechias

EZECHIEL (Ezéchiel, élis), Proph. Apr. 10. R. M.
6 B. C. One of four Major Prophets, supposedly put
to death in Babylon. *Sig.* Heb. strength of God.
Pron. ē-zē'kǐ-ĕl.
(ā-zā'kē-ál), Lat.
(ā-tsā'kē-ál), Du., Ger.
Ézéchiel (ā-zā-shē-āl'), Fr. Ezechiel.
Ezekias (ĕz-ē-kī'ás), var. Ezechias
Ezequias (ā-thā'kē-äs), Sp. Ezechias
Ezequiel (ā-thā-kē-āl'), Sp. Ezechiel
Ezra (ĕz'rá), var. Esdras

F

Fabia (fā'bǐ-á), fem. Fabian
Fabiaan (fä'bē-än), Du., Fabian

FABIAN (Fabiánus, i), P. M. Jan. 20. R. M.
3 Cent. Layman divinely pointed out for Papacy.
Sig. Lat. bean grower. *Pron.* fā'bǐ-ăn.
Fabiano (fä-bē-ä'nō). It. Fabian
Fabianus (fä-bē-ä'nŭs), Lat. Fabian
Fabien (fä-bē-ăn'), Fr. Fabian
Fabio (fä'bē-ō), It. Fabius

FABIUS (Fábius, ii), M. Jul. 31. R. M.
4 Cent. Soldier beheaded at Caesarea. *Sig.* Lat. bean
grower. *Pron.* fā'bǐ-ŭs.
(fä'bē-ŭs), Lat.

FAITH (Fídes, ĕi), V. M. Aug. 1. R. M.
  2 Cent. Daughter of St. Sophia, martyred at 12 yrs.
  In art shown holding sword. *Pron.* fāth.
  Also V. M., at Aden, 3 Cent. Oct. 6. In art shown
  holding gridiron or also a sword.

Fanchette (fän-shĕt′), Fr. dim. Frances
Fanchon (fän-shôǹ′), Fr. dim. Frances
Fannie, Fanny (făn′nĭ), dim. Frances
Farrel (făr′rĕl), var. Fergus

FAUSTA (Faústa, æ), V. M. Sept. 20. R. M.
  4 Cent. Cyzicus. Martyred at 13 yrs. *Sig.* Lat.
  lucky. *Pron.* făs′tà.
  (fŏw′stä), Lat.

FAUSTINA (Faustína, æ), V. Jan. 18.
  6 Cent. With sister, St. Liberata, built convent of
  St. Margarita at Cosio. *Sig.* Lat. lucky. *Pron.*
  făs-tī′nà.
  (fŏws-tē′nä), Lat., It.
Faustine (fōs-tēn′), Fr. Faustina
  (fŏws-tē-nē), Ger.

FAUSTINUS (Faustínus, i), M. Feb. 15. R. M.
  2 Cent. Brother of St. Jovita, beheaded at Brescia.
  Sig. Lat. lucky. *Pron.* făs-tī′nŭs.
  (fŏws-tē′nŭs), Lat.
  Also 4 Cent. disciple of St. Felix, Bishop of Martano,
  C. Jul. 29.
Fausto (fŏws′tō), It. Faustus

FAUSTUS (Faústus, i), M. Jul. 16. R. M.
  3 Cent. Rome. Crucified and shot with arrows. *Sig.*
  Lat. lucky. *Pron.* făs′tŭs.
Fay (fā), dim. Faith
Febe (fā′bā), It. Phoebe

FEBRONIA (Febrónia, æ), V. M. June 25. R. M.
4 Cent. Assyria. *Pron.* fĕ-brō′nĭ-à.
(fä-brō′nē-ä), Lat.
Federica (fä-dä-rē′kä), It., Sp. Frederica
Federico (fä-dä-rē′kō), Port. Sp. Frederick
Federigo (fä-dä-rē′gō), It. Frederick
Fedliminus (fäd-lē-mē′nŭs), Lat. Felim
Fedor (fä′dōr), Rus. Theodore
Fedora (fä-dō′rä), Rus. Theodora
Felice (fä-lē′chä), It. Felix

FELICIA (Felícia, æ), M. Apr. 27.
(d. u.) Nicomedia. *Sig.* Lat. happy. *Pron.* fĕ-lĭsh′à.
(fä-lē′chē-ä), Lat., It.

FELICIAN (Feliciánus, i), M. June 9. R. M.
4 Cent. Rome. With St. Priscus, his brother, both
aged, thrown to lions and miraculously saved,
afterwards beheaded. *Sig.* Lat. happy. *Pron.*
fĕ-lĭsh′ăn.
Félicie (fä-lē-sē′), Fr. Felicia
Félicien (fä-lē-sē-ăṅ′), Fr. Felician

FELICISSIMUS (Felicíssimus, i), M. Aug. 6.
3 Cent. Deacon of Pope Sixtus II. *Sig.* Lat. very
happy. *Pron.* fĕ-lĭ-sĭs′sĭ-mŭs.
(fä-lē-chē′sē-mŭs), Lat.
Felicita (fä-lē′chē-tä), It. Felicitas.

FELICITAS (Felícitas, átis), M. Mar. 6. R. M.
3 Cent. Carthage. Maiden thrown to wild beasts
with St. Perpetua. *Sig.* Lat. happiness. *Pron.*
fĕ-lĭ′sĭ-tàs.
(fä-lē′chē-täs), Lat.

FELICITAS OF ROME, M. Nov. 23. R. M.
  (d. u.) Widow martyred with her seven sons. Also
  called Felicity. In art shown holding book and
  palm, or with sword having seven blades.
Félicitée (fä-lē-sē-tä'), Fr. Felicitas.
Felicity (fĕ-lĭ'sĭ-tĭ), var. Felicitas

FELIM (Fedlimínus, i), B. C. Aug. 13
  6 Cent. Disciple of St. Columba, and brother of six
  saints, B. of Kilmore. *Sig.* Celt. ever good. *Pron.*
  fĕ'lĭm.
Felipa (fä-lē'pä), It., Sp. Philippa
Felipe (fä-lē'pä), Sp. Philip
Felippe (fä-lēp'pä), Port., Philip
Felisa (fä-lē'sä), Sp. Felicia

FELIX I (Félix, ícis), P. M. May 30. R. M.
  3 Cent. *Sig.* Lat. happy. *Pron.* fē'lĭks.
  (fä'lĭks), Lat., Ger., Du.
  (fä'lēks), Sp.

FELIX OF CANTALICIO, C. May 18. R. M.
  16 Cent. Capuchin laybrother who lived by begging.
  Called "Brother Deo Gratias."

FELIX OF DUNWICH, B. C. Mar. 8. R. M.
  7 Cent. Burgundian missioner to Anglo-Saxons.

FELIX OF MILAN, M. Jul. 12. R. M.
  4 Cent. Martyred with St. Nabor.

FELIX OF NOLA, M. Jan. 14. R. M.
  3 Cent. Syrian priest delivered from torturers by an
  angel.

FELIX OF ROME, M. Aug. 30. R. M.
  4 Cent. Priest martyred with St. Adauctus.

FELIX OF VALOIS, C. Nov. 4 and 20. R. M.
13 Cent. Of royal family, changed name from Hugh,
and with St. John of Matha founded Order of
Holy Trinity (Trinitarians) for ransom of cap-
tives. Beheld Blessed Virgin wearing habit of his
Order. In art shown near fountain at which deer
is drinking. *Pron.* väl-wä'.
Félix (fä-lēks'), Fr. Felix
Feliz (fä-lēz'), Port. Felix
Feo (fä'ō), Rus. cont. Theodore; It. cont. Matthew
Feodor (fä-ō-dōr'), Pol., Rus. Theodore
Feodora (fä-ō-dō'rä), Rus. Theodora
Ferdie (fĕr'dē), dim. Ferdinand

FERDINAND (Ferdinándus, i), K. C. May 30. R. M.
13 Cent. Nephew of Blanche of Castille, King of
Spain, Castile and Leon, cousin of St. Louis IX of
France. In art shown as armed knight with grey-
hound, or as king with cross on breast. *Sig.* Ger.
brave. *Pron.* fĕr'dĭ-nănd.
(fär-dē-näṅ'), Fr.
(fĕr'dē-nänt), Ger.
Ferdinanda (fĕr-dĭ-nän'dà), fem. Ferdinand
Ferdinando (fĕr-dē-nän'dō), It. Ferdinand
Ferdinandus (fĕr-dē-nän'dŭs), Lat. Ferdinand

FERGUS (Fer'gus, i), B. C. Nov. 21.
8 Cent. Salzburg. *Sig.* Celt. man's strength. *Pron.*
fĕr'gŭs.
Fernand (fâr-nŏṅ'), Fr. Ferdinand.
Fernanda (fĕr-nän'dä), It., Port., Sp. Ferdinanda
Fernando (fĕr-nän'dō), It., Port., Sp. Ferdinand
Fernão (fĕr-nŏwṅ'), Port. Ferdinand
Ferrand (fĕr-räṅ'), Fr. Ferdinand
Ferrando (fĕr-rän'dō), It. Ferdinand

Ferrer (fĕr'rĕr), *see* St. Vincent.

Ferry (fĕr-rē'), Fr. Frederick

FIACRE (Fiácrius, ii), C. Aug. 30. R. M.
> 6 Cent. Irish anchoret near Meaux, France, patron of gardeners and of Paris cab-drivers. In art shown with shovel. *Sig.* Celt. eagle. *Pron.* fyä'kr'.

Fiacrius (fē-ä'krē-ŭs), Lat. Fiácre.

Fidèle (fē-dāl'), Fr. Fidelis

FIDELIS OF SIGMARINGEN (Fidélis, is), M. Apr. 24. R. M.
> 17 Cent. Austrian lawyer who became a Capuchin and preached in Switzerland, where he was put to death by Protestants. Called "advocate of poor." In art shown with club set with spikes. *Sig.* Lat. faithful. *Pron.* fē-dā'lĭs.

(fē-dā'lĭs), Lat.

Fides (fē'dāz), Lat. Faith

Fifine (fē-fēn'), Fr. fam. Josephine

Filemone (fē-lä-mō'nä), It. Philemon

Filep (fē'lĕp), Hung. Philip

Fileto (fē-lä'tō), It., Philetus

Filiberto (fē-lē-bĕr'tō), It. Philibert

Filide (fē'lē-dä), It. Phyllis

Filip (fē'lĭp), Pol., Sw. Philip
> (fē-lēp'), Rus. Philip

Filippa (fē-lēp'pä), It. Philippa

Filippina (fĭl-ĭp-pē'nä), It., Sw. Philippa

Filippo (fē-lēp'pō), It. Philip

FILLAN (Foelánus, i), Ab. Feb. 3
> 8 Cent. Son of St. Kentigern. Evangelized Scotland. *Pron.* fĭl'ăn.

Filomena (fē-lō-mā'nä), It. Philomena

FINAN (Finánus, i), B. C. Feb. 17
7 Cent. Monk of Iona, B. of Northumbria. *Sig.*
Celt. fair offspring. *Pron.* fĭn'ăn.
Finanus (fē-nä'nŭs), Lat. Finan

FINBAR, FINBARR (Finbárus, i), B. C. Sep. 25.
6 Cent. Founded monasteries of Courgane-Barra and
Cork. Native of Connaught, first B. of Cork.
Pron. fĭn'bär.
Finbarus (fĭn-bä'rŭs), Lat. Finbar.
Fineo (fē-nä'ō), It. Phineas

FINIAN, FINNIAN (Finniánus, i), B. C. Dec. 12.
6 Cent. Son of King of Munster, B. of Killaloe,
Apostle of Isles of Arran and Hebrides. *Sig.* Celt.
fair offspring. *Pron.* fĭn'ĭ-ăn.
Finien (fē-nyăń'), Fr. Finian
Finnianus (fĭn-nē-ä'nŭs), Lat. Finnian

FINTAN (Fintánus, i), Ab. Feb. 17. R. M.
6 Cent. Founder of Monastery of Clonenagh. *Sig.*
Celt. white. *Pron.* fĭn'tăn.
Fintanus (fĭn-tä'nŭs), Lat. Fintan
Fiorenza (fē-ō-rĕn'zä), It. Florence

FIRMIN (Firmínus, i), B. C. Aug. 18. R. M.
5 Cent. Metz. *Sig.* Lat. solid, stable. *Pron.* fēr-măń'.
Firminus (fēr-mē-nŭs), Lat. Firmin
Fisher, *see* John

FLANNAN (Flannánus, i), B. C. Dec. 18
7 Cent. First B. Killaloe. *Pron.* flăn'ăn.
Flannanus (flä-nä'nŭs), Lat. Flannan

FLAVIA (Flávia, æ), V. M. May 7. R. M.
1 Cent. Niece of Emperor Domitian, burned **at**
stake. *Sig.* Lat. yellow. *Pron.* flä'vĭå.
(flä'vē-ä), Lat.

FLAVIAN (Flaviánus, i), M. Dec. 22. R. M.
4 C. Husband of St. Dafrose, father of Sts. Bibiana
and Demetria. *Sig.* Lat. yellow. *Pron.* flā′vĭ-ăn.
Also B. C., Pat. of Antioch, 6 Cent. Jul. 4.
Flavianus (flä-vē-ä′nŭs), Lat. Flavian
Flavien (flä-vē-ăṅ′), Fr. Flavian

FLAVIUS (Flávius, ii), M. June 22. R. M.
1 Cent. Roman senator and consul. *Sig.* Lat. yellow.
Pron. flā′vĭ-ŭs.
(flä′vē-ŭs), Lat.
Flo (flō), dim. of Florence, Flora

FLORA (Flóra, æ), V. M. Nov. 24. R. M.
(d. u.) Seville. *Sig.* Lat. flowers. *Pron.* flō′rȧ.
(flō′rä), Lat., It.
Flore (flōr), Fr. Flora

FLORENCE (Floréntia, æ), M. Nov. 10. R. M.
(d. u.) Caesarion. *See* also Florentina. *Sig.* Lat.
blooming, flourishing. *Pron.* flŏr′ĕns.

FLORENCE (Floréntius, ii), M. Jul. 25.
3 Cent. Roman soldier. *Sig.* Lat. blooming. Also
3 Cent. B. Vienne, Gaul. Jan. 3.
Florence (flō-rŏṅs′), Fr. Florence
Florencia (flō-rĕn′thē-ä), Sp. Florence (fem.)
Florencio (flō-rĕn′thē-ō), Sp. Florence (masc.)

FLORENTINA (Florentína, æ), V. June 20. R. M.
7 Cent. Sister of Sts. Leander, Fulgentius and Isidore. Also var. of Florence. *Sig.* Lat. blooming.
Pron. flō-rĕn-tī′nȧ.
(flō-rĕn-tē′nä), Lat.

FLORENTINE (Florentínus, i), B. C. Oct. 16. R. M.
4 Cent. Treves. *Sig.* Lat. blooming. *Pron.* flō′rĕn-tīn.
(flō-rĕn-tēn′), Fr.
Florentinus (flō-rĕn-tē′nŭs), Lat.
Florentius (flō-rĕnt′sē-ŭs), Lat. Florence (masc.)
Florenz (flō-rĕnts′), Du., Dan., Ger., Sw. Florence

FLORIAN (Floriánus, i), M. May 4. R. M.
4 C. Roman soldier. Invoked against fire and
drought. In art shown with right hand resting on
mill-stone or pouring water on burning house. *Sig.*
Lat. blooming. *Pron.* flô′rĭ-ăn.
Florianus (flō-rē-ä′nŭs), Lat. Florian

FLORIBERT (Floribértus, i), B. C. Apr. 25.
8 Cent. Liége. Son of St. Hubert. *Pron.* flôr′ĭ-bĕrt.
(flō-rē-bâr′), Fr.
Floribertus (flō-rē-bâr′tŭs), Lat. Floribert
Florrie, Flory (flôr′rĭ), dim. Florence, Flora, Florian.
Floss (flŏs), **Flossie** (flŏs′sē), dim. Florence, Flora.
Foligno (fō-lē′nyō), *see* St. Angela.
Fortunat (fōr-tü-nä′), Fr. Fortunatus

FORTUNATA (Fortunáta, æ), V. M. Oct. 14. R. M.
Caesarea, under Diocletian. *Sig.* Lat. lucky. *Pron.*
fôr-tū-nä′tà.
(fōr-tōō-nä′tä), Lat.
Fortunato (fōr-tōō-nä′tō), It. Fortunatus

FORTUNATUS (Fortunátus, i), C. June 1. R. M.
4 Cent. holy parish priest in Italy. *Sig.* Lat. lucky.
Pron. fôr-tū-nä′tŭs.
(fōr-tōō-nä′tŭs), Lat.
Fortuné (fōr-tü-nä′), Fr. Fortunatus
Foster (fŏs′tĕr), var. Vedast.

FOUR CROWNED MARTYRS: Sts. Severus, Severianus, Carpophorus and Victorinus, Nov. 8. R. M.

FOURTEEN HOLY HELPERS:
Achatius, M., June 22
Barbara, V. M., Dec. 4
Blase, B. M., Feb. 3
Catherine, V. M., Nov. 25
Christopher, M., Jul. 25
Cyriac, M., Aug. 8
Denis, B. M., Oct. 9
Erasmus, B. M., June 2
Eustace, M., Sep. 20
George of Lydda, M., Apr. 23
Giles, Ab., Sep. 1
Margaret, V. M., Jul. 20
Pantaleon, M., Jul. 27
Vitus, M., Jun. 15

FRANCES OF ROME (Francísca, æ), Wid. Mar. 9. R. M.
15 Cent. Founder of Congregation (Order of Oblates of St. Benedict) devoted to penance and good works, permitted to see her Guardian Angel. In art shown with basket of bread and angel at side. *Sig.* Fr. free. *Pron.* frăn'sĕz.

Frances de Chantal (dĕ shäṅ-täl'), *see* Jane.
Francesca (fräṅ-chĕs'kä), It. Frances
Francesco (frän-chĕs'kō), It. Francis
Francina (frăn-sē'nà), Du. Frances
Francine (fräṅ-sēn'), Fr. Frances

FRANCIS OF ASSISI (Francíscus, i), C. Oct. 4 (death), Sep. 17 (Stigmata), R. M.
13 Cent. Founder of Friars Minor (Franciscans),

Poor Clares and Third Order. Called "poor man of Assisi"; received "Stigmata," or impression of Wounds of Our Lord. In art shown with birds, with Stigmata or embracing large crucifix. *Sig.* Fr. free. *Pron.* frȧn'sĭs—ăs-sĭs'ĭ.

FRANCIS BORGIA, C. Sept. 30 and Oct. 10. R. M. 16 Cent. Duke of Gandia, entered Society of Jesus and became third Superior General. In art shown baptizing Indians or Japanese. *Pron.* bôr'jȧ.

FRANCIS CARACCIOLO, C. June 4. R. M. 17 Cent. Founder of Regular Clerks Minor. In art shown with monstrance in hand. *Pron.* kä-rät-chē-ō'lō.

Francis Clet, *see* John Francis (Bl.)

FRANCIS JEROME, C. May 11, R. M. Italian Jesuit; labored in Naples, 18 Cent.

FRANCIS OF PAULA, C. Apr. 2. R. M. 15 Cent. A Calabrian, Founder of Hermits of St. Francis, or Minims. *Pron.* pạ'lä.

Francis Regis (rē'jĭs), *see* St. John.

FRANCIS OF SALES, B. C. D. Jan. 29 and Dec. 28. R. M. 17 Cent. born at Annecy, B. of Geneva. Converted 8000 Calvinists in 2 years, wrote "Introduction to a Devout Life." With St. Jane Frances de Chantal founded Visitation Order. In art shown with heart in hand or with Sacred Heart in a glory above him. *Pron.* sälz.

FRANCIS SOLANO OR SOLANUS, C. Jul. 14. R. M. 17 Cent. Franciscan who labored in Peru and Paraguay. *Pron.* sō-lä'nō (or nŭs).

FRANCIS XAVIER, C. Dec. 3. R. M.
16 Cent. One of original band of Society of Jesus.
Apostle to Indies. Labored in Japan. Patron of
Catholic Missions. In art shown with pilgrim's
staff and beads or holding lily. *Pron.* zăv′yĕr.

Francisca (frän-chēs′kä), Lat. Frances
(frän-thēs′kä), Sp.
Francisco (frän-sēs′kō), Port. Francis
(frän-thēs′kō), Sp.
Franciscus (frän-chēs′kŭs), Lat. Francis
(frän-sēs′kŭs), Ger.
Franciska (frän-sēs′kä), Ger. Frances
Franciskus (frän-sēs′kŭs), Ger. Francis
Franco (frän′kō), It. dim. Francis
François (frŏṅ-swä′), Fr. Francis
Françoise (frŏṅ-swäz′), Fr. Frances
Frank (frănk), dim. Francis
Frankie (frănk′ē), dim. Francis
Franko (frän′kō), It. dim. Francis
Frans (fräns), Sw. Francis
Frants (fränts), Dan., Nor. Francis
Franz (fränts), Ger. Francis
Franziska (frän-tsēs′kä), Ger. Frances
Franziskus (frän-tsēs′kŭs), Ger. Francis
Fred (frĕd), dim. Frederick
Freda (frē′dȧ), dim. Frederica
Freddie (frĕd′dĭ), dim. Frederick
Frédéric (frā-dā-rēk′), Fr. Frederick
Frederic (frĕd′ĕr-ĭk), var. Frederick
Frederica (frĕd-ĕr-ī′kȧ), fem. Frederick
(frā-dā-rē′kä), Port., Sp.
Frederic (frĕd′ĕr-ĭk), var. Frederick

FREDERICK (Friderícus, i), B. M. Jul. 18. R. M.
9 Cent. B. Utrecht, labored in Friesland. In art
shown pierced with two swords. *Sig.* Ger. peaceful
ruler. *Pron.* frĕd'ĕr-ĭk.
Frederico (frä-dä-rē'kō), It., Port., Sp. Frederick
Fredericus (frä-dä-rē'kŭs), Lat. var. Frederick
Frederik (frä'dĕr-ĭk), Du., Dan. Frederick
Frédérique (frä-dä-rēk'), Fr. Frederica
Fredrick (frĕd'rĭk), Sw. Frederick
Frida (frē'dä), Ger. dim. Frederica
Fridericus (frē-dä-rē'kŭs), Lat. Frederick

FRIDESWIDE (Frideswínda, æ), V. Oct. 19. R. M.
8 Cent. Daughter of Prince of Oxford, Abb. of
Monastery of St. Mary at Oxford, patroness of
city and University of Oxford. In art shown
crowned, holding book and sceptre. *Sig.* Teut.
peace, strength. *Pron.* frē-dĕs-vē'dĕ.
Frideswinda (frē-däz-wĭn'dä), Lat. Frideswide
Fridli (frĕd'lē), Swiss, Frederick

FRIDOLIN (Fridolínus, i), C. Mar. 6
7 Cent. Missionary with St. Fillan in Netherlands.
Sig. Teut. peace. *Pron.* frē'dō-lĭn.
Fridolinus (frē-dō-lē'nŭs), Lat. Fridolin
Friedel (frē'dĕl), Ger. dim. Frederick
Friederike (frē-dä-rē'kĕ), Du., Ger., Sw. Frederica
Friedrich (frēd'rĭk), Ger. Frederick

FRIGIDIAN (Frigidiánus, i), B. C. Mar. 18.
6 Cent. Son of King of Ulster, B. of Lucca. *Pron.*
frĭ-jĭ'dĭ-ăn.
Frigidianus (frē-jē-dē-ä'nŭs), Lat. Frigidian
Fritz (frētz), Ger. dim. Frederick
Fritzi (frēt'zē), Ger. dim. Frederica

FULGENCE (Fulgéntius, ii), B. C. Jan. 1. R. M.
  6 Cent. Ruspa. Theological writer. In art shown
  with church in hand. *Sig.* Lat. shining. *Pron.*
  fül-zhäns'.
  (fül-zhäns'), Fr.
Fulgentius (fül-jĕnt'sē-ŭs), Lat. Fulgence
Fursaeus (fōōr-sä ŭs), Lat. var. Fursey
Furseus (fōōr-sä'ŭs), Lat. Fursey

FURSEY (Furséus, i), Ab. Jan. 16. R. M.
  7 Cent. Ab. at Tuam, also built monastery of Lagny
  near Paris. *Pron.* fûr'sē.

G

Gabby (găb'bĭ), dim. Gabriel, Gabriella
Gabe (gäb), dim. Gabriel

GABRIEL, THE ARCHANGEL (Gabriel, élis), Mar.
  24. R. M. Announced to Zachary the birth of John
  the Baptist, then to the Blessed Virgin that she
  was to be the Mother of God. In art shown with
  flowing robes, bearing lily. *Sig.* Heb. man of God.
  Pron. gā'brĭ-ĕl.
  (gä-brē-äl'), Fr., Port., Sp.
  (gä'brē-äl), Ger. Lat.

GABRIEL LALEMANT, M. Sep. 26
  17 Cent. Priest, Jesuit, martyred near Ontario, Can.
  Canonized 1930. *Pron.* läl-môn'.
Gabriel Perboyre (pâr-bwär'), *see* John Gabriel (Bl.)

GABRIEL POSSENTI (of the Sorrowful Mother),
  C. Feb. 27. R. M.
  19 Cent. Passionist Brother, died at age of 24,
  devoted to the Passion. Canonized by Pope
  Benedict XV, 1920. Called the "modern Aloysius." *Pron.* pŏs-sĕn'tē.

Gabriela (gā-brĭ-ĕl'ȧ), fem. Gabriel
Gabriele (gä-brē-ā'lā), It. Gabriel
Gabriella (gā-brĭ-ĕl'lȧ), fem. Gabriel
Gabrielle (gä-brē-āl'), Fr. Gabriella
Gabriello (gä-brē-ĕl'lō), It. Gabriel
Gaetan (gä-ä-täṅ'), Fr. Cajetan
Gaetano (gä-ä-tä'nō), It. Cajetan
Galfred (gäl'frĕd), Du. Geoffrey
Galfridus (gäl-frē'dŭs). Lat. Godfrey

GALL (Gállus, i), Ab. Oct. 16. R. M.
7 Cent. Irish missioner who with St. Columban
founded monastery at Luxeuil, then retired to
Switzerland to abbey which bears his name. *Sig.*
Celt. stranger. *Pron.* gạl.
Gallus (gä'lŭs), Lat. Gall

GAMALIEL (Gaméliel, élis), C. Aug. 3. R. M.
Pharisee who taught St. Paul. *Sig.* Heb. recompense
of God. *Pron.* gȧ-mä'lĭ-ĕl.
Gameliel (gä-mä'lē-ĕl), Lat. Gamaliel.
Garcia (gär-thē'ä), Sp. Gerald
Garnier (gär-nyä'), *see* St. Charles
Garret, Garrett, (găr'rĕt), var. Gerard, Gerald

GASPAR DEL BUFALO (Gaspar, áris), (Bl.), C.
Dec. 29
18 Cent. Founder of Society of Precious Blood.
Gaspar also name of one of Magi. *Sig.* Per. treas-
ure-master. *Pron.* gäs'pär.
(gäs'pär), Lat.
Gaspar (gäs-pär'), Port., Sp. Casper
Gaspard (gäs-pär'), Fr. Casper
Gasparo (gäs'pä-rō), It. Casper
Gasparro (gäs-pär'rō), It. Casper

Gasparus (gäs-pä′rŭs), Lat. Gaspar

Gaston (gȧs′tŏn), *see* Vedast

Gatty (găt′ĭ), cor. Gertrude

Gaudens (gạ′dĕnz), var. Gaudentius

GAUDENTIUS (Gaudéntius, ii), B. C. Oct. 25. R. M.
5 Cent. Brescia. *Sig.* Lat. rejoicing. *Pron.* gạ-dĕn′-shŭs.
(gou-dĕnt′sē-ŭs), Lat.

Gaudenzio (gou-dĕnt′sē-ō), It. Gaudentius

Gauthier, Gautier (gō-tyā′), Fr. Walter

GEBHARD (Gebhär′dus, i), B. C. Aug. 27
10 Cent. Constance. *Sig.* Teut. strong giver. *Pron.* gāb′härt.

Gebhardus (gĕb-här′dŭs), Lat. Gebhard

GEDEON (Gédeon, ónis), Sep. 1. R. M.
Judge of Old Testament. *Sig.* Heb. destroyer. *Pron.* gĕd′ē-ŏn.
(gĕ′dā-ŏn), Lat.

Gédéon (zhā-dā-ōn′), Fr. Gedeon

Gedeone (jā-dā-ō′nä), It. Gedeon

Geertruida (här-troi′dä), Du. Gertrude

GELASIUS I (Gelásius, ii), P. C. Nov. 21. R. M.
5 Cent. Rome. *Sig.* Gr. laugher. *Pron.* jĕ-lā′sĭ-ŭs.
(jā-lä′sē-ŭs), Lat.

GEMINIANUS (Geminiánus, i), M. Sep. 16. R. M.
4 Cent. Rome. *Pron.* jĕ-mĭn-ĭ-ăn′ŭs.
(jā-mē-nē-ä′nŭs), Lat.

Gene (jēn), dim. Eugene

GENEROSA (Generósa, æ), M. Jul. 17. R. M.
Carthage under Vigellius. *Sig.* Lat. generous. *Pron.* gĕn-ĕ-rō′sȧ.
(jā-nä-rō′sä), Lat.

Generoso (jā-nā-rō′sō), It. Generosus

GENEROSUS (Generósus, i), Ab. Jul. 17. R. M.
  6 Cent. Poitiers. *Sig.* Lat. generous. *Pron.* jĕn-ĕ-rō′-
  sŭs. (jā-nā-rō′sŭs), Lat.

GENESIUS (Genésius, ii), M. Aug. 25. R. M.
  4 Cent. Rome. Patron of actors. *Pron.* jĕ-nē′sĭ-ŭs.
  (jā-nā′sē-ŭs), Lat.

GENEVIEVE (Genovéfa, æ), V. Jan. 3. R. M.
  5 Cent. Saved Paris from Huns by prayer. Patron
  of Paris. In art shown with lighted candle in hand.
  Pron. jĕn′ē-vēv.

Gennario (jā-nä′rē-ō), It. Januarius

Genovefa (jā-nō-vā′fä), It., Lat. Genevieve

Geoffrey (jĕf′frĭ), var. Gerald

Geoffroi, Geoffroy (zhō-frwä′), Fr. Geoffrey, Godfrey

Geofredo (hā-ō-frā′dō), Sp. Geoffrey

Georg (gā-ôrk′),Dan., Ger., Sw. George

GEORGE (Geórgius, ii), M. Apr. 23. R. M.
  4 Cent. Officer in Roman army, converted, tortured
  and decapitated. One of three patrons of England.
  In art, shown on horseback, vanquishing dragon.
  Sig. Gr. landholder, husbandman. *Pron.* jôrj.
  (zhôrzh), Fr.

Georges (zhôrzh), Fr. George

Georgette (zhôr-zhĕt′), Fr. Georgia

GEORGIA (Geor′gia, æ) V. Feb. 15
  Clermont. Also fem. George. *Pron.* jôr′ja.
  (jā-ôr′jĭ-ä), Lat.

Georgiana (jôr-jĭ-ăn′à), dim. Georgia

Georgie (jôr′jĭ), dim. George, Georgia
  (zhôr-zhē′), Fr. Georgia

Georgienne (zhôr-zhyĕn'), Fr. dim. Georgia
Georgina (jôr-jē'nà), dim. Georgia
Georgine (jôr-jēn'), dim. Georgia
(zhôr-zhēn'), Fr.
(gā-ôr-gē'nē), Ger.
Georgius (jā-ôr'jē-ŭs), Lat. George
Georgy (jôr'jĭ), dim. George, Georgia

GERALD (Geráldus, i), B. C. Mar. 13
7 Cent. Mayo. *Sig.* Ger. strong with spear. *Pron.*
jĕr'ăld.
Geralda (jĕ-răl'dà), fem. Gerald
Géralde (zhā-räld'), Fr. Gerald
Geraldine (jĕr'ăl-dĭn), fem. Gerald
Geraldus (jā-räl'dŭs), Lat. Gerald

GERARD MAJELLA (Gerárdus, i), C. Oct. 16. R. M.
18 Cent. Redemptorist lay-brother canonized by
Pius X in 1904. *Sig.* Ger. strong with spear. *Pron.*
jĕr'ärd màjĕl'là.
(hā'rärt), Du.
Also B. of Toul, 10 Cent. Apr. 23.
Gérard (zhā-rär'), Fr. Gerard
Gerardo (jā-rär'dō), It., Sp. Gerard
Gerardus (jā-rär'dŭs), Lat. Gerard
Géraud (zhā-rō'), Fr. Gerald
Geremia (jā-rā-mē'ä), It. Jeremias
Gerhard (gĕr'härt), Dan., Ger., Sp., Sw. Gerard
Gerhardina (gĕr-här-dē'nä), Ger. Geraldine
Germain (zhâr-măṅ'), Fr. Germanus
Germaine (zhâr-mān'), Fr. Germana

GERMANA (Germána, æ), V. June 15. R. M.
16 C. Pibrac, France. *Pron.* jĕr-măn'à.
Germano (jĕr-mä'nō), It. Germanus

GERMANUS (Germánus, i), B. C. May 28. R. M.
6 Cent. B. of Paris, "Father of the poor." *Pron.*
jĕr-măn′ŭs.
Also 4 Cent., B. M., B. of Besançon, Oct. 11.
Also 5 Cent. B. of Auxerre, Jul. 31.
Gerold (gā′rōlt), Ger. Gerald
Geronimo (jä-rōn′ē-mō), It. Jerome
(hä-rō′nē-mō), Sp.

GERONTIUS (Geróntius, ii), M. Jan. 19. R. M.
Sig. Gr. old man. *Pron.* jĕ-rŏn′sĭ-ŭs.
(jä-rŏnt′sē-ŭs), Lat.
Gerrit (jēr′ĭt), var. of Gerard
Gertie (gĕr′tē), dim. Gertrude
Gertraud (gĕr′trout), Ger. Gertrude
Gertrud (gĕr′trōōt), Dan., Ger., Sw. Gertrude
Gertruda (jĕr-trōō′dä), It., Gertrude

GERTRUDE (Gertrúdis, is), V. Nov. 15. R. M.
14 Cent. Great mystical writer at Benedictine monastery of Hefta. Favored with visions and first
apostle of devotion to the Sacred Heart. In art
shown with seven rings on right hand and heart in
left. *Sig.* Ger. spear maiden. *Pron.* gĕr′trüd.
(zhâr-trüd′), Fr.
Gertrudes (zhâr-trōō′dĕs), Port. Gertrude
Gertrudis (gĕr-trōō′dĭs), Lat. Gertrude
(hĕr-trōō′dēs), Sp.
Gerty (gĕr′tē), dim. Gertrude
Gervaas (hĕr′väs), Du. Gervase
Gervais (zhĕr-vā′), Fr. Gervase

GERVASE (Gervásius, ii), M. June 19. R. M.
1 Cent Martyred with brother, St. Protase, at
Milan. Sons of St. Vitalis. Mentioned in Litany

of Saints. *Sig.* Teut. war eagnerness. *Pron.*
jĕr'vās.

Gervasio (hĕr-vä'sē-ō), Sp. Gervase
Gervasius (jĕr-vä'sē-ŭs), Lat. Gervase
Gherardo (gä-rär'dō), It. Gerard
Giacinta (jä-chēn'tä), It. Hyacintha
Giacinto (jä-chēn'tō), It. Hyacinth
Giacobba (jä-kōb'bä), It. fem. Jacob
Giacobbe (jä-kōb'bä), It. Jacob
Giacomina (jä-kō-mē'nä), It. fem. James
Giacomo (jä'kō-mō), It. James
Giacopo (jä'kō-pō), It. James or Jacob
Gian (jän), It. John
Gianbattista (jän-bät-tēs'tä), It. John the Baptist
Gianni (jän'nē), It. John
Giannina (jä-nē'nä), It. Joan
Giannino (jä-nē'nō), It. John
Gideon (gĭd'ē-ŏn), var. Gedeon
Gil (gĭl), dim. Gilbert, Gilberta
  (hēl), Sp. Giles

GILBERT (Gilbértus, i), Ab. C. Feb. 4. R. M.
  12 Cent. Founder of Gilbertines at Sempringham.
  In art shown with church in hand. *Sig.* Ger. yellow bright—famous. *Pron.* gĭl'bĕrt.
  (zhēl-bâr'), Fr.
  (gēl'bert), Ger.
Gilberta (gĭl-bĕr'tá), fem. Gilbert
Gilberto (jēl-bĕr'tō), It. Gilbert
  (hēl-bĕr'tō), Sp.
Gilbertus (gĭl-bēr'tŭs), Lat. Gilbert

GILES (Aegídius, ii), Ab. Sep. 1. R. M.
  6 Cent. South of France. Famous for his miracles.

In art shown with wounded hart. *Sig.* Gr. a kid.
Pron. jīlz.

Gilles (zhēl), Fr. Giles
Gioachimo (jō-ä-kē'mō), It. Joachim
Giobbe (jōb'bä), It. Job
Giofreddo (jōf-frĕd'dō), It. Geoffrey
Giorgia (jōr'jä), It. Georgia
Giorgio (jōr'jō), It. George
Giosafat (jō'sä-fät), It. Jehosaphat
Gioseffo (jō-sĕf'fō), It. Joseph
Giosiade (jō-sē-ä'dä), It. Josias
Giosuè (jō-sōō-ä'), It. Josue
Giotto (jŏt'tō), It. Godfrey
Giovanna (jō-vän'nä), It. Joan, Jane
Giovannetta (jō-vän-nĕt'tä), It. dim. Joan
Giovannetto (jō-vän-nĕt'tō), It. dim. John
Giovanni (jō-vän'nē), It. John
Giralda (jē-räl'dä), It. Geraldine
Giraldo (jē-räl'dō), It. Gerald
Giraud, Girauld (zhē-rō'), Fr. Gerard
Girolamo (jē-rōl'ä-mō), It. Jerome
Gisbert (gēz'bĕrt), Ger. Gilbert
Giselbert (gē-zĕl-bĕrt), Ger. Gilbert
Gisella (zhē-sĕl-la), Fr. Elizabeth
Giuda (jōō'dä), It. Jude
Giuditta (jōō-dēt'tä), It. Judith
Giulietta (jōō-lē-ĕt'tä), It. Juliet
Giulia (jōō'lē-ä), It. Julia
Giuliana (jōō-lē-ä'nä), It. Juliana
Giuliano (jōō-lē-ä'nō), It. Julian
Giulio (jōō'lē-ō), It. Julius
Giuseppa (jōō-sĕp'pä), It. Josephine
Giuseppe (jōō-sĕp'pä), It. Joseph
Giuseppina (jōō-sĕp-pē'nä), It. Josephine

Giusta (jōōs′tä), It. Justa
Giustina (jōō-stē′nä), It. Justine
Giustino (jōō-stē′nō), It. Justin
Giusto (jōōs′tō), It. Justus
Gladys (glä′dĭs), Welsh form of Claudia

GODARD, GODDARD (Godehárdus, i), B. May 4
  11 Cent. Hildesheim. *Sig.* Ger. pious, virtuous. *Pron.*
  gŏd′ärd.
  (gō-där′), Fr.
Godardus (gō-där′dŭs), Lat. var. Godard
Godefridus (gō-dä-frē′dŭs), Lat. Godfrey
Godefroi, Godefroy (gō-dĕ-frwä′), Fr. Godfrey
Godehardus (gō-dä-här′dŭs), Lat. Godard
Godelième (gō-dĕ-lē-äv′), Fr. Godeleva
GODELEVA (Godele′va, æ) M. Jul 6.
  11 Cent. Flanders. *Pron.* gŏd-ĕ-lē′va.
  (gō-dä-lä′vä), Lat.
Godewijn (hō-dĕ-wĭn′) Du. Godwin

GODFREY (Godefrídus, i), B. C. Nov. 8. R. M.
  12 Cent. Amiens. Also called Geoffrey. In art shown
  serving sick. *Sig.* Ger. at peace with God. *Pron.*
  gŏd′ frĭ.
Godfried (gŏt′frēt), Du., Ger. Geoffrey, Godfrey.
Godofredo (gō-dō-frä′dō), It., Sp., Port. Godfrey

GODWIN (Godwínus, i), C. Apr. 15.
  12 Cent. Disciple of St. Bernard. *Sig.* A. S. good in
  war. *Pron.* gŏd′wĭn.
Godwinus (gŏd-wē′nŭs), Lat. Godwin
Goetz (gĕts), Ger. Godfrey
Goffredo (gōf-frä′dō), It., Port., Sp. Godfrey
Gofredo (gōf-frä′dō), Sp. Godfrey
Gonzaga (gŏn-zä′gà), *see* St. Aloysius

GONZALES (Gundisal'vus, i), B. C. Jan. 26.
(d. u.) Coimbra. *See also* St. Peter. *Pron.* gŏn-thä'läs
Gonzalez (gŏn-thä'läth), var. Gonzales

GORDIAN (Gordiánus, i), M. May 10. R. M.
4 Cent. Roman judge, convert. *Pron.* gôr'dĭ-ăn.
Gordianus (gôrdē-ä'nŭs), Lat. Gordian
Gordien (gôr-dē-ăṅ), Fr. Gordian

GORGONIUS (Gorgónius, ii), M. Sep. 9. R. M.
4 Cent. Nicomedia, officer under Diocletian. *Pron.*
gôr-gō'nĭ-ŭs.
(gôr-gō'nē-ŭs), Lat.
Gotard (gō-tär'), Fr. Godard
Gottfried (gŏt'frēt), Dan., Ger. Godfrey
Gotthard (gŏt'härt), Ger. Godard
Gottlieb (gŏt'lēp), Du., Ger. Theophilus, Theodosius,
Amadeus

GRACE (Grátia, æ), Jul. 5.
(d. u.) Cornwall. Also called Engratia. *Sig.* Lat.
grace, favor. *Pron.* gräs.
(gräs), Fr.
Gracie (grā'sē), dim. Grace
Gratia (grā'shĭ-à), var. Grace
(grät'sē-ä), Lat.

GRATIAN (Gratiánus, i), M. Oct. 23.
4 Cent. Shepherd beheaded in Picardy. *Sig.* Lat.
thanks. *Pron.* grā'shăn.
Gratien (grä-sē-ăṅ'), Fr. Gratian
Grazia (grät'sē-ä), It. Grace
Greg (grĕg), dim. Gregory
Grégoire (grā-gwär'), Fr. Gregory
Gregor (grā'gōr), Dan., Ger. Gregory

GREGORIA (Gregória, æ), M. Nov. 17.
(d. u.) Heraclea. *Sig.* Gr., watchful. *Pron.* grĕ-gŏ'-rĭ-à.
(grä-gō'rē-ä), Lat.
Gregorio (grä-gō'rē-ō), It., Port. Sp., Gregory
Gregorius (grä-gō'rē-ŭs), Lat., Ger., Gregory

GREGORY THE GREAT (Gregórius, ii), I, P. C. D. Mar. 12. R. M.
7 Cent. Son of Senator, prefect of Rome; as Pope reformed clergy, sent St. Augustine to England, regulated ecclesiastical chant; one of four great Doctors of Latin Church. In art shown in papal robe with dove near ear. *Sig.* Ger., watchful. *Pron.* grĕg'ō-rĭ.
Also B. M. Oct. 1

GREGORY II, P. C. Feb. 11. R. M.
Benedictine, 8 Cent., sent St. Boniface to Germany.

GREGORY III, P. C. Dec. 10. R. M.
Syrian, 8 Cent.

GREGORY VII, 11 Cent. P. C. May 25. R. M.
Hildebrand, reformer of Church, humbled Emperor Henry IV at Canossa, died in exile at Salerno.

GREGORY X, 13 Cent. P. C. Jan. 10. R. M.

GREGORY ILLUMINATOR, B. C. Sept. 30. R. M.
Apostle of Armenia. 4 Cent.

GREGORY NAZIANZEN, B. C. D. May 9. R. M.
First B. of Nazianzen, 4 Cent. Friend of St. Basil. Patriarch of Constantinople, voluminous writer, surnamed the Theologian. *Pron.* nă-zĭ-ăn'zĕn.

GREGORY OF NYSSA, B. C. Mar. 9. R. M.
4 Cent. Brother of St. Basil, Theological writer. *Pron.*
nĭs'sà.

GREGORY THAUMATURGUS, B.C., Nov. 17, R.M.
3 Cent. Neo-Caesarea. Called "Miracle-worker" or
"Wonder-worker". Said to have removed mountain
by prayer. *Pron.* thŏw-mă-tûr'gŭs.
Greta (grā'tä), Lith., Margaret
Gretchen (grĕt'kĕn), Ger. dim. Margaret
Griffith (grĭf'fĭth), Welsh for Rufus
Griffithius (grĭ-fĭ'thē-ŭs), Lat. Griffith
Grignon de Montfort (grē-ynŏn dĕ mōn-fôr'), *see*
   Louis (Bl.).
Gritty (grĭt'tĭ), dim. Margaret
Gualter (gwăl-târ'), Port. Walter
Gualterio (gwăl-tä'rē-ō), Sp. Walter
Gualtiero (gwäl-tē-ā'rō), It. Walter
Guarinus (gwä-rē'nŭs), Lat. Warren

GUDULA (Gúdula, æ), V. Jan. 8
8 Cent. Brabant. Daughter of St. Amalberga. Patron
of Brussels. In art shown holding lantern. *Sig.*
Teut. war. *Pron.* gū'dū-là
   (gōō'dŭ-lä), Lat.
Guernard (gĕr-när'), Fr. Werner
Guglielma (gōōl-yĕl'mä), It. Wilhelmina
Guglielmo (gōōl-yĕl'mō), It. William
Guido (gwē'dō), Dan., Sw., It., Guy
   (gē'dō), Du., Ger., Sp., Lat.
Guilbert (gēl-bâr'), Fr. Gilbert
Guilelmo (gēl-yĕl'mō), Sp. William
Guilherme (gēl-yär'mä), Port. William
Guillaume (gē-yōm'), Fr. William

Guillelmina (gēl-yĕl-mē'nä), Sp. Wilhelmina
Guillelmine (gē-yĕl-mēn'), Fr. Wilhelmina
Guillemette (gē-yĕ-mĕt'), Fr. Wilhelmina
Guillermo (gē-yär'mō), Sp. William
Gundelindis (gŭn-dä-lĭn'dĭs), Lat. Gwendolin

GUNTHER (Gúnther, ĕri), C. Oct. 9
    11 Cent. Hermit at Hersfeld. Cousin of St. Stephen
    of Hungary. *Pron.* gŭn'thĕr
    (gŭn'thĕr), Lat.
Gunthramnus (gŭn-thräm'nŭs), Lat. Guntran

GUNTRAN (Gunthram'nus), K. C. Mar. 28. R. M.
    6 Cent. King of Orleans. *Sig.* Teut. war raven. *Pron.*
    gŭn'trăn
Gus (gŭs), dim. August, Augustine
Gussie, Gussy (gŭs'sē), dim. Augusta
Gustavus (gŭs-tä'vŭs), cor. August
Gustus (gŭs'tŭs), dim. August
Guy (gī), var. Vitus
    (gē), Fr.
Gwen (gwĕn), dim. Gwendoline. Also used for Blanch

GWENDOLEN, Gwendolin, Gwendoline (Gunde-
    líndis, is), Ab. Mar. 28
    8 Cent. Sister of St. Eugenia, Alsace. *Sig.* Celt. white
    browed. *Pron.* gwĕn'dō-lĕn or lĭn.
Gwendolyn (gwĕn'dō-lĭn), var. Gwendolen

H̤

Hab (hăb), cor. Herbert

HABACUC (*indecl.*) Proph. Jan. 15. R. M.
    One of the twelve minor Prophets. *Sig.* Heb. embrac-
    ing. *Pron.* hăb'á-kŭk

Habakuk, Habakkuk (hăb'á-kŭk), var. of Habacuc
Habeel (há-bēl'), Ar. Abel
Habîl (hä-bēl'), Ar. Abel
Hadassa, Hadassah (hă-dăs'á), var. of Esther
Hadria (hā'drĭ-á), var. of Adria
Hadrian (hā'drĭ-ăn), var. of Adrian
Hadrianus (hä-drē-ä'nŭs), Lat. Hadrian
Hal (hăl), dim. Henry
Hank (hănk), Henry
Hanna (hăn'nà), var. of Anne
    (hän'nä), Du., Dan., Sw. Anne
Hanne (hän'nē), Dan. Anne
Hans (häns), Ger., Sw., fam. John
Hansel (hän'sĕl), John
Harald (hä'räld), Dan. Harold
Harding (härd'ĭng), see St. Stephen
Haribert (hăr'ĭ-bĕrt), var. of Herbert

HAROLD (Haróldus, i), M. Mar. 17
    12 Cent. Infant put to death by Jews at Gloucester.
    Sig. A. S. champion, general. Pron. hăr'ŏld.
    Also 10 Cent. K. of Denmark, M. Nov. 1.
    (ä-rŏld'), Fr.
Haroldus (hä-rōl'dŭs), Lat. Harold
Haroon (hä-rōōn'), Ar. Aaron
Harriet (hăr'rĭ-ĕt), dim. Henrietta
Harriot (hăr'rĭ-ŏt), dim. Henrietta
Harry (hăr'rĭ), var. of Henry

HARTMANN (Hartmánnus, i), (Bl.), B. C. Dec. 23
    12 Cent. B. of Brixen. Pron. härt'măn
Hartmannus (härt-mä'nŭs), Lat. Hartmann

Harûn (hä-rōōn'), Ar. Aaron
Hattie, Hatty (hăt'tĭ), dim. Henrietta
Hawkin (hą'kĭn), var. Henry
Hawkins (hą'kĭnz), var. Henry
Heberto (ā-bĕr'tō), Sp. Herbert

HEDDA (Hed'da, æ), B. C. Jul. 7. R. M.
    8 Cent. B. of West Saxons. *Pron.* hĕd'dȧ.
    (hĕd'dä), Lat.

HEDWIG (Hedwígis, is), Wid. Oct. 17. R. M.
    13 Cent. Dutchess of Poland. After death of hus-
    band, retired to a Cistercian convent. In art shown
    with church and statue of Our Lady in hands.
    Sig. Teut. war refuge. *Pron.* hĕd'wĭg
Hedwige (ād-wēzh'), Fr. Hedwig
Hedwigis (hĕd-wē'jis), Lat. Hedwig

HEGESIPPUS (Hegesip'pus, i), C. Apr. 7. R. M.
    2 Cent. Ecclesiastical writer, father of Church history.
    Pron. hĕ-jĕ-sĭp'pŭs
    (hā-jā-sĭp'pŭs), Lat.
Heine (hī'nä), Ger. dim. Henry
Heinrich (hīn'rĭk), Ger. Henry
Heinz (hints), Ger. dim. Henry

HELEN (Hélena, æ), Emp. Wid. Aug. 18. R. M.
    4 Cent. Mother of Constantine the Great. Credited
    with discovery of the True Cross. In art shown
    crowned, holding open book or also supporting
    large cross. *Sig.* Gr. light. *Pron.* hĕl'ĕn.
Helena (hĕ'lā-nä), Lat. Helen
    (hĕl'ĕ-nȧ), Eng. var. of Helen
    (ā-lā'nä), Sp. Helen
Hélène (ā-lān'), Fr. Helen

Helene (hĕ-lā′nē), Ger. Helen
Helerius (hĕ-lā′rē-ŭs), Lat. Helier

HELIER (Helérius, ii), M. Jul. 16
  6 Cent. Hermit in Isle of Jersey. *Sig.* Lat. cheerful.
Héloïse (ā-lō-ēz′), Fr. Louise

Helpers, Fourteen Holy, *see* Fourteen
Hen (hĕn), dim. Henry
Hendrik (hĕn′drĭk), Du., Dan. Henry
Henny (hĕn′nĭ), dim. Henry
Henoch (hē′nŏk), var. of Enoch
Hénoch (ā-nŏk′), Fr. Enoch
Henri (äṅ-rē′), Fr. Henry
Henrica (hĕn-rĭ′kȧ), Ger. Henrietta
Henricus (hĕn-rē′kŭs), Lat. Henry
Henrietta (hĕn-rĭ-ĕt′tȧ), fem. Henry. *Sig.* Teut. home
    ruler
Henriette (äṅ-rē-ĕt′), Fr. Henrietta
  (hĕn-rē-ĕt′tē), Du. Ger.
Henrik (hĕn′rĭk), Sw. Henry
Henrika (hĕn-rĭk′ä), Sw. Henrietta
Henrique (ĕn-rē′kā), Port. Henry
Henriqueta (ĕn-rē-kā′tä), Sp. Port., Henrietta

HENRY I (Henrícus, i), Emp. Jul. 15. R. M.
  11 Cent. Husband of St. Cunegunde. Example of
  justice, charity to poor, and zeal for religion. Emp.
  of Germany. In art shown with Cathedral of Bamberg in hand. *Sig.* Teut. chief of a house. *Pron.*
  hĕn′rĭ.

HENRY SUSO (Bl.), C. Mar. 2.
  14 Cent. Constance. Mystical writer, Dominican,
  favored with visions and ecstasies.

HERBERT (Heribértus, i), C. Mar. 20.
> 7 Cent. Hermit, disciple of St. Cuthbert. In art shown with church in hand. *Sig.* Teut. bright warrior. *Pron.* hĕr'bĕrt.
> Also 11 Cent. B. of Cologne; Mar. 16. R. M. (ār-bär'), Fr.

Herberta (hĕr-bĕr'tá), fem. Herbert
Herberto (ĕr-bĕr'tō), Port. Herbert
Heribertus (hĕ-rē-bâr'tŭs), Lat. Herbert

HERMAN JOSEPH (Herman'nus, i) (Bl.). Apr. 7.
> 13 Cent. Premonstratensian contemplative at Cologne, mystical writer. In art shown presenting an apple to picture of Blessed Virgin. *Sig.* Ger. warrior. *Pron.* hĕr'măn.

Hermann (hĕr'män), Du., Ger., Sw. Herman

HERMES (Hermes, étis), M. Aug. 28.
> 2 Cent. Roman magistrate. *Sig.* Gr. of the earth. *Pron.* hĕr'mĕs.

Hernanda (âr-nän'dä), Sp. fem. Ferdinand
Hernando (âr-nän'dō), Sp. Ferdinand
Herold (hā'rōlt), Du. Harold
Hester, Hesther (hĕs'tĕr), var. Esther
Hetty (hĕt'tĭ), dim. Henrietta, Esther
Hezekiah (hĕz-ĕ-kī'á), var. Ezechias
Hieronimo (ē-ä-rō'nē-mō), Port. Jerome

HIERONYMA (Hierónyma, æ), V. M. Sept. 6.
> (d. u.) *Sig.* Gr. holy name. *Pron.* hī-ĕ-rŏn'ĭ-má (hē-ä-rō'nē-mä), Lat.

Hiéronyme (yâr-ō-nēm'), Fr. Jerome
Hieronymus (hē-ä-rō'nē-mŭs), Lat., Ger. Jerome
Hilaire (ē-lār'), Fr. Hilary

HILARIA (Hilária, æ), M. Aug. 12. R. M.
(d. u.) Mother of St. Afra, Augsburg. *Sig.* Lat. cheerful. *Pron.* hĭ-lā'rĭ-à
(hĭ-lä'rē-ä), Lat.

Hilario (ē-lä'rē-ō), Sp., Port. Hilary

HILARION (Hilárion, ónis), Ab. Oct. 21. R. M.
4 Cent. Solitary of Cyprus. In art shown holding an hour glass, or vanquishing dragon by sign of cross. *Sig.* Lat. cheerful. *Pron.* hĭ-lā'rĭ-ŏn
(hĭ-lä'rē-ŏn), Lat.

Hilarius (hĭ-lä'rē-ŭs), Du., Ger., Lat. Hilary

HILARY (Hilárius, ii), B. C. D. Jan. 14. R. M.
4 Cent. Bishop of Poitiers, writer, champion against Arianism. Called the "Athanasius of West." Invoked against snakes. In art shown holding open Book of Gospels. *Sig.* Lat. cheerful. *Pron.* hĭl'à-rĭ.

HILDA (Hĭlda, æ), V. Nov. 17.
7 Cent. Ab. Whitby, Northumbrian princess. In art shown holding model of her abbey. *Sig.* Teut. battle maid. *Pron.* hĭl'dà.
(hĭl'dä), Lat.

Hilde (hĭl'dē), Ger. Hilda

Hildebrand (hĭl'dĕ-brănd), *see* St. Gregory VII.

HILDEGARD, HILDEGARDE (Hildegárdis, is), V. Sep. 17. R. M.
11 Cent. Benedictine, Ab. Bingen. Had gift of prophecy, wrote "Book of Revelations". In art shown with church in hand. *Sig.* Teut. battle maid protection. *Pron.* hĭl'dĕ-gärd.

Hildegardis (hĭl-dĕ-gär'dĭs), Lat. Hildegard

Hiltrud (hēl'trōōd), Ger. Hiltrude

HILTRUDE (Hiltrúdis, is), V. Sep. 27. R. M.

8 Cent. Nun at Hainault; led austere life. In art shown with lamp, book and crown of roses. *Pron.* hĭl'trūd

Hiltrudis (hĭl-trōō'dĭs), Lat. Hiltrude

Hiob (hē'ŏp), Ger. Job

Hippolyte (ē-pō-lēt'), Fr. Hippolytus

HIPPOLYTUS (Hippólytus, i), M. Aug. 13. R. M. 3 Cent. Rome. *Sig.* Gr. horse destruction. *Pron.* hĭ-pŏl'ĭ-tŭs.
Also 3 Cent. B. Porto, M. Aug. 22 (hē-pō'lē-tŭs), Lat.

Hiskia (hĭs'kē-ä), Du. Ezechias

Hodge (hŏj), dim. Roger

Hodgkin (hŏj'kĭn), dim. Roger

Homfroi (ŏn-frwä'), Fr. Humphrey

HOMOBONUS (Homobónus, i), C. Nov. 13. R. M. 14 Cent. Merchant of Cremona. Patron of merchants. *Sig.* Lat. good man. *Pron.* hō-mō-bō'nŭs. (hō-mō-bō'nŭs), Lat.

Honora (hō-nō'rà), var. Honoria

HONORATA (Honoráta, æ), V. Jan. 11. R. M. 5 Cent. Sister of St. Epiphanius, lived at Pavia. *Sig.* Lat. honored. *Pron.* hŏn-ō-rā'tà (hō-nō-rä'tä), Lat.

HONORATUS (Honorátus, i), B. C. May 16. R. M. 7 Cent. B. Amiens. *Sig.* Lat. honored. *Pron.* hŏn-ō-rā'tŭs (hō-nō-rä'tŭs), Lat.

Honoré (ō-nō-rā'), Fr. Honorius

Honorée (ō-nō-rā'), Fr. Honoria

HONORIA (Honória, æ), V. M. Low Sunday Companion of St. Ursula. *Sig.* Lat. honorable. *Pron.*

hŏ-nō'rĭ-á.
(hō-nō'rē-ä), Lat.

HONORIUS (Honórius, ii), B. C. Sep. 30. R. M.
7 Cent.   Benedictine, Archb. Canterbury.   In art
shown holding a baker's peel. *Sig.* Lat. honorable.
Pron. hŏ-nō'rĭ-ŭs.
(hō-nō'rē-ŭs), Lat.

HOPE (Spes, éi), V. M. Aug. 1. R. M.
(d. u.) Rome. *Pron.* hōp.

HORMISDAS (Hormísdas, æ), P. C. Aug. 6. R. M.
6 Cent.   Healed schism between Eastern and Western
Churches. *Pron.* hôr-mĭz'dás
(hōr-mĭz'däs), Lat.

HORTENSE (Horténsius, ii), B. C. Jan. 11
(d. u.)   *Sig.* Lat. gardener. *Pron.* hôr'tĕns
(ôr-täns'), Fr. Hortensia
Hortensia (hôr-tĕn'shà), fem. Hortense
Hortensius (hôr-tĕn'sē-ŭs), Lat. Hortense
Hosea (hō-zē'à), var. Osee

HUBERT (Hubértus, i), B. C. Nov. 3. R. M.
8 Cent.   Nobleman, B. of Maestricht, patron of hunters.   In art shown with stag having crucifix between
horns. *Sig.* Ger. bright in spirit. *Pron.* hū'bĕrt.
(hōō'bĕrt), Ger.
(ü-bâr'), Fr.
Huberta (hū-bĕr'tà), fem. Hubert
Huberto (ōō-bĕr'tō), Sp., Port. Hubert
Hubertus (hōō-bâr'tŭs), Lat. Hubert

HUGH (Húgo, ónis), B. C. Nov. 17. R. M..
· 12 Cent. Carthusian. B. of Lincoln. In art shown
with angel protecting him from lightning.   *Sig.*
Du. mind, soul. *Pron.* hū.

Hugibert (hōō′gē-bĕrt), Ger. var. Hubert
Hugo (hū′gō), var. Hugh
  (hōō′gō), Lat., Du., Dan. Sw.
  (ōō′gō), Sp., Port.
Hugues (üg), Fr. Hugh

HUMBERT (Humbértus, i), (Bl.), C. Mar. 4
  12 Cent. Count of Savoy. *Sig.* Teut. support of
  brightness. *Pron.* hŭm′bĕrt.
  Also C., 7 Cent. disciple of St. Amandus. Sep. 7
Humberta (hŭm-bĕrt′à), fem. Humbert
Humberto (ŭm-bĕr′tō), Sp. Humbert
Humbertus (hŭm-bâr′tŭs), Lat. Humbert
Humfrey (hŭm′frē), var. Humphrey
Humfrid (hōŏm′frĭd), Ger., Sw. Humphrey
Humfridus (hŭm-frē′dŭs), Lat. Humphrey
Humfried (hŭm′frēt), Du., Ger. Humphrey
Humfroi (ŏn-frwä′), Fr. Humphrey
Humph (hŭmf), dim. Humphrey
Humphredus (hŭm-frä′dŭs), Lat. var. Humphrey

HUMPHREY (Onúphrius, ii), C. June 12. R. M.
  4 Cent. Egyptian solitary. *Sig.* A. S. protector of the
  home. *Pron.* hŭm′frĭ
Humphridus (hŭm-frē′dŭs), Lat. var. Humphrey
Humphry (hŭm′frĭ), var. Humphrey
Hunfredo (ŏŏn-frä′dō), Sp. Humfrey

HYACINTH (Hyacínthus, i), C. Aug. 17. R. M.
  13 Cent. Cracow. Dominican missionary who labored in eastern and northern Europe and Thibet,
  called "Apostle of North". In art shown sailing on
  sea on his cloak. *Sig.* Gr. purple. *Pron.* hī′à-sĭnth.
  Also brother of St. Protus, martyred at Rome, 3 C.,
  Sep. 11. R. M.

HYACINTHA (Hyacíntha, æ), V. Jan. 30. R. M.
16 Cent. Viterbo. Franciscan of Third Order, Oblate of Mary (Saccone), patroness of Viterbo. In art shown holding a scourge. *Sig.* Gr. purple. *Pron.* hĭ-à-sĭnth'à.
(hē-ä-sĭn'thä), Lat.

Hyacinthe (ē-ä-sănt'), Fr. Hyacinth
Hyacinthie (ē-ä-sän-tē'), Fr. Hyacintha
Hyacinthus (hē-ä-sĭn'thŭs), Lat. Hyacinth
Hygin (ē-zhăn), Fr. Hyginus

HYGINUS (Hygínus, i), P. M. Jan. 11. R. M.
2 Cent. Athenian. *Sig.* Gr. health. *Pron.* hĭ-jī'nŭs.
(hē-jē'nŭs), Lat.

I

Iago (ē-ä'gō), Sp. James
Ian (ī'àn or ē'àn), Sc. John
Iberius (ē-bä'rē-ŭs), Lat. Ivor

IDA (Ida, æ), Wid. Sept. 4.
9 Cent. Noblewoman of Court of Charlemagne. Also var. of Ita. *Sig.* Ger. godlike. *Pron.* ī'dà.
(ē'dä), Lat.

Ignace (ēn-yäs'), Fr. Ignatius
Ignacio (ēn-yä'chō), It. Ignatius
(ēg-nä'thē-ō), Sp. Ignatius
(ēg-nä'sē-ō), Port.
Ignatia (ĭg-nä'shà), fem. Ignatius

IGNATIUS OF ANTIOCH (Ignátius, ii), B. M.
Feb. 1. R. M.
2 Cent. Converted by Apostles, friend of St. Polycarp. Thrown to wild beasts. Named in Canon of Mass. Also called Theophoros (God-bearer). *Sig.* Gr. ardent, fiery. *Pron.* ĭg-nä'shŭs.
(ĭg-nät'sē-ŭs), Lat.

IGNATIUS OF CONSTANTINOPLE, B. C. Oct. 23.
R. M.
9 Cent. Son of Byzantine Emperor Michael.

IGNATIUS OF LOYOLA, C. Jul. 31. R. M.
16 Cent. Born in No. Spain, soldier wounded in seige
of Pampelona. Founder of Society of Jesus
(Jesuits). Wrote Book of Spiritual Exercises.
Patron of Retreats. In art shown with I H S on
breast or hand.

Ignaz (ĭg-näts'), Ger. Ignatius

Ignazio (ēn-yät'sē-ō), It. Ignatius

Ik, Ike (īk), dim. Isaac

Iky (ī'kē), dim. Isaac

Ilario (ē-lä'rē-ō), It., Sp., Port. Hilary

Ildefons (ēl'dä-fōns), Ger. Ildephonsus

Ildefonso (ēl-dä-fŏn'sō), Sp. Alphonsus, Ildephonsus

Ildefonsus (ēl-dä-fŏn'sŭs), Lat. Ildephonsus

Ildephonsa (ĭl-dĕ-fŏn'sà), fem. Ildephonsus

Ildephonse (ēl-dĕ-fōns'), Fr. Ildephonsus

ILDEPHONSUS (Ildefónsus, i), B. C. Jan. 23. R. M.
7 Cent. Toledo, ecclesiastical writer. In art shown
with vestments or cope brought to him by Blessed
Virgin. *Sig.* Teut. eager for battle. *Pron.* ĭl-dĕ-
fŏn'sŭs.
(ēl-dä-fŏn'sŭs), Lat.

ILLTYD (Iltútus, i), Ab. Nov. 6.
5 Cent. famous Welsh saint, founder of Monastery of
Llantwit. *Pron.* ĭl'tĭd

Ilse (ĭl'sä), Ger. Adelaide

Iltutus (ēl-tōō'tŭs), Lat. Illtyd

IMELDA (Imélda), (Bl.), V. May 12.
14 Cent. Child of 13 at Dominican convent at Bo-

logna. Received First Communion miraculously.
Called "Flower of Holy Eucharist". In art shown
with Sacred Host appearing over her. *Pron.* ĭ-mĕl'dá

Immanuel (ĭm-mä'nōō-ĕl), Ger. Emmanuel
(ĭm-măn'ū-ĕl), Eng. var. of Emmanuel

Inés (ĭ-nās'), Sp., Port. Agnes

Inez (ĭ-ynĕth'), Sp. Agnes
(ī'nĕz), Eng. var. Agnes
(ē-nyās'), Port.

Inigo (ēn-yē'gō), Sp. Ignatius

INNOCENT I (Innocéntius, ii), P. C. Jul. 28 and Mar.
12. R. M.
5 Cent. Pope during invasion by Goths. In art, an
angel bringing him crown. *Sig.* Lat. guileless.
Pron. ĭn'ō-sĕnt.
(ē-nō-sŏn'), Fr.

Innocente (ēn-nō-chĕn'tā), It. Innocent

Innocentius (ĭn-nō-chĕnt'sē-ŭs), Lat. Innocent

Innocenz (ĭn-nŏt-sĕnts'), Ger. Innocent

Innocenzio (ē-nō-chĕn'zē-ŏ), It. Innocent

Inocencio (ē-nō-thĕn'thē-ō), Sp. Innocent

IRENAEUS (Irenǽ'us, i), B. M. June 28. R. M.
3 Cent. B. Lyons, disciple of St. John the Evangelist.
Wrote many works against heretics. In art shown
with book or casket. *Sig.* Gr. peaceful. *Pron.* ĭ-rĕ-nē'ŭs
(ē-rā-nā'ŭs), Lat.
Also B. M. Mar. 25. Pannonia, 4 Cent.

IRENE (Iréne, es), V. M. Apr. 5. R. M.
4 Cent. Thessalonika. Sister of Sts. Agape and
Chionia, burned at stake. In art shown with idols
at feet. *Sig.* Gr. peaceful. *Pron.* ĭ-rēn'.
(ē-rā'nā), Lat., It.
(ē-rā'nĕ), Ger.

Irène (ē-rän'), Fr. Irene
Irenea (ē-rä'nä-ä), It. Irene
Irénée (ē-rä-nä'), Fr. Irenaeus

IRMINA (Irmína, æ), V. Dec. 24. R. M.
7 Cent. Daughter of K. Dagobert of Austria. In art shown with church in hand. *Pron.* ēr-mī'nà (ēr-mē'nä), Lat.

ISAAC JOGUES (*indecl.* or Isaácus, i), M. Sep. 26.
16 Cent. Jesuit priest slain by Indians near Auriesville, N. Y. Canonized in 1930 by Pope Pius XI. First United States Saint. *Sig.* Heb. laughter. *Pron.* ī'zäk zhōg.
(ē-zä-äk'), Fr.

ISAAC, Patriarch. Aug. 17.
Son of Abraham and Sara, husband of Rebecca, father of Esau and Jacob.
Isaacus (ē-zä-ä'kŭs), Lat. Isaac
Isaak (ē'säk), Ger. Isaac
Isabeau (ē-zä-bō'), Fr. Isabel

ISABEL (Isabélla, æ), V. Aug. 31
13 Cent. French princess, daughter of Louis VIII, became nun. *Pron.* ĭz'à-bĕl.
Also var. Elizabeth
(ē-sä-bĕl'), Sp., Port., Isabel, Elizabeth
Isabella (ē-sä-bĕl'lä), It., Sw., Lat. Isabel
(ĭz-à-bĕl'à), Eng. var. Isabel
Isabelle (ē-sä-bĕl'lĕ), Du., Ger. Isabel
(ē-zä-bĕl'), Fr.
(ĭz'à-bĕl), Eng.
Isacco (ē-säk'kō), It. Isaac
Isaia (ē-sī'ä), It. Isaias
Isaiah (ī-zā'yà), var. Isaias

ISAIAS (Isaías, æ), Proph. M. Jul. 6. R. M.
7 Cent. B. C. One of Major Prophets, called "Evangelist of Old Testament," "Prince Among the Prophets," supposed to have been sawn in two at Jerusalem. *Sig.* Heb. salvation of the Lord. *Pron.* ī-zā'yàs.
(ē-sä-ē'äs), Lat., Sp., Port.
Isaïe (ē-zä-ē'), Fr. Isaias
Isak (ē'säk), Dan., Sw. Isaac
Isbel (ĭs'bĕl), Sc. Isabel

ISCHYRION (Ischy'rion, ónis), M. Dec. 22. R.M.
3 Cent. Egyptian at Alexandria. *Pron.* ĭs-kē'rē-ŏn (ĭs-kē-rē-ŏn), Lat.
Ishak (ĭs-häk'), Ar. Isaac

ISIDORE (Isidórus, i), B. C. D. Apr. 4. R. M.
7 Cent. Brother of Sts. Leonidas, Fulgentius and Florentia. B. Seville, voluminous writer. In art shown with pen and bee-hive. *Sig.* Gr. strong gift. *Pron.* ĭz'ĭ-dōr.
(ē-zē-dōr'), Fr.

ISIDORE, C. May 15.
11 Cent. Madrid. The Farmer; led model life of hard work in fields. Angels did his work while he prayed.
Isidoro (ē-sē-dō'rō), It., Sp. Isidore
Isidorus (ē-zē-dō'rŭs), Lat. Isidore
István (ēsht'vän), Hung. Stephen

ITA (Ita, æ), V. Jan. 15.
7 Cent. Daughter of Irish chieftain of Waterford. Called "Brigid of Munster," famous for prophesies and miracles. Founded monastery near Limerick.

Also called Ida. *Sig.* Celt. thirsty. *Pron.* ē′tȧ.
(ē′tä), Lat.
Ivan (ē-vän′), Rus. John
(ī′văn), Eng.
Ivar (ē′vär), Du. Ives

IVES (Ivo, ónis), Pr. C. May 19. R. M
13 Cent. Franciscan lawyer, patron of jurists. In art
shown with deed in hand. *Sig.* Teut. archer. *Pron.*
īvz.
(ē′vō), Lat.
Ivo (ē′vō), Lat. Ives.

IVOR (Ibérius, ii), B. C. Apr. 23.
5 Cent. Contemporary of St. Patrick, uncle of St.
Abban. *Sig.* Teut. bow bearer. *Pron.* ī′vôr.
Ivory (ī′vō-rĭ), var. of Ivor
Izaak (ē′zäk), Dan., Ger., Pol. Isaac
Izsák (ē′säk), Hung. Isaac

J

Jabreel (jä-brēl′), Ar. Gabriel
Jabríl (jä-brēl′), Ar. Gabriel
Jacinta (hä-thēn′tä), Sp. Hyacintha
Jacinte (hä-thēn′tä), Sp. Hyacinth
Jack (jăk), dim. John

JACOB (*indecl.*), Pat. Aug. 28.
Son of Isaac and Rebecca, husband of Rachel and
founder of the twelve tribes of Israel. *Sig.* Heb.
supplanter. *Pron.* jā′kŏb.
(yä′kōb), Lat.
(zhä-kōb′), Fr.
Jacoba (jȧ-kō′bȧ), fem. James
Jacobo (zhä-kō′bō), Port. James
(hä-kō′bō), Sp. James, Jacob

Jacobus (yä-kō'bŭs), Lat. James
Jacopo (yä'kō-pō), It. Jacob
Jacqueline (zhäk-kĕ-lēn'), Fr. Jacqueline, fem. James, Jacoba
Jacques (zhäk), Fr. James
Jacquette (zhä-kĕt'), Fr. Jacoba
Jago (hä'gō), Sp. James
Jaime (hī'mä), Sp. James
Jakab (yŏk'ŏb), Hung. James
Jake (jāk), dim. Jacob
Jakob (yä'kōp), Du., Dan., Pol., Sw., Ger. Jacob, James.
Jakobine (yä-kō-bē'nĕ), Ger. Jacqueline
Jakub (yä'kōōb), Pol. James

JAMES THE GREATER (Jacóbus, i), Ap. Jul. 25. R. M.
Brother of St. John the Evangelist, one of first three called by Jesus, one of witnesses of Transfiguration and Agony in Garden. Preached in Judea and Spain, martyred in Jerusalem, and body brought to Compostella. Patron of Spain. In art shown with pilgrim's staff. *Sig.* Heb. supplanter. *Pron.* jāmz.

JAMES THE LESS. Ap. May 1. R. M.
Cousin of Our Lord, First Bishop of Jerusalem. Thrown from top of Temple at Jerusalem by Jews and stoned to death, then head crushed by fuller's club, with which he is shown in art.
Jamie (jā'mĭ), dim. James
Jan (yän), Du., Pol. John

JANE FRANCES FREMIOT DE CHANTAL (Joánna, æ), Wid. Aug. 21 and Dec. 13. R. M.
17 Cent., Dijon, directed by St. Frances de Sales,

founded Order of Nuns of Visitation. In art shown
holding heart with I H S on it. *Sig.* Heb. grace of
the Lord. *Pron.* jăn frā-mē-ō′ dĕ shän-täl′.

Janet (jă-nĕt′ or jăn′ĕt), dim. Jane, Joan

János (yä′nŏsh), Hung. John

JANUARIUS (Januárius, ii), B. M. Sep. 19. R. M.
4th Cent. Bishop of Beneventum. Each year on his
feast in the Cathedral at Naples, his blood, con-
tained in a precious vessel, liquefies. In art shown
as bishop with Vesuvius behind him. *Sig.* Lat.
January. *Pron.* jăn-ū-ā′rĭ-ŭs.
(yä-nōō-ä′rē-ŭs), Lat.

Janvier (zhän-vyâr′), Fr. Januarius

JARED (*indecl.*), Pat. Mar. 1.
Old Testament. Father of Enoch. *Sig.* Heb. descent.
Pron. jä′rĕd.

JARLATH (Jarláthus, i), B. C. June 6
6 Cent. B. of Tuam, founder of Schools of Cloyne
and Tuam. *Pron.* jär′läth

Jarlathus (yär-lä′thŭs), Lat. Jarlath

Jarret (jär′rĕt), var. of Gerald

Jaspar (jăs′păr), var. Casper

Jasper (jăs′pĕr), var. Casper
(yäs′pĕr), Du.

Jayme (zhī′mä), Port. James

Jeames (jēmz), dim. James

Jean (zhŏn), Fr. John
Baptiste (bä-tēst′), Fr. John the Baptist
(jēn), Eng. Joan, Jane.

Jeanne (zhän), Fr. Jane, Joan
(jēn), Eng.

Jeannette (zhä-nĕt′), Fr. Jane, Joan
(jē-nĕt′), Eng.

Jeff (jĕf), dim. Geoffrey
Jeffery, Jeffrey (jĕf'frĭ), var. Geoffrey
Jem (jĕm), dim. James
Jemmy (jĕm'mĭ), dim. James
Jenkin (jĕnk'ĭn), var. John
Jennie, Jenny (jĕn'nĭ), var. Joan
Jeremiah (jĕr-ĕ-mī'à), var. Jeremias

JEREMIAS (Jeremías, æ), Proph. M. May 1. R. M.
   One of Major Prophets. Martyred in Egypt. Author
   of Lamentations chanted during Holy Week.
   Sig. Heb. exalted of the Lord. *Pron.* jĕr-ĕ-mī'às.
   (yā-rā-mē'äs), Lat., Ger.
   (hā-rā-mē'äs), Sp.
Jérémie (zhā-rā-mē'), Fr. Jeremias
Jeremy (jĕr'ĕ-mĭ), var. Jeremias
Jerom (yā'rōm), Ger. Jerome

JEROME (Hierónymus, i), Pr., C. D. Sep. 30. R. M.
   5 Cent. Bethlehem. Translated Scriptures into Latin,
   the Vulgate. In art shown with writing implements
   and lion or in robes of cardinal. *Sig.* Gr. holy name.
   Pron. jĕ-rōm' or jĕr'ŏm.

JEROME AEMILIAN, C. Jul. 20 and Feb. 8. R. M.
   16 Cent. Venice. Founder of Congregation of
   Regular Clerks for care of orphans.
Jérôme (zhā-rōm'), Fr. Jerome
Jeromo (hā-rō'mō), Sp. Jerome
Jeronimo (hā-rō'nē-mō), Sp. Jerome
   (zhā-rō'nē-mō), Port.
Jeronymus (yā-rō'nē-mŭs), Dan. Jerome
Jerry (jĕr'rĭ), dim. Jerome, Jeremiah
Jesper (yĕs'pĕr), Dan. Jasper, Casper

JESSE (*indecl.*). Dec. 29.
  Ancestor of Our Lord. *Sig.* Heb. wealth. *Pron.*
  jĕs'sē.
Jessica (jĕs'sĭ-kà) var. Joan or Jane
Jessie (jĕs'sē), var. Joan or Jane

JESUS CHRIST
  Nativity, Dec. 25
  Circumcision, Jan. 1
  Epiphany, Jan. 6
  Flight into Egypt, Jan. 7
  Transfiguration, Aug. 6
  Dedication of Basilica of Our Savior at Rome,
    Nov. 10
  Finding of Holy Cross at Jerusalem, May 3
  Most Precious Blood, Jul. 1
  Exaltation of Holy Cross, Sept. 14
  The King, last Sunday in Oct.
Jezajas (yā-zä'yäs), Du. Isaias
Jill (jĭl), dim. Julia
Jim (jĭm), dim. James
Jimmy (jĭm'mĭ), dim. James
Jo (jō), dim. Josephine

JOACHIM (*indecl.*), C. Aug. 16 and Mar. 20. R. M.
  Father of Blessed Virgin, husband of St. Anne. *Sig.*
  Heb. God will judge. *Pron.* jō'à-kĭm.
  (yō'ä-kĭm), Lat.

JOAN OF ARC (Joánna, æ), V. May 30. R. M.
  15 Cent. Born Domremy, beheld visions of St. Cath-
    erine and St. Michael, which directed her to lead
    the French army against the English and save her
    King, Charles VII. Betrayed to English and
    burned at stake. Called "Maid of Orleans". One of

patrons of France. Canonized in 1920 by Benedict
XV. *Sig.* Heb. the Lord's grace. *Pron.* jō'an or
jō-ăn'.

Joanna (jō-ăn'nȧ), var. Joan
(yō-ä'nä), Lat.

Joannes (yō-än'nāz), Lat. John

João (zhō-ŏwṅ'), Port. John

Joaquin (hō-ä-kēn'), Sp. Joachim.

JOB (*indecl.*), Pat. May 10. R. M.
Holy man of Old Testament whom God permitted
Satan to try by severe temptations, but whose
patience was finally rewarded. *Sig.* Heb. afflicted.
Pron. jōb.
(yōb), Sw., Lat. Job
(zhōb), Fr.

Jock (jŏk), dim. John

Joe (jō), dim. Joseph

JOEL (Jo'ël, élis), Proph. July 13. R. M.
8 B. C. One of minor prophets. *Sig.* Heb. The Lord is
God. *Pron.* jō'ĕl.
(yō'ĕl), Lat.
(zhō-ĕl'), Fr. Joel

Jogues (zhōg), *See* St. Isaac

Johan (yō'hän), Sw. John

Johann (yō'hän), Dan., Ger., John

Johanna (jō-hăn'nȧ), var. Joan, Jane
(yō-hän'nä), Ger., Sw.

Johannes (yō-hän'nāz), Lat., Ger., John

JOHN THE BAPTIST (Joánnes, is—Baptísta, æ).
Nativity June 24; Beheading Aug. 29. R. M.
Precursor of Our Lord, son of Sts. Zachary and Eliz-
abeth. Sanctified in his mother's womb. Last and

greatest of Prophets. In art shown clothed in skins baptizing Our Lord or bearing a banner or cross. *Sig.* Heb. precious gift of God.   *Pron.* jŏn.

JOHN BAPTIST DEI ROSSI, Pr. C. May 23. R. M.
17 Cent. A model priest, labored among poor and suffering of Rome.

JOHN BAPTIST DE LA SALLE, Pr. C. May 15 and Apr. 7. R. M.
18 Cent. Rheims. Founder of Brothers of Christian Schools (Christian Brothers). Canonized in 1900 by Pope Leo XIII.

JOHN BAPTIST MARY VIANNEY, Pr. C. Aug. 9.
18 Cent. Curé of Ars, great director of souls, drawing as many as 20,000 people a year to Ars. Canonized in 1925 by Pius XI. Model and patron of parish priests.

JOHN BERCHMANS, C. Aug. 13. R. M.
17 Cent. Diest. Jesuit who died at age of 22. Noted for his modesty and purity; patron of altar-boys.

JOHN OF BEVERLY, B. C. Oct. 25.
7 Cent. York. Teacher of St. Bede.

JOHN BOSCO, C. Jan. 31.
19 Cent. Piedmont. Founder of Salesian Society for care of orphan boys. Canonized by Pius XI in 1934.

JOHN OF BRIDLINGTON, C. Oct. 8.
14 Cent.

JOHN OF BRITTO (Bl.). M. Feb. 4
17 Cent. Portuguese missioner in Hindustan.

JOHN CANTIUS, C. Oct. 20 and Dec. 24. R. M.
15 Cent. Kenty, diocese of Cracow. Practiced rigorous abstinence, famous for zeal and charity. Patron of Poland.

JOHN CAPISTRAN, C. Mar. 28 and Oct. 23. R. M.
15 Cent. Franciscan, at Capistrano. Had great devotion to Holy Name; preached crusade against Turks. *Pron.* căp'ĭs-trăn.

JOHN CHRYSOSTOM, B. C. D. Jan. 27 and Sept. 14. R. M.
4 Cent. Antioch. B. of Constantinople, ecclesiastical writer, great orator (Chrysostom means golden-mouthed), died in exile. Patron of Christian orators. *Pron.* krĭs'ŏs-tŏm.

JOHN CLIMACUS, Ab. Mar. 30. R. M.
6 Cent. Syria. Ab. of Monastery at Mt. Sinai. Wrote book "Ladder (Climax) to Paradise," whence his surname. *Pron.* klĭm'ă-kŭs.

JOHN of THE CROSS, C. Nov. 24 and Dec. 14. R. M.
16 Cent. Mystical writer, founder of Discalced Carmelites.

JOHN DAMASCENE, C. D. Mar. 27 and May 6. R. M.
8 Cent. Born Damascus, ecclesiastical writer, last of Greek Fathers, defender of holy images against the emperor. *Pron.* dă'mả-sēn.

JOHN DE BRÉBEUF, C. M. Sep. 26
16 Cent. Jesuit. Pr. martyred in Ontario, Can. Canonized by Pope Pius XI in 1930. *Pron.* brā-bẽf'.

JOHN EUDES, C. Aug. 19
17 Cent. Ri, France. Founder of Congregation of Jesus and Mary (Eudists), and Sisters of Our Lady

of Charity, also of Houses of Good Shepherd. Devoted to the Sacred Heart of Jesus. *Pron.* ĕd or ūdz.

JOHN THE EVANGELIST, Ap. Dec. 27: May 6 (before Latin Gate), R. M.
The disciple whom Jesus loved. Writer of fourth Gospel and Apocalypse, banished to Isle of Patmos. Cast into boiling oil but unharmed (commemorated by second feast). Only Apostle not martyred. In art shown with eagle or with chalice and serpent.

JOHN FISHER, B. M. June 23
15 Cent. Cardinal, B. of Rochester. Beheaded at Tyburn under Henry VIII, whose tutor he was.

JOHN FRANCIS CLET (Bl.), M. Feb. 17
French Vincentian missionary slain in China in 1820. *Pron.* clā.

JOHN FRANCIS REGIS, C. June 16
17 Cent. Jesuit priest of great fervor and austerity, devoted to plague-stricken at Toulouse.

JOHN GABRIEL PERBOYRE (Bl.), M. Sept. 11
19 Cent. Puech, France. Vincentian missionary strangled on cross in China, 1840. *Pron.* pâr-bwär'.

JOHN OF GOD, C. Mar. 8.
16 Cent. Portugal. Devoted life to care of sick poor. Founded Order of Charity for Service of Sick. Patron of hospitals and of sick.

JOHN GUALBERT, Ab. Jul. 12. R. M.
11 Cent. Florence. Founder of Order of Vallombrosa.

JOHN LALANDE, C. Sep. 26
Martyred near Auriesville, N. Y., in 1646. Canonized 1930. *Pron.* lä-länd.

JOHN LEONARD, C. Oct. 6.
16 Cent. Rome. Founder of Clerks Regular of Mother of God. Canonized by Pope Pius XI.

JOHN OF MATHA, C. Feb. 8. R. M.
13 Cent. Provence. With St. Felix of Valois founded Trinitarian Order for ransom of captives. In art shown with fetters in hand.

JOHN NEPOMUCENE, M. May 16. R. M.
14 Cent. Prague. Martyred for refusing to reveal a confession. In art shown with padlock or finger on lips. *Pron.* nĕ-pŏm'ū-sēn.

JOHN OF ST. FACUNDO, C. June 12. R. M.
15 Cent. Spain. Augustinian hermit devoted to the Mass, celebrated preacher. *Pron.* fä-kŭn'dō.

JOHN THEOPHANE VENARD (Bl.), M., Feb. 3 and 13.
Went from Seminary of Foreign Missions, France, to China, martyred in 1861. Beatified in 1909. *Pron.* thē'ō-fān vä-när'.

Johnnie, Johnny (jŏn'nĭ), dim. John

Jonah (jō'nȧ), var. Jonas

JONAS (Jónas, æ), Proph. Sep. 21. R. M.
8 B. C. Minor Prophet, type of Christ. *Sig.* Heb. dove. *Pron.* jō'nȧs.
(zhō-näs'), Fr.

Jordain (zhôr-dăṅ'), Fr. Jordan

JORDAN (Jordánus, i) (Bl.), Feb. 15
13 Cent. Second Superior General of Dominican Order. *Sig.* Heb. descender. Pron. jôr'dăn.

Jordanus (yôr-dä'nŭs), Lat. Jordan

Jorge (hŏr'hā), Sp. George
 (zhōr'zhā), Port.

JOSAPHAT (*indecl.*), B. M. Nov. 14. R. M.
 16 Cent. Poland. Basilian, Archb. Polotsk, martyred by heretics. *Pron.* jŏs'á-făt.

José (hō-sā'), Sp. Joseph
 (zhō-zā'), Port.

Josef (hō-sĕf'), Sp. Joseph

Josefa (hō-sā'fä), Sp. Josephine

Josefina (hō-sā-fē'nä), Sp. Josephine

Josefita (hō-sā-fē'tä), Sp. Josephine

JOSEPH (*indecl.*), C. Mar. 19. R. M. Also solemnity,
 third Wed. after Easter.
 Spouse of Blessed Virgin, Foster-Father of Our Lord,
 Patron of happy death and of Universal Church.
 In art shown holding rod bearing lily, or with
 Child Jesus in arms. *Sig.* Heb. He shall add.
 Pron. jō'zĕf.
 (yō'zĕf), Ger.
 (zhō-zĕf'), Fr.

JOSEPH BENEDICT COTTOLENGO, C. Apr. 30
 18 Cent. Piedmont. Devoted to poor and distressed,
 founded many Orders for their aid. Canonized by
 Pope Pius XI, 1934. *Pron.* kŏt-tō-lĕng'gō.

JOSEPH CALASANCTIUS, Pr. C. Aug. 27. R. M.
 17 Cent. Spain. Founder of Clerks Regular of
 Mother of God of the Pious Schools, or Piarists.
 Pron. kä-lä-sänk'sē-ŭs.

JOSEPH OF CUPERTINO, Pr. C. Sep. 18. R. M.
 17 Cent. Franciscan, devoted to Mass, often in
 ecstasy. *Pron.* kōō-pâr-tē'nō.

Josepha (jō-sē'fà), fem. Joseph
Josèphe (zhō-zĕf'), Fr. Josepha
Josephina (yō-zā-fē'nä), Port. Josephine
Josephine (jō'zĕf-ēn), fem. Joseph
Joséphine (zhō-zĕ-fē'nĕ), Fr. Josephine
Josephus (yō-sā'fŭs), Lat. Joseph
Josh (jŏsh), dim. Josue
Joshua (jŏsh'ū-à), var. Josue
Josiah (jō-sī'à), var. Josias

JOSIAS (*indecl.*), K. June 23.
    Old Testament. King of Juda. *Sig.* Heb. given of the
    Lord. *Pron.* jō-sī'ăs.
Josie (jō'zē), dim. Joseph, Josepha
Josua (yō'sŏŏ-ä), Du., Ger., Sw. Josue

JOSUE (*indecl.*) Sep. 1. R. M.
    Patriarch, successor of Moses, led Israelites into
    Promised Land. *Sig.* Heb. God of salvation. *Pron.*
    jŏsh'ū-ĕ.
Josué (zhō-sü-ā'), Fr. Josue
Jourdain (zhōōr-dăṅ'), Fr. Jordan
Jovanna (zhō-vän'nä), Port. Joan

JOVIAN (Joviánus, i), M. Aug. 24.
    (d. u.) Antioch. *Pron.* jōv'ĭ-ăn.
Jovianus (yō-vē-ä'nŭs), Lat. Jovian
Jovien (zhō-vyăṅ'), Fr. Jovian

JOVITA (Jovíta, æ), M. Feb. 15. R. M.
    2 Cent. Martyred with his brother St. Faustinus at
    Brescia. *Pron.* jō-vē'tà.
    (yō-vē'tä), Lat.
Jovite (zhō-vēt'), Fr. Jovita
Joyce (jois), cor. of Jucunda
Jozé (zhō-zā'), Port. Joseph

Jozef (yō'zĕf), Pol. Joseph
Jozy (jō'zĭ), dim. Josephine
Jozsef (yō'sĕf), Hung. Joseph
Juan (hōō-än'), Sp. John
Juana (hōō-än'ä), Sp. Jane or Joan
Juanita (hōō-ä-nē'tä), Sp. Jane or Joan
Juanito (hōō-ä-nē'tō), Sp. dim. John

JUCUNDA (Jucúnda, æ), V. Nov. 25. R. M.
    (d. u.) Reggio. *Sig.* Lat. joyful. *Pron.* jū-kŭn'dà.
    (yōō-kŭn'dä), Lat.

JUCUNDUS (Jucúndus, i), B. C. Dec. 30
    5 Cent. Aosta. *Sig.* Lat. joyful. *Pron.* jū-kŭn'dŭs.
    (yōō-kŭn'dŭs), Lat.
Judas (yōō'däs), Lat., Ger., Jude
    (jū'dàs), var. Jude

JUDE THADDEUS (Júdas, æ), Ap. Oct. 28. R. M.
    Son of Cleophas and Mary, brother of James the
    Less and cousin of Jesus. Preached Gospel with
    St. Simon; both martyred in Persia, and share
    same feast. Patron in desperate cases. In art shown
    with halberd, or boat in hand. *Sig.* Heb. praise.
    Pron. jūd thă'dē-ŭs.
    (zhüd), Fr.
Judie (jū'dē), dim. Judith

JUDITH (*indecl.*), Sep. 14.
    Saved Jewish people against Assyrians by slaying
    their general Holofernes. Considered as one of
    Judges. *Sig.* Heb. praised. *Pron.* jū'dĭth.
    (zhü-dēt'), Fr.
    (yōō'dēt), Ger.
Judithe (zhü-dēt'), Fr. Judith
Judy (jū'dĭ), dim. Judith

Jule (jūl), dim. Julian, Julius
Jules (zhül), Fr. Julius

JULIA (Júlia, æ), V. M. Jul. 21. R. M.
3 Cent. Troyes, France. *Sig.* Lat. soft-haired. *Pron.*
jūl'yȧ.
(yōō'lĭ-ä), Lat.
(hōō'lē-ä), Sp.
(zhōō'lē-ä), Port.

JULIA BILLIART (Bl.), V. Apr. 8.
19 Cent. Beauvais. Founder of Sisters of Notre
Dame de Namur. Beatified by Pius X. *Pron.* bē-
yär'.

JULIAN (Juliánus, i), M. Jan. 9. R. M.
4 Cent. With wife, St. Basilissa. *Sig.* Lat. soft-
haired. *Pron.* jū'lĭ-ăn.
(yōō'lē-än), Ger.
(hōō-lē-än'), Sp.

JULIANA FALCONIERI (Juliána, æ), V. June 19.
R. M.
13 Cent. Florence. Noblewoman who entered Order
of Servites, and devoted to the Blessed Sacrament.
Founded Order of Mantellate. *Sig.* Lat. soft-haired.
Pron. jū-lĭ-ăn'ȧ făl-kō-nē-ā'rē.
(hōō-lē-ä'nä), Sp.
(yōō-lē-ä'nä), Lat.
(zhōō-lē-ä'nä), Port.

JULIANA OF CORNILLON, (Bl.) V. Apr. 5.
13 C. Augustinian nun of Liége who obtained the
institution of the Feast of Corpus Christi.
Juliane (yōō-lē-ä'nĕ), Du., Ger., Juliana
Juliano (hōō-lē-ä'nō), Sp. Julian

Julianus (yōō-lē-ä′nŭs), Lat., Ger., Julian
Julião (zhōō-lē-own̄), Port., Julian
Julie (zhü-lē′), Fr. Julia
   (yōō′lē-ĕ), Ger.
Julien (zhü-lē-ăn̄′), Fr. Julian
Julienne (zhü-lē-ĕn′), Fr. Juliana
Juliet (jū′lĭ-ĕt), dim. Julia, Julitta
Julietta (hōō-lē-ĕt′tä), Sp. Julia, Julitta
Julio (hōō′lē-ō), Sp. Julius
   (zhōō′lē-ō), Port.

JULITTA (Julítta, æ), M. Jul. 30. R. M.
   4 Cent. Caesarea   *Pron.* jū-lĭt′ä
   (yōō-lĭt′tä), Lat.

JULIUS (Július, ii), M. Jul. 1. R. M.
   (d. u.) Britain. *Sig.* Gr. soft-haired. *Pron.* jūl′yŭs.
   (yōō′lĭ-ŭs), Lat., Du., Ger.
June (jūn), fem. Junius

JUNIUS (Június, ii), Dea. C. Oct. 6.
   7 Cent. Lindisfarne. Pupil of St. Cuthbert. *Pron.*
   jūn′yŭs.
   (yōō′nĭ-ŭs), Lat.
Just (jŭst), Justin, Justus
   (yŏŏst), Ger. Justus
Juste (zhüst), Fr. Justus

JUSTIN MARTYR (Justínus, i), Apr. 14. R. M.
   2 Cent. Rome. Pagan philosopher converted to Faith,
   great apologist. *Sig.* Lat. just. *Pron.* jŭs′tĭn.
   (zhüs-tăn̄′), Fr.
   (yŏŏs′tēn), Ger.

JUSTINA (Justína, æ), V. M. Sep. 26. R. M.
    4 Cent. Martyred with St. Cyprian at Nicomedia.
    Sig. Lat. just. *Pron.* jŭs-tī'nȧ.
    (yōō-stē'nä), Lat.
    (hŏŏs-tē'nä), Sp.
Justine (zhüs-tēn'), Fr. Justina
    (yōōs-tē'nĕ), Ger.
Justino (hŏŏs-tē'nō), Sp. Justin
    (jōōs-tē'nō), It.
Justinus (yōō-stē'nŭs), Lat. Justin
Justo (hōōs'tō), Sp. Justus

JUSTUS (Jústus, i), B. C. Nov. 10. R. M.
    7 Cent. Canterbury. *Sig.* Lat. just. *Pron.* jŭs'tŭs.
    (yōōs'tŭs), Lat., Ger.

JUTTA (Jútta, æ) (Bl.), Wid. Jan. 13.
    13 Cent. Served lepers at Huy. Also called Yvette.
    Sig. Heb. praise. *Pron.* jŭt'ȧ.
    (yōō'tä), Lat.

JUVENAL (Juvenális, is), B. C. May 3. R. M.
    4 Cent. Narni. *Pron.* jōō'vĕn-ăl.
Juvenalis (yōō-vä-nä'lĭs), Lat. Juvenal

JUVENTIUS (Juvéntius, ii), B. C. Sep. 12 and Feb. 8.
    R. M.
    2 Cent. Pavia. *Pron.* jū-vĕn'sĭ-ŭs.
    (yōō-vĕnt'sē-ŭs), Lat.

K

Kajetan (kä'yä-tän), Ger. Cajetan
Kallistus (kä-lēs'tŭs), Ger. Callistus
Kanut (kä-nōōt'), Ger. Canute
Kanute (kȧ-nūt'), var. Canute

Karel (kä'rĕl), Du. Charles
Karina (kä-rē'nä), Scand. Catherine
Karl (kärl), Ger., Sw. Charles
Karolina (kä-rō-lē'nä), Sw. Caroline
Karoline (kä-rō-lē'nĕ), Ger. Caroline
Karsten (kärs'tĕn), Du. Christian
Kasimir (kä'zē-mēr), Ger. Casimir
Kasimira (kä-zē-mē'rä), Ger. fem. Casimir
Kaspar (käs'pär), Ger. Casper
Kasper (käs'pĕr), Du., Sw. Casper
Katarina (kä-tä-rē'nä), Sw. Catherine
Kate (kāt), dim., Catherine
Katharina (kăth-à-rē'nȧ), Eng. Catherine
Katharine (kä-tä-rē'nĕ), Ger. Catherine
　(kăth'à-rĭn), Eng.
Kathleen (kăth'lēn), var. Catherine
Kathryn (kăth'rĭn), var. Catherine
Katie (kā'tē), dim. Catherine
Katinka (kä-tēnk'ä), Rus. Catherine
Katrina (kä-trē'nä), Lith. Catherine
Katrine (kăt'rĭn), dim. Catherine
Kean (kēn), var. Kenny
Ken (kĕn), dim. Kenneth, Kenelm

KENELM (Kenélmus, i), C. Jul. 17.
　9 Cent. Mercian prince who became king as child
　and was put to death by sister. *Pron.* kĕ'nĕlm.
Kenelmus (kä-nĕl'mŭs), Lat. Kenelm.
Kenneth (kĕn'nĕth), name of Kenny in Scotland.
Kenny (kĕn'nĭ), var. Canice

KENTIGERN (Kentigérnus, i), B. C. Jan. 14.
　6 Cent. First B. Glasgow, driven to Wales, founded
　monastery of St. Asaph. *Sig.* Celt. head chief.
　Pron. kĕn'tĭ-gērn.

Kester (kĕs'tēr), dim. Christopher

KEVIN (Coemgénus, i or Kevi'nus, i), Ab. June 3.
7 Cent. Founded Monastery at Glendalough. One
of patrons of Dublin. *Sig.* Celt. comely. *Pron.*
kĕ'vĭn.
Kevinus (kā-vē'nŭs), Lat. Kevin.

KEYNA (Kéyna, æ) V. Oct. 8.
5 Cent. Welsh recluse at Somersetshire *Pron.* kā-nȧ.
(kā'nä), Lat.

KIERAN (Kyránus, i), Ab. C. Sept. 9.
6 Cent. Founded Monastery of Clonmacnoise.
Also called Kyran.   *Pron.* kĭ'răn.
Also 5 Cent. labored with St. Patrick, became first
B. of Ossory. Patron of Miners. Called "first-
born of Saints of Ireland." Mar. 5.
Kieranus (kē-ā-rä'nŭs), Lat. var. Kieran

KILIAN (Kiliánus, i), B. M. Jul. 8.
7 Cent. Irish missionary to South Germany. First
B. of Wurzburg. Also spelled Killian. *Pron.*
kĭl'yăn.
Kilianus (kĭ-lē-ä'nŭs), Lat. Kilian.
Kilien (kē-lyăn'), Fr. Kilian
Killian (kĭl'yăn), var. Kilian
Kit (kĭt), dim. Catherine, Christina, Christopher
Kittie, Kitty, (kĭt'tĭ), dim. Catherine
Klaas (kläs), Du. Nicholas
Klara (klä'rä), Ger., Sw. Clara
Klas (kläs), Ger. Dan. Nicholas
Klaudia (klou'dē-ä), Sw. Claudia
Klaudius (klou'dē-ŭs), Sw. Claudius
Klaus (klous), cor. of Nicholas
Klementina (klä-mĕn-tē'nä), Lith. Clementine

Klothilde (klō-tēl'dē), Ger. Clothilde
Knut (knōōt), Ger., Norse, Canute
Koenraad (kōōn'rät), Du. Conrad
Konrad (kōn'rät), Ger., Sw. Conrad
Konradine (kŏn-rä-tē'nĕ), Ger. fem. Conrad
Konstantijn (kŏn'stän-tīn), Du. Constantine
Kornelis (kōr-nä'lĭs), Du. Cornelius
Kornelius (kōr-nä'lē-ŭs), Du., Ger. Cornelius
Kosmas (kŏz'mäs), Ger. Cosmas
Kris (krĭs), Du. dim. Christian
Krispijn (krĭs'pīn), Du. Crispin
Krispin (krĭs-pēn'), Sw. Crispin
Kristina (krēs-tē'nä), Lith. Christina
Kristine (krēs-tē'nĕ), Du., Nor. Christina
Kristofer (krĭs'tō-fĕr), Sw. Christopher
Kunegunde (kōō-nä-gōōn'dē), Ger. Cunegunda
Kuno (kōō'nō), Ger. cont. Conrad
Kurt (kûrt), Ger. Constantine
Kyran (kĭ'răn), var. Kieran
Kyranus (kē-rä'nŭs), Lat. Kieran

L

LADISLAS (La'dislaus, ăi), K. June 27. R. M.
11 Cent. K. of Hungary. *Sig.* Slav. ruling well. *Pron.*
lă'dĭs-läs.
Ladislaus (lä'dĭs-lŏws), Lat. Ladislas
Laetitia (lā-tĭ'shà), var. of Lettice

LAMBERT (Lambértus, i), B. C. Sep. 17. R. M.
7 Cent. B. of Maestricht. *Sig.* Ger. rich with land.
Pron. lăm'bĕrt.
Also, M., at Saragossa (d. u.), Apr. 16.
(läm'bĕrt), Ger.
(lŏṅ-bår'), Fr.

Lamberto (läm-bĕr'tō), Sp., It. Lambert
Lambertus (läm-bâr'tŭs), Lat. Lambert
Lancelot (lăn'sĕ-lŏt), Ladislas
  (lŏns-lō'), Fr.
Lancelote (län-sä-lō'tä), Port. Lancelot
Lancilotto (län-chē-lŏt'tō), It. Lancelot
Landbert (länt'bĕrt), Ger. Lambert
Landericus (län-dä'rē-kŭs), Lat. Landry

LANDRY (Landéricus, i), B. C. June 10
  7 Cent. B. of Paris, founder of first Hotel-Dieu, or
  hospital, in Paris. *Pron.* lăn'drĭ.
Lantry (lăn'trĭ), Ir. Lawrence

LARGUS (Lárgus, i), M. Aug. 8 and Mar. 16. R. M.
  4 Cent. Martyred with Sts. Cyriacus and Smaragdus.
  Pron. lär'gŭs.
  (lär'gŭs), Lat.
Larkin (lär'kĭn), Ir. Lawrence
Larry (lăr'rĭ), dim. Lawrence
Lars (lärs), Du., Sw. Lawrence

LASERIAN (Laseriánus, i), B. C. Apr. 18.
  7 Cent. B. of Leighlin, Ire. *Pron.* lä-sē'rĭ-ăn.
Laserianus (lä-sä-rē-ä'nŭs), Lat. Laserian.
Launcelot (lạn'sĕ-lŏt), var. Lancelot
Laura (lạ'rȧ), fem. Lawrence
  (lŏw'rä), It.
Laure (lōr), Fr. Laura
Laurence (lä'rĕns), var. Lawrence
  (lō-räns'), Fr. Laurentia
Laurencho (lŏw-rĕn'shō), Port. Lawrence
Laurens (low'rĕns), Du. Lawrence
Laurent (lō-rŏn'), Fr. Lawrence

LAURENTIA (Lauréntia, æ), M. Oct. 8. R. M.
(d. u.) Converted by her slave at Ancona. *Sig.* Lat.
crowned with laurel. *Pron.* lô-rĕn'shȧ.
(lŏw-rĕnt'sē-ä), Lat.
Laurentius, (lŏw-rĕnt'sē-ŭs), Lat. Lawrence
Laurenz (lŏw'rents), Du., Ger. Lawrence
Lauretta (lô-rĕt'tȧ), dim. Laura
Laurie (lạ'rĭ), Sc. Lawrence
Laurinda (lạ-rĭn'dȧ), var. Laura
Lauritz (lŏw'rĭtz), Dan. Lawrence

LAWRENCE (Lauréntius, ii), Dea. M. Aug. 10. R. M.
3 Cent. Deacon of Pope Sixtus II and treasurer of the
Church. Asked by Emperor to give up the treas-
ure, he gathered his poor about him and said:
"Here are my treasures." Scourged, placed on
rack and gridiron. In art shown with gridiron. *Sig.*
Lat. crowned with laurel. *Pron.* lạ'rĕns.

LAWRENCE OF BRINDISI, C. Jul. 22. R. M.
17 Cent. Capuchin, traveled all over Europe converting souls. *Pron.* brĕn-dē'sē.

LAWRENCE JUSTINIAN, B. C. Sep. 5 and Jan. 8.
R. M.
15 Cent. B. of Venice and first Patriarch; mystical
writer.

LAWRENCE O'TOOLE, B. C. Nov. 14.
12 Cent. Archb. of Dublin, of royal blood.
Lawrie (lạ'rĭ), Sc. Lawrence
Lazare (lä-zär'), Fr. Lazarus
Lazarillo (lä-thä-rēl'yō), Sp. Lazarus
Lazaro (lä'thä-rō), Sp. Lazarus
(lät'sä-rō), It.
(lä'sä-rō), Port.

LAZARUS (Lázarus, i), B. C. Dec. 17. R. M.
Disciple of Our Lord, who raised him from dead. B.
of Marseilles. *Sig.* Heb. God will help. *Pron.*
lăz′à-rŭs.
(lä′zä-rŭs), Lat.
Lazzaro (lät′sä-rō), It. Lazarus

LEA (Léa, æ), Wid. Mar. 22
4 Cent. Rich Roman who lived life of penance. *Sig.*
Heb. weary. *Pron.* lē′à.
(lä′ä), Lat.
Leah (lē′ä), var. Lea

LEANDER (Leánder, dri), B. C. Feb. 27. R. M.
6 Cent. B. of Seville, brother of Sts. Fulgentius and
Isidore. *Sig.* Gr. lion man. *Pron.* lē-ăn′dĕr.
(lä-än′dĕr), Lat.
Léandre (lä-än′dr′), Fr. Leander
Leandro (lä-än′drō), It., Sp. Leander
Leanor (lä-ä-nōr′), Sp. Eleanor
Léger (lä-zhâr′), Fr. Leodegar

LELIA (Lélia, æ), V. Aug. 11
5 Cent. Limerick. Sister of St. Munchin. *Pron.*
lē′lĭ-à.
(lä′lē-ä), Lat.
Lena (lē′nà), dim. Helena or Magdalen
Lenore (lä-nōr′), Fr. Helena
(lä-nō′rĕ), Ger.

LEO I, THE GREAT (Léo, ónis), P. C. D. Apr. 11
R. M.
5 Cent. Scourge of heretics, met Attila, the Hun, before Rome and saved civilization; condemned
Nestorius for denying the human nature of Christ.
Sig. Lat. lion. *Pron.* lē′ō.
(lä′ō), Lat.

LEO II, P. C., July 3. R. M.
7 Cent. Sicily. Improved Church chant.

LEOCADIA (Leocádia, æ), V. M. Dec. 9. R. M.
4 Cent. Toledo
(lä-ō-kä'dē-ä), Lat.
Leon (lä-ōn'), Sp. Leo or Leon
Léon (lä-ŏn'), Fr. Leo or Leon

LEODEGAR (Leodegárus, i), B. M. Oct. 2. R. M.
Autun. *Pron.* lēō'dĕ-gär.
Leodegarus (lä-ō-dä-gä'rŭs), Lat. Leodegar.

LEONARD OF PORT MAURICE (Leonárdus, i), C.
Nov. 26. R. M.
18 Cent. Franciscan, devoted to Passion, promoter
of Way of Cross. *Sig.* Ger. brave as lion. *Pron.*
lĕn'ărd.
(lä'ō-närt), Du.
Léonard (lä-ō-när'), Fr. Leonard
Leonardo (lä-ō-när'dō), It., Sp., Port. Leonard
Leonardus (lä-ō-när'dŭs), Lat. Leonard
Léonce (lä-ōns'), Fr. Leontius
Leone (lä-ō'nä), It. Leo or Leon
Leonhard (lä'ŏn-härt), Ger. Leonard

LEONIDAS (Leónides, æ), M. Jan. 28. R. M.
4 Cent. Egypt. *Sig.* Gr. like a lion. *Pron.* lē-ŏn'ĭ-dàs.
Leonides (lä-ō'nē-dāz), Lat. Leonidas

LEONILLA (Leonílla, æ), M. Jan. 17. R. M.
2 Cent. Put to death with three grandsons. *Pron.*
lē-ō-nĭl'à.
(lä-ō-nĭl'lä), Lat.
Leonor (lä-ō-nōr'), Sp. Eleanor
Leonora (lä-ō-nō'rä), Du., It. Eleanor
(lē-ŏ-nō'rà), Eng.

Léonore (lā-ō-nōr'), Fr. Helen

LEONTIA (Leóntia, æ), M. Dec. 6. R. M.
6 Cent. Africa. *Sig.* like a lion. *Pron.* lē-ŏn'sĭ-à.
(lā-ŏnt'sē-ä), Lat.

LEONTIUS (Leóntius, ii), B. C. Mar. 19 R. M.
4 Cent. Saintes. *Sig.* like a lion. *Pron.* lē-ŏn'sĭ-ŭs.
(lā-ŏnt'sē-ŭs), Lat.

LEOPOLD (Leopóldus, i), C. Nov. 15. R. M.
12 Cent. Margrave of Austria. *Sig.* Gr. bold for the
people. *Pron.* lē'ō-pōld.
(lā'ō-pōlt), Ger.
Léopold (lā-ō-pōld'), Fr. Leopold
Leopoldo (lā-ō-pōl'dō), It., Port., Sp. Leopold
Leopoldus (lā-ō-pōl'dŭs), Lat. Leopold
Létice (lā-tēs'), Fr. Letitia
Leticia (lā-tē'thē-ä), Sp. Letitia
Letitia (lē-tĭsh'à), from Lat. Laetitia, meaning joy.
Probably refers to the five joys of Blessed Virgin.
Letizia (lā-tēt'sē-ä), It. Letitia
Lett, Letty (lĕt'ĭ), cor. Letitia
Lettice (lĕt'tĭs), cor. Letitia
Leupold (loi'pōlt), Ger. Leopold
Lew (lū), Lewie (lū'ē), dim. Louis
Lewis (lū'ĭs), var. of Louis
Lia (lē'ä), It. Lea
Libby (lĭb'bĭ), Elizabeth

LIBERATUS (Liberátus, i), M. Aug. 17. R. M.
5 Cent. Ab. of African monastery. *Sig.* Lat. freed.
Pron. lĭ-bĕ-rā'tŭs.
(lē-bā-rä'tŭs), Lat.
Liboire (lē-bwär'), Fr. Liborius

LIBORIUS (Libórius, ii), B. C. Jul. 23. R. M.
4 Cent. B. of Le Mans. *Pron.* lĭ-bō′rĭ-ŭs.
(lē-bō′rē-ŭs), Lat.
Lidia (lē′dē-ä), It. Lydia

LIDWINA (Lidwína, æ), V. Apr. 14
15 Cent. Schiedham, Holland. Led life of patience
under bodily suffering. *Pron.* lĭd-wī′nà.
(lĭd-wē′nä), Lat.
Liguori (lē-gwō′rē), *see* St. Alphonsus.
Lil (lĭl), Lilian, Lillian (lĭl′ĭ-ăn), Elizabeth
Lilly (lĭl′lĭ), Elizabeth
Lin (lăṅ), Fr. Linus
Lina (lī′nà), Caroline

LINUS (Línus, i), P. M. Sep. 23. R. M.
1 Cent. Successor of St. Peter. Mentioned in
Canon of Mass. *Sig.* Gr. flaxen-haired. *Pron.*
lī′nŭs.
(lē-nŭs), Lat.

LIOBA (Lióba, æ), V. Sept. 28
8 Cent. Labored with St. Boniface in Germany.
Abbess of Bischoffsheim. *Pron.* lī-ō′bà.
(lē-ō′bä), Lat.
Lionardo (lē-ō-när′dō). It. Leonard
Lionel (lī′ō-nĕl), dim. Leo. *Sig.* Lat. young lion.
Lionello (lē-ō-nĕl′lō), It. Lionel
Lionellus (lē-ō-nĕl′lŭs), Lat. dim. Leo
Lisa (lī′zà), Elizabeth
Lisette (lē-zĕt′), Fr. Louise

LIVINUS (Livínus, i), B. M. Nov. 12. R. M.
   7 Cent. Irishman who labored in Flanders, martyred
   by pagans. *Pron.* lǐ-vī'nŭs.
   (lǐ-vē'nŭs), Lat.
Liz (lǐz), **Lizzie** (lǐz'zǐ), Elizabeth
Lodewijk (lō'dĕ-wīk), Du. Louis
Lodovico (lō-dō-vē'kō), It. Louis
Lois (lō'ǐs), form of Louise or Aloysia
Longin (lōn-zhăṅ'), Fr. Longinus

LONGINUS (Longínus, i), M. Mar. 15. R. M.
   1 Cent. Caesarea. Centurion who pierced side of
   Christ. *Pron.* lŏn-jǐ'nŭs.
   (lŏn-jē'nŭs), Lat.
Lora (lôr'à), var. Laura
Lorenz (lō'rĕnts), Dan., Ger., Lawrence
Lorenzo (lō-rĕn'thō), Sp. Lawrence
   (lō-rĕnt'zō), It. (lō-rĕn'zō), Eng.
Loreto, Loretto (lō-rĕt'ō), B.V.M., Our Lady of Loreto
Loretta (lô-rĕt'tà), var. Laura or Loretto
Lottie (lŏt'tǐ), Charlotte
Lou (lōō), **Louie** (lōō'ǐ), Louis, Louise

LOUIS IX (Ludovícus, i), K. C. Aug. 25. R. M.
   13 Cent. King of France, noted for justice and charity; took part in two Crusades; died of plague at
   Tunis. *Sig.* Ger. bold warrior. *Pron.* lōō'ǐs.
   (lōō-ē'), Fr.

LOUIS BERTRAND, C. Oct. 9. R. M.
   16 Cent. Dominican, preached in Spain and South
   America. Apostle of Colombia. S. A. *Pron.*
   bĕr-träṅ'.

LOUIS GRIGNON DE MONTFORT (Bl.), Apr. 28.
18 Cent. Founder of Society of Priests of Holy Ghost, and of the Daughters of Wisdom. Devotional writer. *Pron.* grē-nyŏn'dĕ môn-fôr'.

LOUIS OF TOULOUSE, B. C. Aug. 19. R. M.
13 C. Franciscan, B. of Toulouse, nephew of Louis IX.
Louisa (loō-ē'zȧ), Louise

LOUISE DE MARILLAC (Ludovíca, æ), Wid. Mar. 15.
17 Cent. With St. Vincent de Paul founded Daughters of Charity. Canonized by Pius XI, 1934
Pron. loō-ēz'dĕ mä-rē-yäk'.
(loō-ēz'), Fr.
Loyola loi-ō'lȧ), *see* St. Ignatius
Luc (lük), Fr. Luke
Luca (loō-kä), It. Luke

LUCAN (Lucánus, i), M. Oct. 30. R. M.
5 Cent. near Paris. *Pron.* lū'kăn.
Lucanus (loō-kä'nŭs), Lat. Lucan
Lucas (loō'käs), Lat., Sp. Ger., Port. Luke
Luce (lüs), Fr. Lucius
Lucia (loō-chē'ä), It. (loō'chē-ä), Lat. Lucy
(lū'shĭ-ȧ), Eng.
(loō'thē-ä), Sp.
(loō'sē-ä), Port.

LUCIAN (Luciánus, i), Pr. M. Jan. 7. R. M.
4 Cent. Antioch. *Sig.* Lat. light. *Pron.* lū'shăn.
Luciano (loō-chä'nō), It. Lucian
Lucianus (loō-chē-ä'nŭs), Lat. Lucian
Lucie (lü'sē-ĕ), Du., Ger. Lucy
(lü-sē'), Fr., (lū'sĭ), Eng. dim.

Lucien (lü-sē-ăṅ'), Fr. Lucian
Lucile (lü-sēl'), Fr. Lucilla

LUCILLA (Lucílla, æ), M. Aug. 25, Oct. 31, Dec. 8.
R. M.
3 Cent. Rome. *Sig.* Lat. light. *Pron.* lū-sĭl'là.
(lōō-chē'lä), Lat.
Lucille (lü-sēl'), Fr. Lucilla
Lucinda (lū-sĭn'dà), Lucy
Lucio (lōō'chō), It. Lucius
(lōō'thē-ō), Sp.
(lōō'sē-ō), Port.

LUCIUS (Lúcius, ii), P. M. Mar. 4. R. M.
3 Cent. Governed Church for 1 year. *Sig.* Lat. born
at daybreak. *Pron.* lū'shŭs.
(lōō'chē-ŭs), Lat.
Also 2 Cent. King of So. Wales. Dec. 3.
Lucrece (lū'krēs), Lucretia
(lōō-krā'thē-ä), Sp. Lucretia
Lucrèce (lü-krās'), Fr. Lucretia

LUCRETIA (Lucrétia, æ), V. M. Nov. 23. R. M.
4 Cent. Merida. *Sig.* Lat. gain, light. *Pron.* lū-krē'-
shà.
(lōō-krāt'sē-ä), Lat.
Lucrezia (lōō-krāt'sē-ä), It. Lucretia

LUCY (Lúcia, æ), V. M. Dec. 13, R. M.
4 Cent. Sicilian, martyred at Syracuse. In art shown
with lamp, or eyes on dish. Mentioned in Canon
of Mass. *Sig.* Lat. light. *Pron.* lū'sĭ.
Also M. at Rome. Sep. 16.

LUDGER (Ludgérus, i), B. C. Mar. 26. R. M.
9 Cent. Apostle of Saxony, 1st. B. of Munster. *Sig.*
Teut. people's spear. *Pron.* lŭd'gēr.

Ludgerus (lŭd-gā'rŭs), Lat. Ludger

LUDOLF (Ludol'fus), B. C. Mar. 29.
13 Cent. Premonstratensian, B. of Ratzeburg.
Pron. lū'dŏlf.

Ludolfus (lōō-dŏl'fŭs), Lat. Ludolf
Ludolphe (lü-dŏlf'), Fr. Ludolf
Ludovic (lū'dō-vĭk), var. of Louis
Ludovico (lōō-dō-vē'kō), It. Louis
Ludovicus (lōō-dō-vē'kŭs), Lat. Louis
Ludovika (lōō-dō-vē'kä), Ger., Sw. Louise
Ludwig (lōŏt'vĭk), Ger., Sw. Louis
Luigi (lōō-ē'jē), It. Louis
Luigia (lōō-ē'jä), It. Louise
Luis (lōō-ēs'), Sp. Louis
Luisa (lōō-ē'sä), It., Sp. Louise
Luise (lōō-ē'zĕ), Ger. Louise
Luitpold (lōō'ēt-pōlt), Ger. Leopold
Luiz (lōō-ēs'), Port. Louis
Luiza (lōō-ē'sä), Port. Louise
Lukas (lōō'käs), Ger. Luke
Lukats (lōō'kätch), Hung. Luke

LUKE (Lúcas, æ), Ev. Oct. 18 and May 9. R. M.
Painter, physician, writer of third Gospel and Acts of
Apostles. Supposed to have painted portrait of
Bl. Virgin which is in Church of St. Mary Major,
Rome. In art shown with easel and brush, or head
of ox, the symbol of sacrifice. *Sig.* Lat. light. *Pron.*
lūk.

LULLUS (Lúllus, i), B. C. Oct. 16. R. M.
8 Cent. B. of Mayence, pupil of Ven. Bede. *Pron.*
lŭl'lŭs.
(lŭl'lŭs), Lat.

Lulu (lū'lū), Louise

LUTGARDE (Lutgárdis, is), V. June 16. R. M.
13 Cent. Belgian nun, mystic. *Sig.* Teut. people's
guard. *Pron.* lŭt'gärd.
Lutgardis (lŭt-gär'dĭs), Lat.
LYDIA (Ly'dia, æ), Aug. 3. R. M.
1 Cent. First convert of St. Paul in Europe. *Pron.*
lĭd'ĭ-à.
(lĭ'dē-ä), Lat.
Lydie (lē-dē'), Fr. Lydia

M

Mab (măb), Mabel, Maud
Mabel (mā'bĕl), Amabilis
Mabella (mā-bĕl'à), Amabilis

MACANISIUS (Macanísius, ii), B. C. Sept. 3.
5 Cent. B. of Connor and Down, baptized and consecrated by St. Patrick. *Pron.* mă-kă-nĭ'shŭs.
(mä-kä-nē'sē-ŭs), Lat.

MACARIUS (Macárius, ii), Pr. C. Jan. 2. R. M.
4 Cent. Hermit of Egypt. *Pron.* mă-kā'rĭ-ŭs.
(mä-kä'rē-ŭs), Lat.

MACARTIN (Macartínus, i), B. C. Mar. 24.
6 Cent. First B. of Clogher. *Pron.* mä-kär'tĭn.
Macartinus (mä-kär-tē'nŭs), Lat. Macartin.
Macharius (mă-kā'rĭ-ŭs), var. Macarius
Maclovius (mä-klō'vē-ŭs), Lat. Malo

MACRINA (Macrína, æ), Wid. Jan. 14. R. M.
4 Cent. Neo-Caesarea. Grandmother of Sts. Basil
and Gregory of Nyssa *Pron.* mà-krī'nà.
(mä-krē'nä), Lat.

Madalena (mä-dä-lä′nä), It. Magdalen
Maddalena (mäd-dä-lä′nä), It. Magdalen
MADELEINE SOPHIE BARAT (Magdaléna, æ),
  V. May 25.
  18 Cent. Joigny. Founder of Religious of Sacred
  Heart. *Pron.* mä-d'län′ sō-fē′ bä-rä′.
  (mä-d'län′), Fr. Magdalen
Madelena (mä-dä-lä′nä), Sp. Magdalen
Madelène (mäd-län′), Fr. Magdalen
Madeline (măd′ĕ-lĭn), var. Magdalen
Madelon (mä-d'lôṅ′), Fr. var. Magdalen
Madge (măj), Margaret
Mae (mä), Mary
Mag (măg), Margaret
Magdalen (măg′dà-lĕn), *see* Mary Magdalen
Magdalena (mäg-dä-lä′nä), Du., Lat., Ger., Sp.
  Magdalen
Magdalene (măg′dà-lēn), var. Magdalen
  (mäg-dä-lä′nĕ), Ger.
Magdelaine (mä-d'län′), Fr. var. Magdalen
Maggie (măg′gĭ), Margaret
Magi (mä′jī), Casper, Melchior, Balthassar
MAGLORIUS (Maglórius, ii), B. C. Oct. 24. R. M.
  6 Cent. Ab. of Lanmeur, Brittany. *Pron.* mà-glō′-
  rĭ-ŭs.
  (mä-glō′rē-ŭs), Lat.
MAGNUS (Mágnus, i), M. Apr. 16
  12 Cent. Governor of the Orkney Islands. *Sig.* Lat.
  great. *Pron.* măg′nŭs.
  (mä′nyŭs), Lat.
Maimie (mä′mĭ), Mary
Maisie (mä′zĭ), Margaret
Malachi (măl′à-kĭ), Malachy

MALACHIAS (Malachías, æ), Proph. Jan. 14. R. M.
Last of Minor Prophets. *Sig.* Heb. messenger of the
Lord. *Pron.* măl-à-kī'ăs.
(mä-lä-kē'äs), Lat. Malachy, Malachias.
Malachie (mä-lä-kē'), Fr. Malachy

MALACHY (Malachías, æ), B. C. Nov. 3. R. M.
12 Cent. Archbishop of Armagh, possessed gifts of
miracles and prophecy. Died at Clairvaux in presence of St. Bernard. In art shown presenting an
apple to a king. *Sig.* Heb. messenger of the Lord.
Pron. măl'à-kĭ.
Malaquias (mä-lä-kē'äs), Sp. Malachy

MALO (Maclóvius, ii), B. C. Nov. 15
7 Cent. Welshman, B. of Aleth. *Pron.* mă'lŏ.
Also M. 3 Cent., soldier of Theban Legion, Oct. 10.

MAMERTUS (Mamértus, i), B. C. May 11. R. M.
5 Cent. Originator of Rogation Days, B. of Vienne.
Pron. mă-mēr'tŭs.
(mä-mâr'tŭs), Lat.
Mandy (măn'dĭ), dim. Amanda
Manoel (mä-nō-äl'), Port. Emmanuel
Manon (mä-nôn'), Fr. Mary

MANSUETUS (Mansuétus, i), B. C. Feb. 19. R. M.
7 Cent. Milan. *Sig.* Lat. meek. *Pron.* män-swē'tŭs.
(män-swä'tŭs), Lat.
Manuel (mä-nōō-äl'). Sp., Port. Emmanuel
Manuela (mä-nōō-ä'lä), Sp. Emmanuela
Marc (märk), Fr. Mark
Marcel (mär-säl'), Fr. Marcellus

MARCELLA (Marcélla, æ), Jan. 31. R. M.
5 Cent. Roman widow, disciple of St. Jerome. *Pron.*
mär-sĕl'lȧ.
(mär-chä'lä), Lat.
Marcelle (mär-sĕl'), Fr. Marcella

MARCELLIAN (Marcelliánus, i), M. June 18. R. M.
3 Cent. Rome. Martyred with brother St. Mark.
Pron. mär-sĕl'yăn.
Marcellianus (mär-chĕl-lē-ä'nŭs), Lat. Marcellian
Marcellin (mär-sä-yăń'), Fr. Marcellinus
Marcellino (mär-chĕl-lē'nō), It. Marcellinus

MARCELLINUS (Marcellínus, i), Pr. M. June 2.
R. M.
Rome, under Diocletian. *Pron.* mär-sĕl-lī'nŭs.
Marcello (mär-chĕl'lō), It. Marcellus

MARCELLUS I (Marcéllus, i), P. M. Jan. 16. R. M.
4 Cent. Pope during last persecution. *Pron.* mär-
sĕl'lŭs.
(mär-chä'lŭs), Lat.
Also M., 1 Cent. Oct. 7.
Marcelo (mär-thä'lō), Sp. Marcellus

MARCIA (Márcia, æ), M. Apr. 14
3 Cent. Umbria. Also fem. Mark, Marcius. *Pron.*
mär'shȧ.
(mär'chē-ä), Lat.
(mär'chä), It.
Marcie (mär-sē'), Fr. Marcia

MARCIUS (Március, ii), M. Mar. 5
(d. u.) Antioch. *Pron.* mär'shŭs.
(mär'chē-ŭs), Lat.
Marco (mär'kō), It. Mark
Marcos (mär'kōs), Sp. Mark
Marcus (mär'kŭs), Lat. Mark

MARGARET OF ANTIOCH (Margaríta, æ), V. M.
Jul. 20. R. M.
3 Cent. One of Fourteen Holy Helpers. In art shown
with open-mouthed dragon under feet. Also called
Marina. *Sig.* Gr. pearl. *Pron.* mär'grĕt.

MARGARET OF CORTONA, Pen. Feb. 22. R. M.
13 Cent. of Third Order of St. Francis. *Pron.* kôr-
tō'na.

MARGARET MARY ALACOQUE, V. Oct. 17. R. M.
17 Cent   Visitation Nun at Paray-le-Monial. After
vision of Our Lord, she spread devotion to Sacred
Heart. Canonized by Benedict XV in 1920. *Pron.*
ä-lä-kōk'.

MARGARET POLE (Bl.), M. May 28.
16 Cent. Mother of Bl. Card. Reginald Pole, Count-
ess of Salisbury, beheaded under Henry VIII.

MARGARET, QUEEN OF SCOTLAND, Wid. June
10 and Nov. 16. R. M.
11 Cent. Wife of Malcolm III, noted for charity.
In art shown with sceptre and book or black cross.
Margaretha (mär-gä-rā'tä), Du. Margaret
Margarethe (mär-gä-rā'tĕ), Ger. Margaret
Margarida (mär-gä-rē'dä), Port. Margaret
Margarita (mär-gä-rē'tä), It., Lat., Sp. Margaret
Margery (mär'jĕr-ĭ), Margaret

Margherita (mär-gä-rē'tä), It. Margaret
Margie (mär'jĭ), Margaret
Margot (mär-gō'), Fr. Margaret
Marguerite (mär-gĕ-rēt'), Fr. Margaret
Mária (mä'rē-ä), Hung. Mary
Maria (mä-rē'ä), It., Ger., Lat., Sp., Port., Sw. Mary
  (mȧ-rī'a), Eng.
Marian (mă'rĭ-ăn), Mary
Mariana (mä-rē-ä'nä), Sp., Port. Mary Anne
Mariane, Marianne (mä-rē-än'), Fr. Mary Anne
Marianna (mä-rē-än'nä), It. Mary Anne

MARIANUS (Mariánus, i), Dea. M. Apr. 30. R. M.
  3 Cent. Numidia. Martyred with St. James, M.
  Pron. mä-rē-ä'nŭs.
  (mä-rē-ä'nŭs), Lat.
Marie (mä-rē'), Fr., Eng. Mary
  (mä-rē'ĕ), Ger., Dan.

MARINA (Marína, æ), V. Jul. 17. R. M.
  (d. u.) Bithynia. *Pron.* mȧ-rē'nȧ.
  (mä-rē'nä), Lat.
Marion (mär'ĭ-ŏn), Mary
  (mä-rē-ôn'), Fr.

MARIUS (Márius, ii), M. Jan. 19. R. M.
  3 Cent. Persian noble, martyred with his wife, St.
  Martha. *Pron.* mä'rĭ-ŭs.
  (mä'rē-ŭs), Lat.
Marjorie, Marjory (mär'jō-rĭ), Margaret

MARK, (Márcus, i), Ev. M. Apr. 25 and Jan. 31. R.M.
  One of Our Lord's disciples, companion of St. Peter,
  writer of Gospel. In art shown with book and
  winged lion, king of beasts, as he stresses the king-
  ship of Christ. Lion is also his symbol.

MARK, M. June 18. R. M.
3 Cent. Rome. Slain with brother St. Marcellian.
Sig. Lat. hammer. *Pron.* märk.
Also 2 Cent., first B. of Jerusalem, Oct. 22.
Also 4 Cent., P. M. Oct. 7. Institutor of pallium.
Governed Church only a few months.
Markus (mär′kŭs), Ger. Mark
Marta (mär′tä), It., Sp. Martha

MARTHA (Mártha, æ), V. Jul. 29. R. M.
Sister of Mary Magdalen and Lazarus, hostess to
Our Lord at Bethany, died at Marseilles. *Sig.*
Heb. ruler of the house. *Pron.* mär′thä.
(mär′thä), Lat., Du., Ger., Port.
Also Persian noblewoman martyred at Rome with
husband, St. Marius, and sons, Sts. Audifax and
Abachum. Jan. 19. R. M.
Marthe (märt), Fr. Martha

MARTIAL (Martiális, is), M. Jul. 10. R. M.
2 Cent. Rome. One of seven sons of St. Felicitas, all
martyrs. *Sig.* Lat. warlike. *Pron.* mär′shăl.
Martialis (märt-sē-ä′lĭs), Lat. Martial

MARTIN I (Martínus, i), P. M. Nov. 12, R. M.
7 Cent. Died in exile. *Sig.* Lat. warlike. *Pron.* mär′
tĭn.
(mär′tēn), Ger.
(mär-tēn′), Sp., Sw.
(mär-tăṅ′), Fr.

MARTIN OF TOURS, B. C. Nov. 11 and Jul. 4. R. M.
4 Cent. Soldier. B. of Tours, apostle and miracle-
worker of Gaul. In art shown dividing cloak with
beggar.

MARTINA (Martína, æ), V. M. Jan. 1 and 30. R. M. 3 Cent. Rome. In art shown with Lictor's fasces and axe. *Sig*. Lat. warlike. *Pron*. mär-tē-nà. (mär-tē'nä), Lat.
Martine (mär-tēn'), Fr. Martina
Martinez (mär-tē'nĕth), Sp. son of Martin.
Martinho (mär-tē'nyō), Port. Martin

MARTINIAN (Martiniánus, i), M. Jul. 2. R. M. 1 Cent. One of wardens of Mamertine prison when St. Peter was imprisoned. *Pron*. mär-tĭ'nĭ-ăn.
Martinianus (mär-tē-nē-ä'nŭs), Lat. Martinian
Martino (mär-tē'nō), It., Sp. Martin
Martinus (mär-tē'nŭs), Lat. Martin
Martyn (mär'tĭn), Eng. var. Martin

MARY (María, æ), Blessed Virgin, Mother of Our Lord. *Sig*. Heb. star of sea. *Pron*. mā'rĭ.
Annunciation, Mar. 25;
Apparition at Lourdes, Feb. 11;
Assumption, Aug. 15;
Good Counsel, Apr. 26;
Guadalupe, Dec. 12;
Help of Christians, May 24;
Holy House of Loretto, Dec. 10;
Immaculate, Conception, Dec. 8;
Lourdes, Feb. 11;
Most Holy Name, Sept. 12;
Most Holy Rosary, Oct. 7;
Most Pure Heart, Sat. after Oct. Corp. Christi;
Mount Carmel, Jul. 16;
Nativity, Sept. 8;
Perpetual Help, June 27;
Presentation, Nov. 21;

Purification, Feb. 2;
Ransom, Sept. 24;
Seven Dolors, Sept. 15;
Snow, Aug. 5;
Visitation, Jul. 2;
Way, May 24

MARY ANNE OF JESUS (Bl.), V. May 16.
   17 Cent. "Lily of Quito," Ecuador, mystic, beatified 1852.

MARY OF THE ANGELS (Bl.), V. Dec. 18.
   17 Cent. Carmelite of Turin, beatified 1865

MARY OF EGYPT, Pen. Apr. 2. R. M.
   4 Cent.

MARY OF THE INCARNATION (Bl.), Wid. Apr. 18.
   16 Cent. Paris. Foundress of French Carmel.

MARY MAGDALEN, Pen. Jul. 22. R. M.
   Sister of Martha and Lazarus, great example of peni-
   tence, bathed feet of Jesus with tears. In art shown
   with box of ointment.

MARY MAGDALEN OF PAZZI, V. May 29.
   17 Cent. Florence. Carmelite mystic, austere in
   mortifications.

MARY MAGDALEN POSTEL, V. Jul. 16.
   18 Cent., Cherbourg. Foundress of Sisters of Christian Schools of Mercy.

MARY SALOME, Oct. 22. R. M.
   Wife of Zebedee, sister-in-law of Blessed Virgin, pres-
   ent at Crucifixion, mother of Sts. John and James.
   Pron. sà-lōm or sà-lō′mē.

Marya (mär'yä), Pol. Mary
Marzia (märt'sē-ä), It. Marcia
Massimiliano (mäs-sē-mē-lē-ä'nō), It. Maximilian
Massimino (mäs-sē-mē'nō), It. Maximin
Massimo (mäs'sē-mō), It. Maximus
Mat (măt), dim. Matthew, Matthias, Martha, Mathilda
Máté (mä'tä), Hung. Matthew
Mateo (mä-tä'ō), Sp. Matthew
Mateusz (mä'tyōōsh), Pol. Matthew
Mathias (mä-tē'äs), Ger. Matthias
Mathieu (mä-tyŭ'), Fr. Matthew

MATHILDA (Mathíldis, is), Wid. Mar. 14.
10 Cent. Wife of Emperor Henry of Germany. *Sig.*
Ger. mighty battle maid. *Pron.* mà-tĭl-dà.
Matilda (mä-tēl'dä), It., Sw. Mathilda
Mathilde (mä-tēld'), Fr. Mathilda
(mä-tĭl'dĕ), Dan., Ger.
Mathildis (mä-tēl'dĭs), Lat. Mathilda
Matias (mä-tē'äs), Sp. Matthias
Matilde (mä-tēl'dä), Sp. Mathilda
Matteo (mät-tä'ō), It. Matthew
Matthaeus (mät-tä'ōōs), Ger., Lat. Matthew
Matthäus (mät-tä'ōōs), Ger., Du. Matthew
Mattheus (mät-tä'ŭs), Du. Matthew

MATTHEW (Matthae'us, i), Ap. Ev. Sep. 21. R. M.
Taxgatherer who left all to follow Jesus. Preached
Gospel in Judea and Ethiopia. Wrote first Gospel.
In art shown with an angel or with purse or bag.
Sig. Heb. gift of Jehovah. *Pron.* măth'yū.

MATTHIAS (Matthías, æ), Ap. M. Feb. 24. R. M.
Chosen by Apostles to replace Judas. In art shown

with axe, lance, or holding sword by point. *Sig.*
Heb. gift of Jehovah. *Pron.* măth-thī'ăs.
(mät-thē'äs), Lat.
Matthieu (mä-tyü'), Fr. Matthew
Matthijs (mä-tīs'), Du. Matthias
Mattia (mät-tē'ä), It. Matthias
Mattie, Matty (măt'tĭ), Matthew, Matthias, Martha,
    Mathilda
Maud (mạd), Mathilda
Maudlin (mạd'lĭn), Magdalen
Maun (mạn), Magdalen
Maur (môr), Fr. Maurus

MAURA (Máura, æ), V. M. Nov. 30. R. M.
    Constantinople. *Pron.* mạ'rà. (mŏw'rä), Lat.
Maureen (mô'rēn), Ir. form of Mary

MAURICE (Maurítius, ii), M. Sept. 22. R. M.
    3 Cent. Officer of Theban Legion. In art shown as
    warrior with banner. *Sig.* Lat. dark-colored.
    Pron. mạ'rĭs.
(mŏ-rēs'), Fr. Maurice
Mauricio (mŏw-rē'thē-ō), Sp. Maurice
Maurisio (mŏw-rē'sē-ō), It. Maurice
Mauritius (mŏw-rēt'sē-ŭs), Lat. Maurice
Maurits (mō'rĭts), Du. Maurice
Mauritz (mō'rĭts), Du. Maurice
Maurizio (mŏw-rēt'sē-ō), It. Maurice

MAURUS (Máurus, i), Ab. Jan. 15. R. M.
    6 Cent. First disciple of St. Benedict at Nursia.
    In art shown with censer in hand. *Pron.* mô'rŭs.
    (mŏw'rŭs), Lat.
Max (măks), Maximilian, Maximian
Maxime (mäk-sēm'), Fr. Maximus

MAXIMILIAN (Maximiliánus, i), B. M. Oct. 12.
R. M.
3 Cent. B. of Lorsch. *Sig.* the great Emil. *Pron.*
măks-ĭ-mĭl′ĭ-ăn.
(mäk-sē-mē′lē-än), Ger.
Maximiliano (mäk-sē-mē-lē-ä′nō), Sp. Maximilian
Maximilianus (mäk-sē-mē-lē-ä′nŭs), Lat. Maximilian
Maximilião (mä-sē-mē-lē-ŏwṅ′), Port. Maximilian
Maximilien (mäk-sē-mē-lē-ăṅ′), Fr. Maximilian

MAXIMIN (Maximínus, i), B. C. Mar. 29
4 Cent. Brother of St. Maxentius and B. of Treves.
Champion of belief in Holy Trinity. *Pron.* măks′-
ĭ-mĭn.
(mäk-sē-măṅ′), Fr.
Maximinus (mäk-sē-mē′nŭs), Lat. Maximin
Maximo (mäk′sē-mō), Sp. Maximus

MAXIMUS (Máximus, i), M. Apr. 14. R. M.
3 Cent. Rome. Jailer of Sts. Tiburtius and Valerian,
converted and martyred. *Sig.* Lat. greatest. *Pron.*
măks′ĭ-mŭs.
(mäk′sē-mŭs), Lat.
May (mā), Mary

MECHTILDIS (Mechtíldis, is), V. Feb. 26.
13 Cent. Cistercian at Hefta; with St. Gertrude first
to propagate devotion to Sacred Heart. *Sig.* Teut.
mighty battle maid. *Pron.* měk-tĭl′dĭs.
(měk-tĭl′dĭs), Lat.

MÉDARD (Medárdus, i), B. C. June 8. R. M.
6 Cent. B. of Noyon and Tournai. *Pron.* mā-där′.
(mä-där′), Fr.
Medardus (mä-där′dŭs), Lat. Medard
Meg (měg), **Meggy** (měg′gĭ), Margaret

MEINRAD (Meinrádus, i), Pr. M. Jan. 21. R. M.
9 Cent. Monk at Reichenau who became recluse at
Einsiedeln, Switzerland. In art shown holding
wooden cup. *Sig.* Teut. mighty council. *Pron.*
mīn'răd.
Meinradus (mā-ĭn-rä'dŭs), Lat. Meinrad

MELANIA THE ELDER (Melánia, æ), Mat. Oct. 8.
4 Cent. Rome. Disciple of St. Augustine. *Sig.* Gr.
black. *Pron.* mĕ-lā'nĭ-à.
(mā-lä'nē-ä), Lat.

MELANIA THE YOUNGER, Mat. Dec. 31. R. M.
4 Cent. Rome. Grand-daughter of above.
Mélanie (mā-lä-nē'), Fr. Melania
Melchiade (mĕl-kē-äd'), Fr. Melchiades

MELCHIADES (Melchíades, is), P. M. Dec. 10 and
Jan. 10. R. M.
4 Cent. Also called Miltiades. *Pron.* mĕl-kī'à-dēz.
(mĕl-kē'ä-dāz), Lat.
MELCHIOR (*indecl.*) Jul. 23.
One of Magi, whose relics are at Cologne. *Sig.* Pers.
king. *Pron.* mĕl'kĭ'ŏr.
Mélèce (mā-lās'), Fr. Meletius

MELETIUS (Melétius, ii), B. C. Feb. 12. R. M.
4 Cent. B. of Antioch. *Sig.* Lat. honied. *Pron.*
mĕ-lē'sĭ-ŭs.
(mā-lāt'sē-ŭs), Lat.

MELLITUS (Mellítus, i), B. C. Apr. 24. R. M.
7 Cent. Archb. Canterbury, Benedictine. *Sig.* Lat.
honey-sweet. *Pron.* mĕl-lē'tŭs.
(mĕl-lē'tŭs), Lat.

MENNAS (Ménnas, æ), M. Nov. 11. R. M.
   3 Cent. Egyptian officer in Roman army, beheaded.
   Pron. mĕn'ás.
   (mĕn'näs), Lat.
Mercedes (mēr-sā'dēz), B. V. M., Our Lady of Mercy
Mercy (mēr'cĭ), Mercedes
Merici (mĕ-rē'chē), *see* Angela
Mertin (mĕr-tăṅ'), Fr. Martin
Meta (mē'tȧ), cor. Margaret
Méthode (mā-tōd'), Fr. Methodius

METHODIUS (Methódius, ii), B. C. Jul. 7. R. M.
   9 Cent. With his brother Cyril, Greeks, Apostles of
   Slavs, credited with originating Slav alphabet.
   Pron. mĕ-thō'dĭ-ŭs.
   (mā-thō'dē-ŭs), Lat.
Micah (mī'kȧ), var. Micheas
Michæas (mē-kā'äs), Lat. Micheas

MICHAEL THE ARCHANGEL (Míchaël, élis),
   Apparition, May 8; Dedication Sept. 29. R. M.
   Conqueror of Lucifer. In 5 Cent. appeared at Mt.
   Gargano, near Naples, and asked that temple be
   built in honor of all the Angels. One of the three
   Angels honored in name by Church. In art shown
   in armor slaying dragon or driving Satan from
   Heaven. *Sig.* Heb. who is like God? *Pron.* mī'kĕl.
   (mē'kä-äl), Lat., Ger.
Michal (mē'käl), Pol. Michael

MICHEAS (Michæ'as, æ), Proph. Jan. 15. R. M.
   Contemporary of Isaias; one of Minor Prophets;
   prophesied birth of Christ in Bethlehem. *Sig.*
   Heb. who is like Jehovah? *Pron.* mĭ-kē'ăs.

Michel (mē-shāl'), Fr. Michael
Michele (mē-kā'lā), It. Michael
Mick (mĭk), dim. Michael
Miguel (mē-gāl'), Port., Sp. Michael
Mihály (mē'häl), Hung. Michael
Mike (mĭk), dim. Michael
Mikhail (mē-kä-āl'), Rus. Michael
Miklos (mē'klŏsh), Hung. Nicholas

MILBURGA (Milbúrgis, is), V. Feb. 23. R. M.
    7 Cent. Sister of St. Mildred of Thanet, daughter of
    King of Mercia, became Abbess of Wenlock,
    Shropshire, Eng. *Sig.* Teut. mild pledge. *Pron.*
    mĭl'bûr-gà.
Milburgis (mĭl-bōōr'jĭs), Lat. Milburga
Milda (mĭl'dà), cont. Mathilda

MILDRED (Mildréda, æ), V. Ab. Jul. 13.
    7 Cent. Mercia. Daughter of St. Emenburga, sister
    of Sts. Milburga and Mildgith. In art, shown as
    abbess, holding lamp. *Sig.* Ger. mild threatener.
    *Pron.*mĭl'drĕd.
Mildreda (mĭl-drā'dä), Lat. Mildred
Milly (mĭl'lĭ), cont. Emily, Amelia, Camilla, Mildred
Miltiades (mĭl-tī'ä-dēz), var. Melchiades
Mina (mē'nà), **Minella** (mĭ-nĕl'là), dim. Wilhelmina
Minette (mē-nĕt'), Fr. Wilhelmina
Minnie (mĭn'nĭ), Mary
Miriam (mĭr'ĭ-ăm), var. Mary
Modeste (mō-dāst'), Fr. Modestus

MODESTUS (Modéstus, i), M. June 15. R. M.
    4 Cent. Husband of St. Crescentia, martyred with
    her and St. Vitus. *Sig.* Lat. modest. *Pron.* mō-
    dĕs'tŭs.
    (mō-dĕs'tŭs), Lat.

Moisè (mō-ē-sä′), It. Moses
Moïse (mō-ēz′), Fr. Moses
Moises (mō-ē-zäz′), Port., Sp. Moses
Mol (mŏl), Mary
Mollie (mŏl′lĭ), **Molly** (mŏl′lĭ), Mary

MONICA (Mónica, æ), Wid. May 4 and Apr. 9. R. M.
4 Cent. Model of wives and mothers; by years of prayers and tears won conversion of her son St. Augustine. Model and Patron of Christian mothers. In art, standing behind the kneeling Augustine. *Pron.* mŏn′ĭ-kȧ.
(mō′nē-kä), Lat.

Monique (mō-nēk′), Fr. Monica
Montfort (mônt-fôr′), *see* Louis Grignon de Montfort.
Moosa (mōō′sä), Ar. Moses
Morgan (môr′găn), var. of Muredach
Moritz (mō′rēts), Du., Ger., Sw. Maurice
(mō′rĭts), Dan.
Morris (mŏr′rĭs), var. Maurice
Mose (mōz), Fr. Moses

MOSES (Móyses, is). Pat. Sep. 4. R. M.
Hebrew prophet; leader chosen by God, lawgiver of Old Testament. Received Ten Commandments from God. *Sig.* Egyptian, drawn out of water. *Pron.* mō′zĕz.

Moyses (mō′ē-zäz), Lat. Moses
(mō-ē-sĕs′), Sp. Port.
Moyzesz (moi′zhĕsh), Pol. Moses
Mozes (mō′zĕsh), Hung. Moses

MUNCHIN (Munchínus, i), B. C. Jan. 2.
5 Cent. Bishop of Limerick of which he is patron. *Pron.* mŭn′kĭn.

Munchinus (mŭn-kē'nŭs), Lat. Munchin

MUREDACH (Muredáchus, i), B. C. Aug. 12
5 Cent. Disciple of St. Patrick, first Bishop of Killala.
Sig. Celt. sea protector. *Pron.* mōōr'dăk.
Muriel (mū'rĭ-ĕl), from Gaelic, Mary
Murtagh (mûr'tä), var. Muredach
Mûsa (mōō'sä), Ar. Moses

MYRON (My'ron, ónis), Pr. M. Aug. 17. R. M.
3 Cent. priest of Greece. *Pron.* mī'rŏn.
(mē'rŏn), Lat.

N

NABOR (Nábor, ŏris), M. July 12. R. M.
4 Cent. martyred with St. Felix at Milan. *Pron.*
nä'bŏr.
Also 4 Cent. Officer in Roman army, June 12
(nä'bôr), Lat.

NAHUM (*indecl.*) Proph. Dec. 1. R. M.
One of Minor Prophets. *Sig.* Heb. consolation. *Pron.*
nä'hŭm.
Nam (năm), Ambrose
Nan (năn), **Nance** (năns), **Nancy** (năn'sĭ), Anne
Nanette (nä-nĕt'), Fr. Anne
(nă-nĕt'), Eng.
Nanny (năn'nĭ), Anne

NAPOLEON (Napóleon, ónis), M. Aug. 15
4 Cent. Alexandria. *Sig.* Gr. lion of forest. *Pron.*
nă-pō'lē-ŏn.
(nä-pō'lä-ŏn), Lat.
Napoléon (nä-pō-lä-ôn'), Fr. Napoleon
Napoleone (nä-pō-lä-ō'nä), It. Napoleon

Narcisse (när-sēs'), Fr. Narcissus
Narcisso (när-chēs'sō), It. Narcissus

NARCISSUS (Narcíssus, i), B. M. Mar. 18. R. M.
4 Cent. Martyred in Spain with St. Felix, his deacon.
Sig. Gr. daffodil. *Pron.* när-sĭs'sŭs.
(när-chē-sŭs), Lat.
Nat (năt), Nathaniel
Natal (nä-täl'), Port., Sp. Natalis
Natale (nä-tä'lä), It. Natalis

NATALIA (Natália, æ), Dec. 1. R. M.
4 Cent. Constantinople. Woman who ministered to
martyrs. *Pron.* nä-tä'lĭ-à.
(nä-tä'lē-ä), Lat.
Natalie (nă'tà-lē), var. Natalia

NATALIS (Natális, is), C. Jan. 27.
6 Cent. Founder of monasticism in Northern Ireland,
associate of St. Columba. *Pron.* nä-tä'lĭs.
(nä-tä'lĭs), Lat. Also Lat. of Noel.
Natan (nä-tän'), Sp. Nathan
Natanael (nä-tä-nä-ĕl'), Sp. Nathaniel

NATHAN (*indecl.*), Proph. Dec. 29.
Prophet who reproved King David. *Sig.* Heb. gift.
Pron. nä'thăn.
(nä-tŏn'), Fr.
Nathanael (nă-thăn'ā-ĕl), supposedly Bartholomew.
Sig. Heb. gift of God.
Nathaniel (nă-thăn'ĭ-ĕl), var. Nathanael.
(nä-tä-nē-ĕl'), Fr. Nathaniel
Natheus (nä'thä-ŭs), Lat. Nathy.

NATHY (Nátheus, i), B. C. Aug. 9.
6 Cent. Son of chieftain of Connaught, B. of Achon-
ry. *Pron.* nä'thĭ.

Nazaire (nä-zâr′), Fr. Nazarius

NAZARIUS (Nazárius, ii), M. Jul. 28. R. M.
4 Cent. Born at Rome, baptized by St. Linus,
preached at Milan, Vienne and Treves. Martyred
with St. Celsus at Milan. *Pron.* nȧ-zā′rĭ-ŭs.
(nä-zä′rē-ŭs), Lat.
Also 4 Cent. M. June 12. Officer in Roman army.

Nazianzen (nă-zĭ-ăn′zĕn), *see* St. Gregory

Neal (nēl), Cornelius

Ned (nĕd), **Neddy** (nĕd′dĭ), Edward, Edmund, etc.

Neemia (nä-ä-mē′ä), It. Nehemias

Nehemiah (nē-hē-mī′à), var. Nehemias

NEHEMIAS (Nehemías, æ), Proph. Jul. 13.
Rebuilt walls of Jerusalem and restored worship of
Jehovah. *Sig.* Heb. comfort of Jehovah. *Pron.*
nē-hē-mī′às.
(nā-hä-mē′äs), Lat.
(nā-ä-mē′äs), Sp.

Néhémie (nā-ä-mē′), Fr. Nehemias

Neil (nēl), Cornelius

Nell (nĕl), **Nellie** (nĕl′lĭ), **Nelly** (nĕl′lĭ), Helen, Ellen,
Eleanor

Nepomucene (nĕ-pŏm′ū-sēn), *see* St. John

Nérée (nä-rä′), Fr. Nereus

NEREUS (Néreus, i), M. May 12. R. M.
1 Cent. Baptized with St. Achilleus by St. Peter.
Sig. Gr. sea-god. *Pron.* nē′rūs.
(nā′rä-ŭs), Lat.

Neri (nâ′rē), *see* St. Philip.

Nest (nĕst), Agnes

NESTOR (Néstor, ŏris), M. Sept. 8. R. M.
4 Cent. A youth at Gaza, Palestine. *Pron.* nĕs′tŏr.
(nĕs′tôr), Lat.

Net (nĕt), **Nettie** (nĕt′tĭ), **Netty** (nĕt′tĭ), Henrietta,
    Antoinette
Nib (nĭb), **Nibbie** (nĭb′ĭ), cor. Isabel
Niccolò (nēk-kō-lō′), It. Nicholas

NICEPHORUS (Nicéphorus, i), M. Feb. 9. R. M.
    3 Cent. Syrian. *Pron.* nĭ-sĕf′ŏ-rŭs.
    (nē-tchā′fō-rŭs), Lat.

NICHOLAS OF TOLENTINO (Nicoláus, ái), C. Sept.
    10. R. M.
    13 Cent. Augustinian zealous for souls in Purgatory.
    In art shown as hermit with stars around head.
    Sig. Gr. victory of the people. *Pron.* nĭk′ō-lăs,
    tō-lĕn-tē′nō.

NICHOLAS OF MYRA, THE GREAT, B. C. Dec. 6
    R. M.
    4 Cent. Archb. Myra, Asia Minor, Patron of children.
    Santa Claus is a corruption of his name. In art
    shown with three balls of gold on book, or three
    purses at feet. *Pron.* mī′rà.
Nick (nĭk), dim. Nicholas
Nicodème (nē-kō-dām′), Fr. Nicodemus

NICODEMUS (Nicodémus, i), C. Aug. 3. R. M.
    1 Cent. disciple of Our Lord, who with St. Joseph of
    Arimathea laid His body in tomb. *Sig.* Gr. victory
    of the people. *Pron.* nĭk-ō-dē′mŭs.
    (nē-kō-dā′mŭs), Lat.
Nicolaas (nē′kō-läs), Du. Nicholas
Nicolao (nē-kō-lä′ō), Port. Nicholas
Nicolas (nē-kō-läs′), Sp. Nicholas
    (nĭk′ō-lăs), Eng.
    (nē-kō-lä′), Fr.

Nicolaus (nē-kō-lä′ŭs), Lat. Nicholas
  (nē′kō-lŏwss), Ger.
Nicole (nē-kōl′), Fr. Nicholas
Nicolò (nē-kō-lō′), It. Nicholas
Nicomède (nē-kō-mäd′), Fr. Nicomedes

NICOMEDES (Nicomédes, is), Pr. M. Sept. 15. R. M.
  1 Cent. Rome. Associate of Sts. Nereus, Achilleus
  and Petronilla, scourged to death. *Pron.* nĭk-ō-mē′-
  dēz.
  (nē-kō-mā′dāz), Lat.
Niklas (nēk′läs), Ger. Nicholas
Nikolai (nē-kō-lä′ē), Rus. Nicholas
Nikolas (nē-kō-läs′), Rus. Nickolas
Nikolaus (nē′kō-lŏwss), Ger. Nicholas
Nils (nĭls), Du., Sw. Nicholas

NILUS (Nílus, i), C. Sept. 26. R. M.
  10 Cent. Basilian monk, founder of Monastery of
  Grottoferrata. *Pron.* nī′lŭs.
  (nē′lŭs), Lat.
Nina (nē′nà), Anne
Ninette (nē-nĕt′), Fr. Anne

NINIAN (Niniánus, i), B. C. Sept. 16. R. M.
  5 Cent. B. of Withern, Ap. of Cumberland and of
  Southern Picts of Scotland. *Pron.* nĭn′ĭ-ăn.
Ninianus (nē-nē-ä′nŭs), Lat. Ninian.
Ninon (nē-nôṅ′), Fr. Anne
Nita (nē′tà), dim. Anita
Noa (nō′ä), Sw. Noe
Noah (nō′à), var. Noe

NOE (*indecl.*), Pat. May 2
  Type of Christ father of Sem, Cham and Japhet.
  Built Ark by order of God and with his family was

saved in the Deluge. *Sig.* Heb. comfort. *Pron.*
nō'ē.

Noé (nō-ā'), Fr. Noe.

NOEL CHABANEL (Natális, is), M. Sept. 26
Martyred in Ontario, Can. 1649. Canonized 1930.
Jesuit priest. *Sig.* Fr. Christmas. *Pron.* nō'ĕl,
shä-bä-nĕl'.

Noël (nō-āl'). Fr. Noel or Natalis. *Sig.* Christmas.

Nol (nōl), Oliver

Nolasco (nō-lăs'kō), *see* St. Peter.

Nooh (nōō), Ar. Noe

Nora, Norah (nō'rȧ), dim. Helen, Honora, Eleanor,
Leonora

NORBERT (Norbértus, i), B. C. June 6. R. M.
12 Cent. Magdeburg. Founder of Premonstratensian
Order, devoted to penance and divine worship,
also care of poor. Revived devotion to Blessed
Sacrament. Archb. Magdeburg. In art shown holding up chalice and Host in right hand. *Pron.*
nôr'bērt. (nôr-bâr'), Fr.

Norberta (nôr-bēr'tȧ), fem. of Norbert

Norbertus (nôr-bâr'tŭs), Lat. Norbert

Noreen (nô-rēn'), Ir. Honora

Notburga (nŏt'bēr-gȧ), var. of Nothburga
(nŏt-bōōr'gä), Lat. of Nothberga

NOTHBURGA (Notbúrga, æ), V. Sept. 13
14 Cent. Tyrolese servant girl, patron of poor and of
hired hands. In art shown carrying bread and sickle.
Sig. Teut. compelling protection. *Pron.* nŏth'bûr-gȧ.

NOTKER (Nótkerus, i), (Bl.), C. Apr. 6.
10 Cent. Monk of St. Gall, Switzerland, great mu-

sician and hymn writer. *Sig.* Teut. compelling spear. *Pron.* nŏt'kĕr.

Notkerus (nŏt'kā-rŭs), Lat. Notker

NOVATUS (Novátus, i), C. June 20. R. M. 2 Cent. Rome. Brother of Sts. Praxedes and Pudentiana. *Pron.* nō-vā'tŭs.
(nō-vä'tŭs), Lat.

Nuh (nōō), Ar. Noe

NYMPHA (Nym'pha, æ), V. M., Nov. 10. R. M. 5 Cent. Iconium. *Sig.* Gr. bride. *Pron.* nĭm'fà.
(nēm'fä), Lat.

O

Obadiah (ō-bà-dī'à), var. of Abdias

Octave (ŏk-täv'), Fr. Octavius

OCTAVIA (Octávia, æ), Apr. 15 (d. u.) Antioch. *Sig.* Lat. eighth-born. *Pron.* ŏk-tä'vĭ-à.
(ŏk-tä'vē-ä), Ger., Lat., Sp.

OCTAVIAN (Octaviánus, i), M. Mar. 22. R. M. 5 Cent. Carthage. *Sig.* Lat. eighth-born. *Pron.* ŏk-tä'vĭ-ăn.

Octaviano (ŏk-tä-vē-ä'nō), It. Octavian

Octavianus (ŏk-tä-vē-ä'nŭs), Lat. Octavian

Octavie (ŏk-tä-vē'), Fr. Octavia

Octavien (ŏk-tä-vē-ăṅ'), Fr. Octavian

Octavio (ŏk-tä'vē-ō), Sp. Octavius

OCTAVIUS (Octávius, ii), M. Nov. 20. R. M. 3 Cent. Soldier of Theban Legion, patron of Turin. *Sig.* Lat. eighth-born. *Pron.* ŏk-tä'vĭ-ŭs.
(ŏk-tä'vē-ŭs), Lat.

Octavus (ŏk-tā'vŭs), var. of Octavius
Odile (ō-dēl'), Fr. Ottilie
Odilia (ō-dĭl'ĭ-à), var. of Ottilie

ODILO (Odĭlo, ónis), Ab. Jan. 1. R. M.
   11 Cent. Ab. Cluny, introduced All Souls' Day. *Sig.*
   Teut. rich. *Pron.* ō-dĭ'lō.
   (ō-dē'lō), Lat.
Odilon (ō-dē-lŏn'), Fr. Otto

ODO (Odo, ónis), B. C. Jul. 4.
   12 Cent. Benedictine, B. of Wilton, Archb. Canterbury. Defended Pope against Henry IV of Germany. *Sig.* Teut. rich. *Pron.* ō'dō.
   Also 10 Cent. Ab. Cluny. Nov. 18. R. M.
   (ō'dō), Lat.
Odoardo (ō-dō-är'dō), var. It. Edward
Odon (ō-dŏn'), Fr. Odo
Odulf (ō-dōōlf), Ger. var. Adolph

OLAF (Olávus, i), K. M. Jul. 29. R. M.
   10 Cent. Norwegian King, converted Sweden. *Sig.*
   Teut. ancestor's relic. *Pron.* ō'läf.
Olavus (ō-lä'vŭs), Lat. Olaf
Ole (ōl), cont. of Olaf

OLGA, Mat. Jul. 11.
   9 Cent. Wife of Igor I, Duke of Kiev, Russia. *Sig.*
   Teut. holy. *Pron.* ŏl'gà.
Olier (ō-lē-âr'), Fr. Oliver
Oliva (ō'lē-vä), Lat. Olive

OLIVE (O'liva, æ), V. June 3. R. M.
   (d. u.) Nun at Anagni, near Rome. *Sig.* Lat. olive.
   Pron. ŏ'lĭv.
   (ō-lēv'), Fr.

OLIVER PLUNKETT (Olivérius, ii), (Bl.), B. M. Jul.
11.
17 Cent. Archb. Armagh, hanged at Tyburn, beati-
fied by Benedict XV, 1920. *Sig.* Lat. olive-tree.
Pron. ŏl'ĭ-vēr.
Oliveiro (ō-lē-vä'rō), Port. Oliver
Oliverio (ō-lē-vä'rē-ō), Sp. Oliver
Oliverius (ō-lē-vä'rē-ŭs), Lat. Oliver
Olivia (ō-lĭv'ĭ-à), var. Olive, also Ger., Lat., It.
Olivie (ō-lē-vē'), Fr. Olive
Olivier (ō-lē-vē-ā'), Fr. Oliver
(ō-lē-vēr'), Du. Sw.
Oliviero (ō-lē-vē-ā'rō), It. Oliver
Ollie (ŏl'lē), dim. Olive
Omfredo (ŏm-frä'dō), It. Humphrey
Onésime (ō-nä-zēm'), Fr. Onesimus
Onesimo (ō-nä'sē-mō), It. Onesimus

ONESIMUS (Onésimus, i), B. M. Feb. 16. R. M.
1 Cent. Slave for whom St. Paul wrote Epistle to
Philemon, B. of Ephesus. *Pron.* ō-nĕz'ĭ-mŭs.
(ō-nä'sē-mŭs), Lat.
Onfroi (ŏṅ-frwä'), Fr. Humphrey
Onofredo (ō-nō-frä'dō), It. Humphrey
Onufrio (ō-nōō'frē-ō), It. Humphrey
Onuphrius (ō-nōō'frē-ŭs), Lat. Humphrey

OPTATUS (Optátus, i). B. C. June 4. R. M.
4 Cent. writer. B. Mileve. *Sig.* Lat. chosen. *Pron.*
ŏp-tä'tŭs.
(ŏp-tä'tŭs), Lat.
Oreste (ō-rāst'), Fr. Orestes

ORESTES (Oréstes, is), M. Nov. 9. R. M.
4 Cent. Noted Cappadocian convert maker. *Sig.*

Gr. mountaineer. *Pron.* ō-rĕs'tēz.
(ō-rās'tāz), Lat.
Orlando (ōr-län'dō), It. Roland
Orsola (ōr'sō-lä), It. Ursula
Ortensia (ōr-tĕn'sē-ä), It. Hortense (fem.)
Ortensio (ōr-tĕn'sē-ō), It. Hortense (masc.)

OSBURGA (Osbúrga, æ), V. Mar. 28.
11 Cent. Ab. Coventry. *Pron.* ŏs'bûr-gà.
(ŏs-boōr'gä), Lat.

OSCAR (Anschárius, ii), B. C. Feb. 3. R. M.
9 Cent. B. of Hamburg and Bremen, converted
Danes and Swedes. In art shown with convert
Danes or with fur pelisse. *Sig.* Celt. bounding
warrior. *Pron.* ŏs'kăr.

OSEE (*indecl.*), Proph. Jul. 4. R. M.
8 B. C. One of 12 minor prophets. *Sig.* Heb. salvation. *Pron.* ō'sē.
Osmond (ŏz'mŏnd), var. of Osmund.
Osmont (ōz-môṅ'), Fr. Osmund

OSMUND (Osmúndus, i), B. C. Dec. 4. R. M.
11 Cent. Norman noble at court of William the
Conqueror, Chancellor of England, B. of Salisbury. *Sig.* Ger. Protection of God. *Pron.* ŏz'-
mŭnd.
Osmunda (ŏz-mŭn'dà), fem. Osmund
Osmundus (ŏz-mŭn'dŭs), Lat. Osmund

OSWALD (Oswáldus, i), B. C. Feb. 28.
10 Cent. Nephew of St. Odo, Archb. York.
Sig. Ger. Power of God. *Pron.* ŏz'wăld.
Also King of Northumbria, M. Aug. 5. R. M.
Oswalda (ŏz-wăl'dà), fem. Oswald

Oswaldus (ŏz-wäl'dŭs), Lat. Oswald

OSWIN (Oswínus, i), K. M. Aug. 20.
7 Cent. King in Northumbria, directed by St. Aidan.
Sig. Teut. divine friend. *Pron.* ŏz'wĭn.
Oswinus (ŏz-wē'nŭs), Lat. Oswin
Oswold (ŏz'wŏld), var. of Oswald
Oswy (ŏs'wĭ), var. Oswin
Othilia (ō-tē'lē-ä), Lat. Ottilia

OTHMAR (Othmárus, i), Ab. Nov. 16.
8 Cent. Benedictine, Ab. St. Gall. *Sig.* Teut. happy
fame. *Pron.* ŏth'mär.
Othmarus (ōth-mä'rŭs), Lat. Othmar
Otho (ō'tō), Lat. Otto
Othon (ō-tōń'), Fr. Otto
Oton (ō-tōn'), Sp. Otto
Otonio (ō-tō'nē-ō), Sp. Otto
Ottavia (ŏt-tä'vē-ä), It. Octavia
Ottaviano (ŏt-tä-vē-ä'nō), It. Octavian
Ottavio (ŏt-tä'vē-ō), It. Octavius

OTTERAN (Otteránus, i), B. C. Oct. 27.
6 Cent. Ab. of Iona, disciple of St. Columba. *Pron.*
ŏt'ĕ-răn.
Otteranus (ŏ-tä-rä'nŭs), Lat. Otteran

OTTILIA, OTTILIE (Othília, æ), V. Dec. 13. R. M.
7 Cent. Patron of Alsace, invoked against blindness.
In art shown with two eyes on a book. *Sig.* Teut.
happy battle maid. *Pron.* ŏt-tĭ'lĭ-á or ŏt'tĭ-lĭ.

OTTO (O'tho, ónis), B. C. Jul. 2. R. M.
Bamberg, Apostle of Pomerania. *Sig.* Teut. rich.
Pron. ŏt'tō.
Ottone (ŏt-tō'nā), It. Otto

Ouen (ōō-ăn'), Fr. Owen

OWEN (Audoë'nus, i), C. Aug. 24.
  7 Cent. Monk at Lichfield, companion of St. Chad.
  Sig. Celt. lamb or young warrior. *Pron.* ō'ĕn.

P

Pablo (pä'blō), Sp. Paul

PACHOMIUS (Pachómius, ii), C. May 9. R. M.
  3 Cent. Founder of community life in Egypt. *Pron.*
  pă-kō'mĭ-ŭs.
  (pä-kō'mē-ŭs), Lat.

PACIFICUS (Pacíficus, i), C. Sept. 24. R. M.
  18 Cent. Priest of Order of Friars Minor. *Sig.* Lat.
  peaceful. *Pron.* pă-sĭ'fĭ-kŭs.
  (pä-tchē'fē-kŭs), Lat.
Paddy (păd'dĭ), dim. Patrick
Pádraic (pä'drĭk), Ir. Patrick
Pál (päl), Hung. Paul

PALLADIUS (Palládius, ii), B. C. Jul. 6.
  5 Cent. First Bishop of Scots. *Pron.* păl-lā'dĭ-ŭs.
  (pä-lä'dē-ŭs), Lat.
Pamphile (pän-fēl'), Fr. Pamphilus.

PAMPHILUS (Pámphilus, i), Pr. M. June 1. R. M.
  4 Cent. Caesarea. *Pron.* păm'fĭ-lŭs.
  (päm'fē-lŭs), Lat.
Pancrace (pän-kräs'), Fr. Pancratius
Pancras (pän'kräs), Pancratius

PANCRATIUS (Pancrátius, ii), M. May 12. R. M.
  4 Cent. Boy of fourteen, one of Fourteen Holy
  Helpers. *Sig.* Gr. ruler of all. *Pron.* păn-krā'shŭs.
  (pän-krät'sē-ŭs), Lat.

Pankratius (pän-krät'sē-ŭs), Ger. Pancratius

PANTALEON (Pantáleon, ónis), M. Jul. 27. R. M.
4 Cent. Physician, of Nicomedia, patron of doctors.
Sig. Gr. all lion. *Pron.* păn-tă'lē-ŏn.
(pän-tä'lä-ŏn), Lat.
Pantaléon (pän-tä-lä-ôn'), Fr. Pantaleon
Paola (pä'ō-lä), It. Paula
Paolina (pä-ō-lē'nä), It. Paulina
Paolo (pä'ō-lō), It. Paul
Pascal (päs-käl'), Fr. Paschal

PASCHAL BAYLON (Paschális, is), C. May 17.
R. M.
16 Cent. Spanish shepherd of Aragon, Franciscan
lay-brother devoted to Blessed Sacrament, patron
of Eucharistic devotions and societies. In art shown
before Blessed Sacrament, with staff and bundle
on ground. *Sig.* Heb. child of Passover. *Pron.*
păs'kăl.
Also 9 Cent. Paschal I, P. C. Feb. 11. R. M.
Paschalis (päs-kä'lĭs), Lat. Paschal.
Pascual (päs-kwäl'), Sp. Paschal
Pasquale (päs-kwä'lä), It. Paschal
Pat (păt), dim. Patrick, Patricia, Martha, Mathilda

PATIENCE (Patiéntia, æ), M. May 1. R. M.
3 Cent. Wife of St. Orentius, with whom she was
martyred. *Sig.* Lat. patience. *Pron.* pā'shĕns.
(pä-syăns'), Fr.
Patientia (pät-sē-ĕnt'sē-ä), Lat. Patience
Patrice (pä-trēs'), Fr. Patrick

PATRICIA (Patrícia, æ), M. Mar. 13. R. M.
4 Cent. Martyred at Nicomedia with husband, St.

Macedonius. *Sig.* Lat. noble. *Pron.* pă-trĭ′shȧ.
(pä-trē′tchē-ä), Lat.

Patricio (pä-trē′thē-ō), Sp. Patrick
(pä-trē′sē-ō), Port.

Patricius (pä-trē′chē-ŭs), Lat. Patrick

PATRICK (Patrícius, ii or Patrítius, ii), B. C. Mar. 17.
R. M.
5 Cent. Received mission from Pope Celestine.
Archb. of Armagh, Patron of Ireland. In art shown
as bishop with shamrock and crozier crushing serpent. *Sig.* Lat. noble, patrician. *Pron.* păt′rĭk.

Patritius (pä-trēt′sē-ŭs), Lat. Patrick

Patrizio (pä-trēt′sē-ō), It. Patrick

Patrizius (pä-trēt-sē-ōŏs), Ger. Patrick

Patty (păt′tĭ), Patrick, Patricia, Martha, Mathilda

PAUL THE APOSTLE (Páulus, i), Conversion, Jan.
25 (June 29 with St. Peter), Commemoration,
June 30. R. M.
Apostle of the Gentiles. Persecutor of Christians,
thrown from horse by light from heaven and converted. Carried Gospel throughout Roman
Empire. Author of many of Epistles. Beheaded
at Rome. In art shown with sword and book of
Gospels or two swords, one up, one down. *Sig.* Lat.
little. *Pron.* pạl.
(pōl), Fr. Paul
(pŏwl), Ger.

PAUL, THE FIRST HERMIT, C. Jan. 10 and 15.
Lower Thebaid, 3 Cent. Life written by St. Jerome.
In art shown with long white beard, near palm
tree, or with raven.

PAUL OF CROSS, C. Apr. 28 and Oct. 18
17 Cent. Genoa. Founder of Order of Passionists.

PAULA (Páula, æ), Jan. 26. R. M.
  5 Cent. Roman noblewoman, mother of St. Eustochia. Entered community of St. Jerome at Bethlehem. In art shown with sponge in hand or with book and black veil. *Sig.* Lat. little. *Pron.* pạ'lä (pŏw'lä), Ger., Lat., Port., Sp.
Paule (pōl), Fr. Paula
Paulin (pō-lăn'), Fr. Paulinus

PAULINA (Paulína, æ), June 6. R. M.
  4 Cent. Martyred with father, St. Artemis, and mother, St. Candida. *Sig.* Lat. little. *Pron.* pạ-lī'nà.
(pŏw-lē'nä), Lat., Port., Sp.
Pauline (pō-lēn'), Fr. Paulina
(pạ-lēn'), Eng.
(pŏw-lē'nĕ), Ger.

PAULINUS (Paulínus, i), B. C. June 22. R. M.
  4 Cent. Bordeaux. Prefect of Rome, senator and consul. Friend of Sts. Martin and Ambrose, B. of Nola. *Sig.* Lat. little. *Pron.* pạ-lī'nŭs.
(pŏw-lē'nŭs), Lat.
Paulo (pŏw'lō), Port. Paul
Paulus (pŏw'lŭs), Lat. Paul
Pavel (pä'vĕl), Rus. Paul
Pawel (pä'vĕl), Pol. Paul
Pearl (pērl), Margaret
Peder (pä'dēr), Dan. Peter
Pedro (pä'drō), Port., Sp. Peter
Peg (pĕg), **Peggie** (pĕg'gĭ), Margaret
Pelagia (Pelágia, æ), Pen. Oct. 8. R. M.
  5 Cent. Jerusalem. *Pron.* pĕ-lä'jĭ-à.
(pĕ-lä'jē-ä), Lat.

Pellegrino (pĕl-lä-grē'nō), It. Peregrine
Penelope (pē-nĕl'ō-pē), Irene. *Sig.* Gr. weaver
Pepi (pĕ'pē), Ger. Paul
Percy (pēr'sĭ), *see* St. Thomas
Pérégrin (pä-rä-grăṅ'), Fr. Peregrine

PEREGRINE (Peregrínus, i), B. M. May 16. R. M.
3 Cent. Auxerre. *Sig.* Lat. stranger. *Pron.* pĕr'ē-grĭn.
Peregrino (pä-rä-grē'nō), Port., Sp. Peregrine
Peregrinus (pä-rä-grē'nŭs), Lat. Peregrine

PERFECTUS (Perféctus, i), Pr. M. Apr. 18. R. M.
9 Cent. Spaniard of Cordova slain by Mohammedans. *Sig.* Lat. perfect. *Pron.* pēr-fĕk'tŭs.
(pâr-fĕk'tŭs), Lat.

PERPETUA (Perpétua, æ), M. Mar. 6. R. M.
3 Cent. Maiden thrown to wild beasts at Carthage
with St. Felicitas. Named in Canon of Mass. In
art shown beside wild cow or with ladder guarded
by dragon. *Sig.* Lat. lasting. *Pron.* pēr-pĕ'tū-à.
(pâr-pĕ'tōō-ä), Lat.
Perpétue (pâr-pä-tü'), Fr. Perpetua
Pete (pēt), dim. Peter

PETER (Pétrus, i), Ap. June 29. Chains, Aug. 1.
Chair, at Antioch, Feb. 22; at Rome, Jan. 18.
Ded. of Bas. of Sts. P. and P. Nov. 18. R. M.
First Pope, the Rock upon which Christ built His
Church, crucified head downwards out of humility,
at Rome. In art shown with two keys of gold and
iron or fish, or crucified head downward.
Sig. Gr. rock. *Pron.* pē'tēr.
(pä'tĕr) Ger.

PETER OF ALCANTARA, C. Oct. 19. R. M.
16 Cent. Spanish Franciscan, mystical writer, adviser of St. Teresa. *Pron.* ăl-kän'tä-rä.

PETER OF ALEXANDRIA, B. M. Nov. 26. R. M.
4 Cent. First to condemn errors of Arius.

PETER CANISIUS, C. D. Apr. 27.
16 Cent. Nimwegen. Jesuit, one of companions of St. Ignatius; preached against Protestantism in Germany. Called "second Apostle of Germany." Author of a Catechism. *Pron.* kă-nē'sē-ŭs.

PETER CELESTINE, P. C. May 19. R. M.
13 Cent. Founder of Celestinian Order of Monks; resigned out of humility after reigning as Pope for four months. *Pron.* sĕl'ĕs-tĭn or sĕ-lĕs'tĭn.

PETER CHRYSOLOGUS, B. C. D. Dec. 4. R. M.
5 Cent. Imola. Archb. Ravenna, eloquent preacher, hence name Chrysologus (golden mouthed). *Pron.* chrĭ-sŏl'ō-gŭs.

PETER CLAVER, C. Sep. 8. R. M.
17 Cent. Spanish Jesuit, labored in South America, Apostle of Negroes, patron of all missions among Negroes. *Pron.* klä'vĕr.

PETER DAMIAN, B. C. D. Feb. 23. R. M.
11 Cent. Ravenna. Hermit of Fonte Avellano, learned writter, Card. B. of Ostia. In art shown with cardinal's hat beside him. *Pron.* dä'mĭ-ăn.

PETER FABER (Bl.), C. Aug. 9.
16 Cent. Jesuit, companion of St. Ignatius. *Pron.* fä'bĕr.

PETER FOURIER, C. Dec. 9. R. M.
16 Cent. Model parish priest of Lorraine, founder of several Congregations. *Pron.* fōō-rē-ā'.

PETER GONZALES, C. Apr. 14.
12 C. Dominican of noble family, labored among sailors in Spain and is their patron. In art shown walking on sea with fire in hand. Also called Elmo. *Pron.* gŏn-thä'lās.

PETER JULIAN EYMARD (Bl.), C. Jan. 19 and Aug. 3
19 Cent. La Mure, France. Founder of Congregation of Fathers of Blessed Sacrament and Sisters-Servants of Blessed Sacrament. Beatified, 1925, by Pius XI. *Pron.* ā-mär'.

PETER THE MARTYR, June 2. R. M.
Priest executed with St. Marcellinus, 4 Cent. Named in Canon of Mass. In art shown with axe in head.

PETER NOLASCO, C. Jan. 31. R. M.
13 Cent. Languedoc. Founder with St. Raymund of Order of Our Lady of Ransom for freeing slaves from Moors. In art shown with chain in hand. *Pron.* nō-läs'kō.

PETER OF VERONA, M. Apr. 29. R. M.
13 Cent. Dominican, model of prayer and penance, slain by Manichaean heretics. *Pron.* vĕ-rō'nȧ.
Peterkin (pē'tēr-kĭn), dim. Peter.

PETRONILLA (Petronĭlla, æ), V. May 31. R. M.
1 Cent. Convert of St. Peter. *Sig.* Gr. rock. *Pron.* pĕ-trō-nĭl'lȧ.
(pā-trō-nē'lä), Lat.
Pétronille (pā-trō-nēl'), Fr. Petronilla
Petrus (pā'trōōs), Ger., Lat., Peter

Phebe (fē'bē), var. Phoebe
Phébé (fā-bā'), Fr. Phoebe
Phelim (fĕ'lĭm), var. Felim
Phemie (fē'mē), Sc. Euphemia
Pheny (fē'nĭ), dim. Josephine
Phil (fĭl), dim. Philip

PHILEMON (Phĭlemon, émonis), M. Nov. 22. R. M.
  1 Cent. Christian to whom St. Paul addressed an
  Epistle. Stoned to death with St. Apphias. *Sig.*
  Gr. loving, friendly. *Pron.* fĭ-lē'mŏn.
  (fē'lā-mŏn), Lat.
Philémon (fē-lā-mōn'), Fr. Philemon

PHILIBERT (Philibértus, i), Ab. Aug. 20. R. M.
  7 Cent. Founder of Abbey of Jumièges. *Sig.* Teut.
  bright will. *Pron.* fĭl'ĭ-bērt.
  (fē-lē-bâr'), Fr.
Philibertus (fē-lē-bâr'tŭs), Lat. Philibert

PHILIP (Philíppus, i), Ap. M. May 1. R. M.
  Preached in upper Asia, martyred in Phrygia. In art
  shown with T-cross or cross on staff. *Sig.* Gr. lover
  of horses. *Pron.* fĭl'ĭp.

PHILIP BENIZI, C. Aug. 23. R. M.
  13 Cent. Florence. Superior General of Servite
  Order, elected Pope, but refused out of humility.
  Pron. bĕ-nē'zē.

PHILIP OF JESUS, C. Feb. 5.
  16 Cent. Spanish Franciscan of Mexico, crucified in
  Japan, of which he was first martyr.

PHILIP NERI, C. May 26. R. M.
  16 Cent. Florence. "Apostle of Rome," founder of
  Oratorians. *Pron.* nâ'rē.

Philipp (fē'lĕp), Ger. Philip

PHILIPPA (Philíppa, æ), M. Sep. 20. R. M.
  3 Cent. Put to death at Pamphylia with son, St. Theodore. *Sig.* Gr. lover of horses. *Pron.* fĭ-lĭp'pȧ.
  (fē-lē'pä), Lat.

Philippe (fē-lĕp'), Fr. Philip

Philippina (fĭ-lĭp-pē'nȧ), dim. Philippa

Philippine (fē-lĭp-pē'nĕ), Ger. Philippa
  (fē-lĕp-pēn'), Fr.

Philippos (fĭ'lĭp-pŏs), Gr. Philip

Philippus (fē-lē'pŭs), Lat. Philip

PHILOMENA (Philoména, æ or Philuména, æ), V. M. Aug. 11
  (d. u.). In art shown with lily, palm and javelin. *Sig.* Gr. daughter of light. *Pron.* fĭl-ō-mē'nȧ.
  (fē-lō-mā'nä), Lat.

Philomène (fē-lō-mān'), Fr. Philomena

Philumena (fē-lōō-mā'nä), Lat. var. Philomena

PHINEAS (Phíneas, æ), Aug. 12
  Jewish high priest, grandson of Aaron. *Pron.* fĭn'ē-ăs.
  (fē'nā-äs), Lat.

Phinéas (fē-nā-äs'), Fr. Phineas

Phinees (fē-nā-ĕs'), Sp. Phineas

PHOCAS (Phócas, æ), M. Mar. 5. R. M.
  Syrian of early Church. Invoked by those bitten by snakes. *Pron.* fō'kăs.
  (fō'käs), Lat.

PHOEBE (Phœ'be, es), Sep. 3. R. M.
  1 Cent. Deaconess commended by St. Paul. *Sig.* Gr. shining. *Pron.* fē'bē.
  (fā'bā), Lat.

Pie (pē), Fr. Pius
Pierce (pērs), var. Peter
Pierre (pyâr'), Fr. Peter
Pierrot (pyâr-rō'), Fr. dim. Peter
Pieter (pē'tēr), Du. Peter
Pietro (pē-ā'trō), It. Peter
Piligrim (pē-lē-grēm), Ger. Peregrine
Pio (pē'ō), It. Pius
Piotr (pyōt'r), Rus., Pol. Peter
Pip (pĭp), dim. Philip

PIUS I (Píus, ii), P. M. Jul. 11. R. M.
2 Cent. *Sig.* Lat. filial, dutiful. *Pron.* pī'ŭs.
(pē'ŭs), Lat.

PIUS V, P. C. May 5. R. M.
16 Cent. Dominican of Bologna. Prayed for victory
over Turks at Lepanto. Reformed Missal and
Breviary.

PLACID (Plácidus, i), M. Oct. 5. R. M.
6 Cent. Disciple of St. Benedict, brother of Sts.
Eutychius, Victorinus and Flavia. *Sig.* Lat. peaceful. *Pron.* plă'sĭd.
Placide (plä-sēd'), Fr. Placid

PLACIDIA (Placídia, æ), V. Oct. 11. R. M.
5 Cent. Verona. *Sig.* Lat. peaceful. *Pron.* plă-sĭd'ĭ-à.
(plä-chē'dē-ä), Lat.
Placidie (plä-sē-dē'), Fr. Placidia
Placidus (plä'chē-dŭs), Lat. Placid
Pol (pŏl), **Polly** (pŏl'lĭ), Mary

POLYCARP (Polycar'pus, i), B. M. Jan. 26. Feb. 23
2 Cent. Converted by St. John the Evangelist.
B. of Smyrna, burned alive. *Sig.* Gr. much fruit.
Pron. pŏl'ĭ-kärp.

Polycarpe (pō-lē-kärp'), Fr. Polycarp
Polycarpo (pō-lē-kär'pō), It. Polycarp
Polycarpus (pō-lē-kär'pŭs), Lat. Polycarp

PONTIANUS (Pontiánus, i), P. M. Nov. 19. R. M.
3 Cent. exiled to Sardinia. *Pron.* pŏn-sĭ-ăn'ŭs.
(pŏnt-sē-ä'nŭs), Lat.
Pontien (pŏn-syăń'), Fr. Pontianus
Pop (pŏp), Robert
Postel (pŏs-těl'), *see* Mary Magdalen
Praxède (präk-säd'), Fr. Praxedes

PRAXEDES (Praxédes, is), V. M. Jul. 21. R. M.
2 Cent. Daughter of Roman senator Pudens, sister of
St. Pudentiana, devoted to martyrs. *Sig.* Gr.
active. *Pron.* präk-sē'dēz.
(präk-sä'dāz), Lat.
Prime (prēm), Fr. Primus

PRIMUS (Prímus, i), M. June 9. R. M.
Brother of St. Felician, with whom he was thrown to
wild beasts, but was saved by miracle, then beheaded. *Sig.* Lat. first. *Pron.* prī'mŭs.
(prē'mŭs), Lat.

PRISCA (Prísca, æ), V. M. Jan. 18. R. M.
3 Cent. Rome. Also called Priscilla. *Sig.* Lat. ancient. *Pron.* prĭs'kà.
(prēs'kä), Lat.

PRISCILLA (Priscílla, æ), Wid. Jan. 16. R. M.
1 Cent. Mother of Senator Pudens and grandmother of Sts. Praxedes and Pudentiana. *Sig.*
Lat. ancient. *Pron.* prĭs-sĭl'là.
(prē-shĭl'lä), Lat.

Priscille (prē-sēl'), Fr. Priscilla
Prisque (prēsk), Fr. Prisca

PROCESSUS (Procéssus, i), M. Jul. 2. R. M.
1 Cent. Slain with St. Martinianus, warden of Mamertine prison when St. Peter was imprisoned. Converted by miracle and baptized by the Apostle. *Pron.* prō-sĕs'ŭs.
(prō-chā'sŭs), Lat.

PROSPER OF AQUITAINE (Prósper, ĕri), B. C. June 25. R. M.
5 Cent. Apologist against Nestorianism and Pelagianism. *Pron.* prŏs'pēr.
(prōs'pâr), Lat.
Protais (prō-tā'), Fr. Protase

PROTASE (Protásius, ii), M. June 19. R. M.
1 Cent. Patron of Milan, brother of St. Gervase. *Pron.* prō'tāz.
Protasius (prō-tä'zē-ŭs), Lat. Protase
Prote (prōt), Fr. Protus

PROTUS (Prótus, i), M. Sept. 11. R. M.
3 Cent. Beheaded with St. Hyacinth, his brother. *Pron.* prō'tŭs.
(prō'tŭs), Lat.

PRUDENCE (Prudéntia, æ), V. May 6.
15 Cent. Of Order of Eremites of St. Augustine. *Sig.* Lat. wise. *Pron.* prü'dĕns.
Prudentia (prōō-dĕnt'sē-ä), Lat. Prudence

PRUDENTIUS (Prudéntius, ii), B. C. Apr. 28. R. M.
9 Cent. Tarazona, Spain. *Sig.* Lat. wise. *Pron.* prü-dĕn'shŭs,
Prudy (prü'dĭ), **Prue** (prü), dim. Prudence

PUDENS (Púdens, éntis), M. May 19. R. M.
2 Cent. Roman Senator, father of Sts. Praxedes and
Pudentiana. *Pron.* pū'dĕnz.
(pōō'dĕnz), Lat.

PUDENTIANA (Pudentiána, æ), V. May 19. R. M.
2 Cent. Daughter of Senator Pudens, sister of St.
Praxedes, 16 years old. Patron of Philippine
Islands. *Pron.* pū-dĕn-sĕ-ăn'á.
(pōō-dĕnt-sē-ä'nä), Lat.
Pudentienne (pōō-dŏn-sē-ĕn'), Fr. Pudentiana

PULCHERIA (Pulchéria, æ), V. Emp. Sept. 10. R. M.
5 Cent. Byzantium, guardian of the Faith and peacemaker. *Sig.* Lat. beautiful. *Pron.* pŭl-kē'rĭ-á.
(pōōl-kä'rē-ä), Lat.
Pulcherie (pŭl-kä-rē'), Fr. Pulcheria

Q

QUENTIN (Quinctínus, i), M. Oct. 4
6 Cent. At Tours, officer of court of King Cothaire I.
Preferred death rather than sin. *Sig.* Lat. fifth.
Pron. kwĕn'tĭn.
Quinctinus (kwĭnk-tē'nŭs), Lat. Quentin
Quintianus (kwĭnt-sē-ä'nŭs), Lat. var. Quentin
Quintin (kwĭn'tĭn), var. Quentin
Quiricus (kwē'rē-kŭs), Lat. Cyr.

R

RADEGUND, RADEGUNDA (Radegúndis, is), Q.
Aug. 13. R. M.
6 Cent. Queen of France. *Pron.* rä'dĕ-gŭnd or gŭn'dà.
Radegundis (rä-dä-gŭn'dĭs), Lat. Radegund
Radulphus (rä-dŭl'fŭs), Lat. Ralph

Rafael (rä-fä-äl'), Sp. Raphael
Rafaele (rä-fä-ä'lä), **Raffaele** (räf-fä-ä'lä), It. Raphael.
Raimond (rä-mōṅ'), Fr. Raymund
Raimondo (rī-moōn'dō), It. Raymund
Raimund (rī'moŏnt), Ger. Raymond

RALPH (Radúlphus, i), B. C. June 21.
 9 Cent. French, of royal blood. Archb. of Bruges.
 Sig. Teut. house wolf. *Pron.* rălf.
Ramon (rä-mōn'), Sp. Raymund
Randal (răn'dăl), var. Ralph
Raolfo (rä-ōl'fō), It. Ralph
Raoul (rä-oōl'), Fr. Ralph

RAPHAEL THE ARCHANGEL (Ráphaël, élis), Oct.
 24. R. M.
 Guardian of young Tobias on his journey. One of the
    three angels honored by the Church. In art shown
    with boy Tobias carrying fish. *Sig.* Heb. healing of
    God. *Pron.* rä'fä-ĕl. (rä'fȧ-äl), Ger. Lat.
Raphaël (rä-fä-ĕl'), Fr. Raphael
Rastus (răs'tŭs), dim. Erastus
Ray (rä), dim. Raymund
Raymond (rä-mōṅ'), Fr. Raymund
 (rä'mŏnd), var. of Raymund

RAYMUND NONNATUS (Raymúndus, i), C. Aug.
 31. R. M.
 13 Cent. Spain. Cardinal. Member of Order of Our
    Lady of Ransom for redemption of captives. *Sig.*
    Teut. wise potection. *Pron.* rä-mŭnd.

RAYMUND OF PENNAFORT, C. Jan. 23. R. M.
 13 Cent. Spanish noble, General of Dominican Order.
    With St. Peter Nolasco founded Order of Our
    Lady of Ransom. Noted canonist.

Raymundo (rī-mōōn'dō), Sp. Raymond
Raymundus (rä-ē-mŭn'dŭs), Lat. Raymund
REGINA (Regína, æ), V. M. Sept. 7. R. M.
3 Cent. Autun. *Sig.* Lat. queen. *Pron.* rĕ-jē'na.
(rä-jē'nä), Lat.
Régine (rä-zhēn'), Fr. Regina
REGINALD (Regináldus, i), (Bl.) C. Feb. 12
13 Cent.   One of first Dominicans, professor at
University of Paris. *Sig.* Ger. strong ruler. *Pron.*
rĕj'ĭ-nāld.
Reginaldus (rä-jē-näl'dŭs), Lat. Reginald
Regis (rē'jĭs), *see* St. John Francis
Regnauld, Regnault (rĕh-nō'), Fr. Reginald
Reichard (rī'kärt), Ger. Richard
Reinaldo (rä-ē-näl'dō), Sp. Reginald
Reinalt (rī'nält), Ger. Reginald
Reine (rån), Fr. Regina
Reinhold (rīn'hōlt), Dan., Ger., Sw. Reginald
Reinold (rī'nōlt), Du. Reginald
Reinwald (rīn'wält), Ger. Reginald
REMBERT (Rembértus, i), B. C. Feb. 4 and June 11.
R. M.
9 Cent. Flanders. Labored with St. Oscar in Scandi-
navia. Archb. Bremen. *Sig.* Teut. splendor of
judgment. *Pron.* rĕm'bĕrt.
Rembertus (rĕm-bâr'tŭs),   Lat. Rembert.
Rémi (rä-mē'), Fr. Remigius
REMIGIUS (Remígius, ii), B. C. Jan. 13 and Oct. 1.
5 Cent. Laon.   Apostle of Franks, converted and
baptized Clovis, first king of France. Archb. Rheims
at 22 years, governed for 70 years. *Pron.* rĕ-mĭ'-
jĭ-ŭs.
(rä-mē'jē-ŭs), Lat. Remigius

Rémy (rä-mē'), Fr. Remigius

Renata (rē-nä'tá), fem. of Renatus

Renato (rä-nä'tō), It. Renatus

RENATUS (Renátus, i), B. C. Nov. 12
    5 Cent. B. of Angers. *Sig.* Lat. reborn. *Pron.*
    rē-nä'tŭs.
    (rä-nä'tŭs), Lat.

Renaud (rĕ-nō'), Fr. Reginald, Reynold

René (rĕ-nä'), Fr. Renatus

RENÉ GOUPIL (Renátus, i), C. M. Sep. 26
    17 Cent. Brother of Society of Jesus, martyred near
    Auriesville, N. Y. Canonized 1930. *Pron.* rĕ-nä'
    gōō-pēl'.

Renée (rĕ-nä'), Fr. Renata, fem. of Renatus

REPARATA (Reparáta, æ), V. M. Oct. 8. R. M.
    3 Cent. Palestinian maiden. When beheaded, dove
    flew up from body. *Pron.* rĕ-pà-rä'tá.
    (rä-pä-rä'tä), Lat.

Réparate (rä-pä-rät'), Fr. Reparata

RESPICIUS (Respícius, ii), M. Nov. 10. R. M.

Reta (rē'tá), cor. Margaret

Retta (rĕt'á), cor. Margaret

Reuben (rü'bĕn), var. Ruben

Reynaldo (rä-näl'dō), Sp. Reginald

Ricardo (rē-kär'dō), It., Port., Sp. Richard

RICHARD OF CHICHESTER (Richárdus, i), B. C.
    Apr. 3. R. M.
    13 Cent. Chancellor of Oxford, friend of St. Edmund.
    In art shown with book, chalice on side at his feet.
    Sig. Ger. powerful. *Pron.* rĭch'ärd of chĭch'ĕs-tĕr.
    (rē-shär'), Fr.
    (rēk'ärt), Ger.

Also King of England 8 Cent., father of Sts. Willibald, Wunibald and Walburga.   Feb. 7. R. M.

RICHARD FETHERSTONE (Bl.), M. Jul. 30
16 Cent.   Priest hanged at Smithfield.

RICHARD KIRKMAN (Bl.), M. Aug. 22
16 Cent.   Priest martyred at York.

RICHARD REYNOLDS (Bl.), M. May 4
16 Cent.   Bridgettine priest martyred at Tyburn.

RICHARD THIRKILL (Bl.), M. May 29
16 Cent.   Priest martyred at Tyburn.

RICHARD WHITING (Bl.), M. Dec. 1
Abbot of Glastonbury hanged in 16 Cent. under Henry VIII.
Richardus (rē-kär'dŭs), Lat. Richard
Ridolfo (rē-dōl'fō), It. Rudolph, Ralph
Rinaldo (rē-näl'dō), It. Reginald

RITA OF CASSIA (Rĭta, æ), Wid. May 22. R. M.
15 Cent. Augustinian devoted to Passion, known as "Saint of the Impossible." Also cont. of Margaret. In art shown with wound in forehead. *Sig.* Gr. pearl. *Pron.* rē'tà.
(rē'tä), Lat. Rita
Rob (rŏb), dim. Robert

ROBERT (Robértus, i), Ab. June 7. R. M.
Cistercian, Abbot of Newminster. In art shown holding church. *Sig.* Ger. bright in fame. *Pron.* rŏb'ērt.
(rō-bâr'), Fr.
(rō'bĕrt), Ger.

ROBERT BELLARMINE, B. C. D. Mar. 27
16 Cent. Jesuit Cardinal, controversialist, writer, author of catechism. *Pron.* bĕl'är-mĭn or mēn.

ROBERT JOHNSON (Bl.), M. May 28
16 Cent. Priest hanged at Tyburn.
Robertina (rŏ-bēr-tē'nȧ), fem. dim. Robert
Roberto (rō-bēr'tō), It., Port., Sp. Robert
Robertus (rō-bĕr'tŭs), Lat. Robert
Robin (rŏb'ĭn), Robert
Robina (rō-bī'nȧ), fem. Robert

ROCH (Róchus, i), C. Aug. 16. R. M.
14 Cent. Layman of Montpellier, France, devoted to plague-stricken. Patron of sick. In art shown as pilgrim with staff and wallet, or with dog. *Pron.* rōk.
Roche (rōsh), Fr. Roch
Rochus (rō'kŭs), Lat. Roch
Rock (rŏk), var. of Roch.
Roderic (rŏd'ēr-ĭk), var. Roderick
Roderich (rō'dĕ-rĭk), Ger. Roderick

RODERICK (Ruderícus, i), M. Mar. 13. R. M.
9 Cent. Spanish priest put to death by Moors at Cordova. *Sig.* Ger. rich in fame. *Pron.* rŏd'ēr-ĭk.
Roderigo (rō-dä-rē'gō), Sp. Roderick
Roderigue (rō-dâ-rēg'), Fr. Roderick
Rodolfo (rō-dōl'fō), It., Sp. Rudolph, Ralph
Rodolph (rō'dŏlf), Rudolph, Ralph
Rodolphe (rō-dŏlf'), Fr. Rudolph
Rodolpho (rō-dŏl'fō), Port. Rudolph, Ralph
Rodolphus (rō-dŏl'fŭs), Rudolph, Ralph
Rodrigo (rō-drē'gō), It., Sp. Roderick
Rodrigue (rō-drēg'), Fr. Roderick
Roeland (rōō'länt), Du. Roland

ROGER (Rogérus, i), B. C. Dec. 30
   6 Cent. Normandy. *Sig.* Ger. famous with spear.
   Pron. rŏj'ēr.
   (rō-zhā'), Fr.
Rogerio (rō-hā'rē-ō), Sp. Roger
   (rō-zhā'rē-ō), Port.
Rogero (rō-jā'rō), It. Roger
Rogerus (rō-jā'rŭs), Lat. Roger

ROLAND (Rolándus, i), M. June 16
   8 Cent. Fell in battle against Saracens. *Sig.* Ger.
   fame of the land. *Pron.* rō'lănd.
   (rō-län'), Fr.
   (rō'länt), Ger.
Rolando (rō-län'dō), It., Port., Sp. Roland
Rolandus (rō-län'dŭs), Lat. Roland
Roldan (rōl-dän'), Sp. Roland
Roldão (rōl-down'), Port. Roland
Romain (rō-măn'), Fr. Romanus

ROMANUS (Románus, i), Ab. Feb. 28. R. M.
   5 Cent. Brother of St. Lupicinus, founder of monasteries in Jura Mountains. *Sig.* Lat. Roman. *Pron.*
   rō-mä'nŭs. Also M. Aug. 9. Roman soldier converted by St. Lawrence. Also B. M. July 24. Son
   of Vladimir, Duke of Muscovy. Also known as
   Boris. Apostle of Russia.

ROMEO (Romaéus, i), C., O. Carm. Mar. 4.
   14 Cent. Carmelite of Lucca. *Pron.* rō'mē-o.

ROMUALD (Romuáldus, i), Ab. Feb. 7 and June 19
   11 Cent. Of noble family of Ravenna, founder of
   Camaldolese Order. Body incorrupt after 4 cen-
   turies. *Sig.* Teut. famed power. *Pron.* rōm'ōō-äld.

Romualdus (rō-moȯ-äl′dŭs), Lat. Romuald
ROMULUS (Rómulus, i), M. Mar. 24. R. M.
(d. u.) *Pron.* rŏm′ū-lŭs. (rō′moo-lŭs), Lat.
RONALD, M. Aug. 20.
12 C. Chieftain of Orkney murdered by rebels. *Sig.*
Sc. judge power.
Rory (rô′rĭ), Ir. Rufus, Roger
Rosa (rō′sä), It., Sp., Port., Lat. Rose. (rō′zȧ), Eng.
Rose
Rosabel (rŏz′ȧ-bĕl), **Rosabella** (rŏz-ȧ-bĕl′lȧ), Rose,
Rosalia. *Sig.* a fair rose.
ROSALIA (Rosália, æ), V. Jul. 15 and Sept. 4. R. M.
12 C. Palermo. Patroness against pestilence and
earthquake. *Sig.* Lat. rose. *Pron.* rō-zä′lĭ-ȧ.
(rō-zä′lē-ä), Lat.
Rosalie (rō-sä-lē′), Fr. Rosalia. (rŏz′ȧ-lē), Eng.
Rosalind (rŏz′ȧ-lĭnd), Rose
ROSAMOND (Rosamúnda, æ), Wid. Apr. 3
Sig. Teut. famous protection. *Pron.* rŏz′ȧ-mŏnd.
Rosamunda (rō-sä-moon′dä), Sp. Lat. Rosamond
Rosamunde (rō-sä-münd′), Fr. Rosamund

ROSE OF LIMA (Rósa, æ), V. Aug. 24 and 30. R. M.
17 Cent. Patron of Lima, Peru. Spanish Sister of
Third Order of St. Dominic. In art shown with
garland of roses on head. *Sig.* Lat. rose. *Pron.* rōz.

ROSE OF VITERBO, V. Mar. 6 and Sept. 4. R. M.
13 Cent. Mystic of Franciscan Third Order. Died at
18 years of age. In art shown with roses in hand
or apron. *Pron.* vē-tēr′bō.

Rosemonde (rō-z′môṅd′), Fr. Rosamond
Rosina (rōō-sē′nä), Sw. Rose
Rosmonda (rōs-mōn′dä), It. Rosamond
Rowland (rō′lănd), var. of Roland

Roy (roi), Celt. Rufus
Rozamond (rō'zä-mōnt), Port. Rosamond
Rudericus (rōō-dä-rē'kŭs), Lat. Roderick
Rüdiger (rü-dē-gĕr), Ger. Roger
Rudolf (rü'dŏlf), Du., Ger., Sw. Rudolph, Ralph

RUDOLPH (Rudólphus, i) (Bl.), M. Jul. 27
    16 Cent. Jesuit Martyr in Japan. *Sig.* Ger. famous
    wolf or hero. *Pron.* rü'dŏlf.
Rudolphe (rü-dōlf'), Fr. Rudolph
Rudolphus (rōō-dŏl'fŭs), Lat. Rudolph
Ruf (rüf), Fr. Rufus
Rufin (rōō-fēn'), Sw. Griffith
    (rüfăn') Fr. Rufinus

RUFINA (Rufína, æ), V. M. Jul. 10. R. M.
    3 Cent. Suffered death with sister, St. Secunda, to
    preserve virginity. *Sig.* Lat. red. *Pron.* rü-fī'nà.
    (rōō-fē'nä), Lat.
Rufine (rü-fēn'), Fr. Rufina

RUFINUS (Rufínus, i), Dea. M. Apr. 7. R. M.
    4 Cent. Pontus. *Sig.* Lat. red. *Pron.* rü-fī'nŭs.
    (rōō-fē'nus), Lat. Rufinus
    (rü-fē'nŭs), Du. Griffith
Rufo (rōō'fō), It., Sp. Rufus

RUFUS (Rúfus, i), B. C. Nov. 7. R. M.
    4 Cent. Metz. *Sig.* Lat. red, red-haired. *Pron.* rü'-
    fŭs.
    (rōō'fŭs), Lat.
Rugiero, Ruggiero (rōō-jä'rō), It. Roger.

RUMOLD (Rumóldus, i), B. M. July 1. R. M.
    8 Cent. Irish B., Patron of Malines. *Pron.* rŭm'ŏld.
Rumoldus (rōō-mōl'dŭs), Lat. Rumold

RUPERT (Rupértus, i), B. C. Mar. 27. R. M.
8 Cent. French B. of Worms and Salzburg. *Sig.* Teut.
bright fame. *Pron.* rü′pĕrt.
(rü-pâr′), Fr.
Ruperto (roō-pĕr′tō), It., Sp. Rupert
Rupertus (roō-pâr′tŭs), Lat. Rupert
Ruprecht (roō′prĕkt), Ger. Rupert
Rurik (rū′rĭk), Rus. Roderick

RUSTICUS (Rústicus, i), M. Oct. 9. R. M.
1 or 3 Cent. Priest under St. Denis of Paris. *Sig.* Lat.
peasant. *Pron.* rŭs′tĭ-kŭs.
(rŭs′tĭ-kŭs), Lat.
Rutger (rŭt′gĕr), Du. Roger

RUTH (*indecl.*) Sept. 1
Wife of Booz and great-grandmother of King David.
Sig. Heb. beauty. *Pron.* rüth.
Ruy (roō-ē′), Sp. Roderick.

S

SABBAS (Sabbas, æ) Ab. Dec. 5. R. M.
6 Cent. Founder of many monasteries in Palestine.
Pron. săb′bás.
(săb′bäs), Lat.

SABINA (Sabína, æ), M. Aug. 29. R. M.
2 Cent. Wealthy Roman widow. *Pron.* sä-bĭ′nȧ.
(sä-bē′nä), Lat.
Sabine (sä-bēn′), Fr. Sabina
(sä-bē′nĕ), Du., Ger.

SABINUS (Sabínus, i), B. M., Dec. 30. R. M.
4 Cent. Spoleto. *Pron.* sȧ-bĭ′nŭs.
(sä-bē′nŭs), Lat.
Sadie (sā′dē), dim. Sarah
Sal (săl), dim. Sarah.

Salamon (shŏl′ŏ-mōn), Hung. Solomon
Salesius (sä-lä′sē-ŭs), Lat. de Sales, *see* St. Francis.
Sally (săl′lĭ), dim. Sarah
Salomão (sä-lō-mŏwṅ′), Port. Solomon

SALOME (*indecl.*), June 29
 9 Cent. Recluse at Altaich, Bavaria. *See also* St.
 Mary. *Sig.* Heb. peaceful. *Pron.* sȧ-lōm′or sȧ-lō′mē.
 (sä-lō′mĕ), Ger.
Salomé (sä-lō-mä′), Fr. Salome
Salomo (sä-lō-mō), Du. Solomon
Salomon (sä-lō′mōn), Pol. Solomon
 (sä-lō-mōn′), Fr., Ger., Sp., Port.
 (sä′lō-mōn), Lat.
Salomone (sä-lō-mō′nä), It. Solomon

SALVATOR (Salvátor, óris), M. Dec. 18.
 (d. u.) Africa. *Sig.* Lat. savior. *Pron.* säl-vä′tôr.
 (säl-vä′tōr), Lat.

SALVIAN (Salviánus, i), Pr. C. Jul. 22.
 5 Cent. Pr. at Marseilles. *Pron.* săl′vĭ-ăn.
Salvianus (săl-vē-ä′nŭs), Lat. Salvian

SALVIUS (Sálvius, ii), B. C. Jan. 11. R. M.
 7 Cent. B. of Amiens. *Pron.* săl′vĭ-ŭs.
 (săl′vē-ŭs), Lat.
Sam (săm), **Sammy** (săm′mĭ), dim. Samuel
Samson (săm′sŏn), var. of Sampson.

SAMPSON (Samp′son, ónis), B. C. Jul. 28. R. M.
 6 Cent. Welsh Ab. Llantwit, B. of Dole, Brittany.
 Sig. Heb. great joy. *Pron.* sămp′sŏn.
 (sämp′sŏn), Lat.
 (säṅ-sōṅ′), Fr.

SAMUEL (Sámuel, élis), Proph. Aug. 20. R. M.
Last and greatest judge of Israel, anointed Kings
Saul and David. *Sig.* Heb. asked of God. *Pron.*
săm'ū-ĕl.
(sä-mü-ĕl'), Fr.
(sä'mōō-äl), Ger., Lat.
(sä-mōō-ĕl'), Sp.
Sámuel (shä'mōō-ĕl), Hung. Samuel
Samuele (sä-mōō-ä'lä), It. Samuel
Sancius (sän'chē-ŭs), Lat. var. Sanctius.

SANCTIUS (Sánctius, ii), M. June 5. R. M.
9 Cent. Spain. *Pron.* sănk'sĭ-ŭs.
(sänkt'sē-ŭs), Lat.

SANCTUS (Sánctus, i), Dea. M. June 2. R. M.
2 Cent. One of 48 martyrs of Lyons. *Sig.* Lat. holy.
Pron. sănk'tŭs.
(sänk'tŭs), Lat.
Sander (săn'dẽr), **Sandy** (săn'dĭ), Sc. dim. Alexander
Sansão (sän-sŏwṅ'), Port. Samson
Sanson (sän'sōn), Sp. Samson
Santiago (sänt-ē-ä'gō), Sp. Saint James
Sara (sä'rà), var. of Sarah
(sä-rä'), Fr.
(sä'rä), Ger., Du,. It., Port., Sp.

SARAH (*indecl.*), Aug. 19.
Wife of Abraham, mother of Isaac. *Sig.* Heb. princess.
Pron. sä'rà.
Saturnin (sä-tür-năṅ'), Fr. Saturninus

SATURNINA (Saturnína, æ), V. M. June 4. R. M.
7 Cent. Pat. of animals. *Pron.* să-tür-nī'nà.
(sä-tōōr-nē'nä), Lat.

SATURNINUS (Saturnínus, i), M. Nov. 29. R. M.
   3 Cent. Rome. *Pron.* să-tûr-nĭ'nŭs.
   (sä-tōōr-nē'nŭs), Lat.
Sawnie (sạ'nĭ), Sc. dim. Alexander

SCHOLASTICA (Scholástica, æ), V. Feb. 10. R. M.
   6 Cent. Sister of St. Benedict and first nun of his
   Order. In art shown with lily or with dove at feet
   or bosom. *Sig.* Lat. scholar. *Pron.* skō-lăs'tĭ-kȧ.
   (skō-läs'tē-kä), Lat.
Scholastique (skō-läs-tēk'), Fr. Scholastica
Sczepan (s'chä'pän), Pol. Stephen
Sebastiaan (sä-bäs'tē-än), Du. Sebastian

SEBASTIAN (Sebastiánus, i), M. Jan. 20. R. M.
   3 Cent. Centurion of Roman army, tied to tree and
   pierced with arrows, then clubbed to death. In
   art shown pierced with arrows. *Sig.* Gr. venerable.
   Pron. sē-băs'chăn.
   (sä-bäs-tē-än'), Ger., Sp.
Sebastião (sä-bäs-te-own'), Port. Sebastian
Sebastiano (sä-bäs-tē-ä'nō), It. Sebastian
Sebastianus (sä-bäs-tē-ä'nŭs), Lat. Sebastian
Sébastien (sä-bäs-tēăn'), Fr. Sebastian
Seconde (sä-kōnd'), Fr. Secundus

SECUNDA (Secúnda, æ), V. M. Jul. 10. R. M.
   3 Cent. Suffered death with sister, St. Rufina, to
   preserve virginity. *Sig.* Lat. second. *Pron.* sĕ-
   kŭn'dȧ.
   (sä-kŭn'dä), Lat.

SECUNDUS (Secúndus, i), Pr. C. May 15
   Ordained by the Apostles, he evangelized Spain.
   Sig. Lat. second. *Pron.* sĕ-kŭn'dŭs
   (sä-kŭn'dŭs), Lat.

Selina (sē-lǐ'nà), var. Celia

SENAN (Senánus, i), B. C. Mar. 8
   6 Cent. B. of Iniscattery, Ire. *Pron.* sē'năn.
Senanus (sā-nä'nŭs), Lat. Senan

SENNEN (*indecl.*), M. Jul. 30. R. M. Persian nobleman
   martyred in 3rd Cent. with St. Abdon. Also var.
   Senan. *Pron.* sĕn'nĕn.

SERAPHIA (Seráphia, æ), V. M. Jul. 29. R. M.
   2 Cent. Spain. *Pron.* sĕ-răf'ĭ-à.
   (sā-rä'fē-ä), Lat.

SERAPHINA (Seraphína, æ), V. Jul. 29. *Pron.* sĕr-
   à-fī'nà.
   (sā-rä-fē'nä), Lat.

SERAPHINUS (Seraphínus, i), C. Oct. 12. R. M.
   16 Cent. Montegranaro. Capuchin lay brother. *Pron.*
   sĕr-à-fī'nŭs.
   (sā-rä-fē'nŭs), Lat.
Serapia (sā-rä'pē-ä), Lat. var. Seraphia.

SERAPION (Serápion, ónis), B. C. Oct. 30. R. M.
   2 Cent. B. of Antioch. *Pron.* sĕ-rä'pē-ŏn.
   (sā-rä'pē-ŏn), Lat.
Sérapion (sā-rä-pē-ôṅ'), Fr. Serapion

SERENA (Seréna, æ), Mat. Aug. 16. R. M.
   3 Cent. Rome. Wife of Emp. Diocletian. *Sig.* Lat.
   calm. *Pron.* sē-rē'nà.
   (sā-rä'nä), Lat., It.
Sereno (sē-rē'nō), var. Serenus

SERENUS (Serénus, i), M. June 28. R. M.
3 Cent. Disciple of Origen. *Sig.* Lat. calm. *Pron.*
sē-rē′nŭs.
(sä-rä′nŭs), Lat.
Serge (sârzh), Fr. Sergius

SERGIUS (Sérgius, ii), M. Oct. 7. R. M.
3 Cent. Syrian. *Pron.* sēr′jĭ-ŭs.
(sâr′jē-ŭs), Lat.
Sevastian (sā-väs-tē-än′), Rus. Sebastian

SETH (*indecl.*), Mar. 1.
Third son of Adam and Eve. *Sig.* Heb. appointed.
Pron. sĕth.

SEVEN HOLY BROTHERS, MM., Jul. 10. R. M.
Januarius, Felix, Philip, Sylvanus, Alexander, Vitalis
and Martial, all martyred in presence of mother,
St. Felicity, 2 Cent.

SEVEN HOLY FOUNDERS OF SERVITE ORDER.
Feb. 12. 13 Cent. Seven citizens of Florence: Bona-
juncta Mannetti, Manettus of Antella, Amideus
Amidei, Uguccio Uguccioni, Sostineus Sostinei and
Alexis Falconieri. Canonized by Leo XIII, 1888.

SEVERIAN (Severiánus, i), B. M. Feb. 21. R. M.
5 Cent. B. of Bethsan, Galilee.
Also 4 Cent. one of Four Holy Crowned Martyrs,
Nov. 8. R. M. *Pron.* sĕ-vĕr′ĭ-ăn.
(sā-vā-rē-ä′nŭs), Lat.

SEVERINUS (Severínus, i), Her. Nov. 27. R. M.
6 Cent. Paris. *Pron.* sĕ-vĕ-rī′nŭs.
(sā-vā-rē′nŭs), Lat.
Also 5 Cent., B. C. San Severino, Jan. 8.

SEVERUS (Sevérus, i), M. Nov. 8. R. M.
One of Four Crowned Martyrs. *Pron.* sĕ-vē'rŭs.
(sā-vā'rŭs), Lat.

Sherwood (shĕr'wŏŏd), *see* Thomas (Bl.)

SIGEBERT (Sigebértus, i), K. M. Jan. 25.
7 Cent. King of East Anglia. *Sig.* Teut. conquering
brightness. *Pron.* sē'gĕ-bĕrt.

Sigebertus (sē-jā-bâr'tŭs), Lat. Sigebert

Sigefroid (sē-zhĕ-frwä'), Fr. Sigfrid.

SIGFRID, (Sigfrídus, i), B. C. Feb. 15
11 Cent. English missionary in Sweden and Norway.
Sig. Teut. conquering peace. *Pron.* sĭg'frĭd.

Sigfridus (sĭg-frē'dus), Lat. Sigfrid

SIGISBERT (Sigisbértus, i), C. Jul. 11
6 Cent. Irish founder of Abbey of Dissentis, Switzerland. *Pron.* sē'jĭs-bĕrt.

Sigisbertus (sē-jĭs-bâr'tŭs), Lat. Sigisbert

Sigismond (sē-zhēs-mōṅ'), Fr. Sigismund

Sigismondo (sē-jēs-mōn'dō), It. Sigismund

SIGISMUND (Sigismúndus, i), K. M. May 1. R. M.
6 Cent. King of Burgundy. *Sig.* Ger. conquering protection. *Pron.* sĭj'ĭs-mŭnd.
(sē'gĭs-mŭnt), Ger.

Sigismundo (sē-hēs-mŏŏn'dō), Sp. Sigismund
(sē-zhēs-mŏŏn'dō), Port.

Sigismundus (sē-jĭs-mŭn'dŭs), Lat. Sigismund

Sigmund (sēg'mŭnt), Ger. Sigismund

Sigrid (sē'grēd), Nor. Serena

SILAS (Sílas, æ), C. Jul. 13. R. M.
1 Cent. Companion of St. Paul. Also contracted form
of Silvan. *Sig.* Lat. living in a wood. *Pron.* sī'lăs.
(sē'läs), Lat.

Silvain (sēl-văń'), Fr. Silvanus

SILVAN (Silvánus, i), Ab. Feb. 28.
    7 Cent. Ab. of Bangor. Also Sylvan and Sillan. *Sig.*
    Lat. living in a wood. *Pron.* sĭl'văn.
    Also 4 Cent. B. of Gaza. May 4.
Silvano (sēl-vä'nō), It., Sp. Silvanus
Silvanus (sēl-vä'nŭs), Lat., Ger. Silvan
Silvère (sēl-vär'), Fr. Silverius

SILVERIUS (Silvérius, ii), P. M. June 20. R. M.
    6 Cent.   Cast into prison by Empress Theodosia.
    Pron. sĭl-vē-rĭ-ŭs.
    (sĭl-vä'rē-ŭs), Lat.
Silvester (sĭl-vĕs'tēr), *see* Sylvester
    (sēl-vĕs'târ), Lat.
Silvestre (sēl-vĕstr'), Fr. Sylvester
    (sēl-vĕs'trā), Sp.
Silvestro (sēl-vĕs'trō), It. Sylvester
Silvia (sĭl'vĭ-à), *see* Sylvia
    (sēl'vē-ä), Lat.
Silvie (sēl-vē'), Fr. Sylvia
Silvio (sēl'vē-ō), It. Silvius

SILVIUS (Sĭlvius, ii), M. Mar. 15.
    (d. u.) With St. Lucius at Nicomedia. *Sig.* Lat. liv-
    ing in a wood. *Pron.* sĭl'vĭ-ŭs.
    (sĭl'vē-ŭs), Lat.
Sim (sĭm), Simon, Simeon
Simão (sē-mŏwń'), Port. Simon
Simeão (sē-mä-ŏwń'), Port. Simeon

SIMEON (Símeon, ónis), B. M. Feb. 18.
    2 Cent. Kinsman of Our Lord, son of Cleophas and

Mary. B. of Jerusalem.   Martyred by crucifixion.
Sig. Heb. hearing with acceptance.   *Pron.* sĭm'ē-ŏn.
(sē'mā-ōn), Lat., Ger.
(sē-mā-ōn'), Sp.

SIMEON STYLITES, C. Jan. 5. R. M.
5 Cent. Syrian, lived life of penance atop a pillar for
37 years.   *Pron.* stĭ-lī'tēz.
Siméon (sē-mā-ōn'), Fr. Simeon
Simeone (sē-mā-ō'nā), It. Simeon

SIMON (Símon, ónis), Ap. Oct. 28. R. M.
1 Cent. Born at Cana.   Preached Gospel with St.
Jude, with whom he was martyred in Persia; called
the Zealot. In art shown with saw.   *Sig.* Heb.
obedient.   *Pron.* sī'mŏn.
(sē'mŏn), Lat., Sw., Ger.
(sē-mon'), Fr.
(sē-mōn'), Sp.
Also infant martyred at Trent, in 15 Cent. Mar. 24.

SIMON STOCK, May 16.
13 Cent. Carmelite General to whom Blessed Virgin
presented Brown Scapular.   Died at Bordeaux.
Simone (sē-mō'nā), It. Simon
Simplice (săn-plēs'), Fr. Simplicius

SIMPLICIUS (Simplícius, ii), P. C. Mar. 10. R. M.
5 Cent.   *Sig.* Lat. guileless.   *Pron.* sĭm-plĭ'sĭ-ŭs.
(sĭm-plē'chē-ŭs), Lat.
Also M., Jul. 29. R. M.   Beheaded with brother, St.
Faustinus, and sister, St. Beatrice, in 4 Cent.
Sis (sĭs), Sisely (sĭs'lĭ), Cecilia
Sismondo (sēs-mōn'dō), Sp. Sigismund
Sixte (sēkst), Fr. Sixtus

SIXTUS II (Síxtus, i), P. M. Aug. 6. R. M.
3 Cent. Also called Xystus. *Sig.* Lat. sixth. *Pron.*
sĭx'tŭs.
(sēx'tŭs), Lat.
Smaragde (smä-rägd'), Fr. Smaragdus.

SMARAGDUS (Smarágdus, i), M. Aug. 8. R. M.
Martyred with Sts. Cyriacus and Largus. Named
in Canon of Mass. *Sig.* Gr.emerald. *Pron.* smä-
räg'dŭs.
(smä-räg'dŭs), Lat.
Sofia (sō-fē'ä), It., Rus., Sp., Sw. Sophie
Solanus (sō-lä'nŭs), *see* St. Francis.
Soliman (sō-lē-män'), Ar. Solomon

SOLOMON (Sálomon, ónis), June 17.
Third King of Israel, son of David and builder of
Temple. *Sig.* Heb. peaceful. *Pron.* sŏl'ō-mŏn.

SOPHIA (Sophía, æ), Wid. M. Sep. 30. R. M.
2 Cent. Mother of Sts. Faith, Hope and Charity.
Sig. Gr. wisdom. *Pron.* sō-fī'á.
(sō-fē'ä), Lat., Ger.
Sophie (sō-fē'), Fr. Sophia. *See also* Madeleine Sophie.
(sō-fē'ĕ), Ger.
(sō'fē), Eng.

SOPHONIAS (Sophonías, æ), Proph. Dec. 3
(sō-fō-nē'äs), Lat. *Pron.* sō-fō-nī'ás.
Sophronia (sō-frō'nĭá), fem. of Sophronius

SOPHRONIUS (Sophrónius, ii), B. C. Mar. 11. R. M.
7 Cent. Patriarch of Jerusalem. *Sig.* Gr. of sound
mind. *Pron.* sō-frō'nĭ-ŭs.
(sō-frō'nē-ŭs), Lat.
Sophronie (sō-frō-nē'), Fr. Sophronia
Sophy (sō'fē), var. Sophia

SOSTHENES (Sósthenes, is), Nov. 28. R. M.
1 Cent. Ruler of synagogue of Corinth, became disciple of St. Paul. *Pron.* sŏs'thē-nēz.
(sŏs'thä-nēz), Lat.

SOTER (Sóter, eris), P. M. Apr. 22. R. M.
2 Cent. *Pron.* sō'tĕr.
(sō'tēr), Lat.

SPIRIDION (Spiri'dion, ónis), B. C. Dec. 14. R. M.
4 Cent. Island of Cyprus. *Sig.* Gr. round basket.
Pron. spĭ-rĭ'dĭ-ŏn.
(spē-rē'dē-ŏn), Lat.
Stacy (stā'sĭ), cor. Eustace, Anastasia
Stanislao (stä-nĭs-lä'ō), It. Stanislaus
Stanislas (stăn'ĭs-läs), var. Stanislaus

STANISLAUS (Stanisláus, ái), B. M. May 7. R. M.
11 Cent. Poland. B. of Cracow. Reproved King Boleslas of Poland for wicked life, who had him slain at altar. *Sig.* Slav. glory of the camp. *Pron.* stăn'ĭs-lŏws.
(stä-nĭs-lä'ŭs), Lat.

STANISLAUS KOSTKA, S. J. C. Aug. 15
16 Cent. A Polish Jesuit seminarian who died as novice at 18 years of age, distinguished for his purity and innocence.
Stefan (stĕf'än), Sw. Stephen
Stefano (stā'fä-nō), It. Stephen
Stella (stĕl'lä), Esther, Estelle, Eustella. *Sig.* Lat. star
Stepan (stä-pän'), Rus. Stephen
Stephan (stäf'än), Dan., Ger., Stephen
Stephana (stĕf'à-nà), fem. Stephen
Stephanie (stä-fä-nē'), Fr. Stephana
(stä-fä'nē-ĕ), Ger.

Stephanus (stā'fä-nŭs), Lat. Stephen

STEPHEN, I. (Stéphanus, i), P. M. Aug. 2. R. M.
3 Cent. Put to death while saying Mass.

STEPHEN HARDING, Ab. Apr. 17. R. M.
12 Cent. One of founders of Cistercian Order at
Citeaux.

STEPHEN OF HUNGARY, K. C. Sept. 2. R. M.
10 Cent. King of Hungary: dedicated kingdom to
Blessed Virgin. *Sig.* Gr. a crown. *Pron.* stē'v'n.

STEPHEN, PROTOMARTYR, Dec. 26. Finding of
Relics of, Aug. 3. R. M.
1 Cent. first deacon, chosen by Apostles, stoned to
death by Jews while St. Paul, then known as Saul,
encouraged them. In art shown as deacon, with
stones nearby or on Gospel in hand. *Pron.* prō'tō
mär'tēr = first martyr.

Steve (stĕv), Stephen
Steven (stā'vĕn), Du. Stephen
Stevie (stē'vĭ), dim. Stephen
Stylites (stī-lī'tēz), see St. Simeon
Sue (sū) dim. Susanna

SUITBERT (Suitbértus, i), B. C. Mar. 1. R. M
7 Cent. Ap. of Frisia. *Pron.* swĭt'bērt.
Suitbertus (swēt-bâr'tŭs), Lat.
Suke (sūk), Susanna
Suky, Sukey (sū'kĭ), Susanna
Suleymân (sōō-lä-män'), Ar. Solomon
Sulpice (sül-pēs'), Fr. Sulpicius

SULPICIUS (Sulpícius, ii), B. C. Jan. 17. R. M.
7 Cent. Archb. Bourges. *Sig.* Lat. red spotted face.
Pron. sŭl-pē'shŭs.
(sŭl-pē'chē-ŭs), Lat.
Susan (sū'zăn), Susanna
Susana (sōō-sä'nä), Sp. Susanna

SUSANNA (Susánna, æ), M. Aug. 11. R. M.
3 Cent. Roman noble maiden. *Sig.* Heb. lily. *Pron.*
sū-zăn'nä.
(sōō-zä'nä), Lat., It.
(sōō-sä'nä), Sp., Port.
Susannah (sū-zăn'nä), var. Susanna
Susanne, Suzanne (sü-zän'), Fr. Susanna
Susie (sū'zē), **Suzy,** (sū'zĭ), dim. Susanna
Swidbert (swĭd'bĕrt), var. Suitbert

SWITHIN (Swithúnus, i), B. C. Jul. 2
9 Cent. Winchester. The translation of his relics
once delayed for forty days by rain, a legend
states, hence the popular notion regarding rain on
his feast. *Sig.* A. S. strong friend. *Pron.* swĭth'ĭn.
Swithun (swĭth'ŭn), var. of Swithin.
Swithunus (swē-thōō'nŭs), Lat. Swithin
Sylvain (sĕl-văn'), Fr. Sylvan.
Sylvan (sĭl'văn), var. Silvanus
Sylvanus (sĭl-vā'nŭs), var. Silvanus

SYLVESTER I (Silvéster, ri), P. C. Dec. 31. R. M.
4 Cent. Pope during "Peace of Constantine." *Sig.*
Lat. bred in the country. *Pron.* sĭl-vĕs'tēr.
(sĕl-vĕs'tēr), Lat.

SYLVESTER, Ab. Nov. 26. R. M.
12 Cent. Founder of Sylvestrines, Congregation of
Hermits, at Fabriano.

Sylvestre (sĕl-vĕs′tr), Fr. Sylvester
    (sĕl-vĕs′trä), Port.

SYLVIA (Sílvia, æ), Wid. Nov. 3. R. M.
    6 Cent. Rome. Mother of St. Gregory the Great.
    Sig. Lat. bred in the country. *Pron.* sĭl′vĭ-á.

Sylvie (sĕl-vē′), Fr. Sylvia

SYMPHORIAN (Symphoriánus, i), M. Aug. 22. R. M.
    2 Cent. Autun. *Pron.* sĭm-fō′rĭ-ăn.

Symphorianus (sēm-fō-rē-ä′nŭs), Lat. Symphorian.

Symphorien (săn-fō-ryăṅ′), Fr. Symphorian

SYMPHOROSA (Symphorósa, æ), M. Jul. 18. R. M.
    Tivoli. Martyred with her seven sons under Hadrian.
    Pron. sĭm-fō-rō′sá.
    (sĕm-fō-rō′sä), Lat.

Symphorose (săṅ-fō-rōs′), Fr. Symphorosa

SYNESIUS (Synésius, ii), M. Dec. 12. R. M.
    3 Cent. Rome. *Pron.* sĭ-nē′sĭ-ŭs.
    (sē-nä′sē-ŭs), Lat.

T

Tabitha (tăb′ĭ-thá), var. Dorcas.
    (tä′bē-thä), Lat.

Taddeo (täd-dä′ō), It. Thaddeus

Tadeo (tä-dä′ō), Sp. Thaddeus

Taffy (tăf′ĭ), Welsh, David

Tam (tăm), Sc. cor. Thomas

Tamás (tŏm′äsh), Hung. Thomas

Tamzine (tăm′zēn), dim. Thomasa

TARCISIUS (Tharcísius, ii), M. Aug. 15. R. M.
    3 Cent. Roman acolyte who, while carrying the
    Blessed Sacrament to the sick, was beaten to death.
    Called the "Martyr of the Holy Eucharist." *Pron.*
    tär-sĭ′shŭs.

(tär-chē′sē-ŭs), var. Lat.
Tave (tāv), **Tavy** (tā′vĭ), dim. Octavia
Ted (tĕd), **Teddy** (tĕd′dĭ), dim. Theodore, Edward,
    Edwin, Edmund
Télesphore (tā-läs-fôr′), Fr. Telesphorus

TELESPHORUS (Telésphorus, i), P. M. Jan. 5. R. M.
    2 Cent. A Greek accredited with introducing Lent,
    also the Gloria in the Mass, and the three Christ-
    mas Masses. In art shown with a chalice with
    three Hosts. *Pron.* tĕ-lĕs′fō-rŭs.
    (tā-läs′fō-rŭs), Lat.

Teobaldo (tā-ō-bäl′dō), It., Sp. Theobald
Teodora (tā-ō-dō′rä), It., Sp. Theodora
Teodorico (tā-ō-dō-rē′kō), It., Sp. Theodoric
Teodoro (tā-ō-dō′rō), It., (tā-ō-thō′rō), Sp. Theodore
Teodosia (tā-ō-dō′sē-ä), It. Theodosia
Teodosio (tā-ō-dō′sē-ō), It., Sp. Theodosius
Teofilo (tā-ō′fē-lō), It., Sp. Theophilus

TERENCE (Teréntius, ii), M. Apr. 10. R. M.
    3 Cent. Carthage. *Sig.* Lat. tender. *Pron.* tĕr′ĕns.
Térence (tā-rŏns′), Fr. Terence
Terencio (tā-rän′thē-ō), Sp. Terence
Terentius (tā-rĕnt′sē-ŭs), Lat. Terence

TERESA (Terésia, æ), V. Oct. 15. R. M.
    16 Cent. Daughter of Alphonsus Sanchez de Cepeda,
    born at Avila. Reformed the Carmelite Order and
    founded 32 convents. A contemplative favored
    with visions, and great mystical writer. In art
    shown with flaming arrow in breast. *Sig.* Gr.
    carrying ears of corn. *Pron.* tĕ-rē′sà.
    (tā-rā′sä), It., Sp.

TERESA OF THE CHILD JESUS, V. Oct. 3.

Teresa Martin, born at Alençon 1873, entered
Carmelite Order at Lisieux at 15 years and died in
1897. Wrote famous Autobiography, and prom-
ised to spend her heaven doing good on earth.
Known as "The Little Flower of Jesus." Canonized in 1925 by Pius XI. Patron of missions. In
art shown scattering roses.

Teresia (tā-rā'sē-ä), Lat. Teresa

Terry (tĕr'rĭ), dim. Terence or Teresa

TERTIUS (Tértius, ii), M. Dec. 6. R. M.

6 Cent. Monk flayed alive in Africa. *Sig.* Lat. third.
Pron. tûr'shĭ-ŭs.
(târt'sē-ŭs), Lat.

Tess (tĕs) **Tessie** (tĕs'sĭ), dim. Teresa

Thaddæus (thä-dā'ŭs), Lat. Thaddeus

Thaddäus (tä-dā'o͞os), Ger. Thaddeus

Thaddeo (täd-dā'ō), Port. Thaddeus

Thaddeus (thăd'dē-ŭs), *see* St. Jude. *Sig.* Syr. the wise.

Thaddy (thă'dĭ), dim. Thaddeus

Tharsice (tär-sēs'), Fr. Tarcisius

Tharcisius (tär-chē'sē-ŭs), Lat. Tarcisius

THECLA (Thécla, æ), V. M. Sep. 23. R. M.

1 Cent. Convert of St. Paul at Iconium. In art
shown surrounded by wild beasts. *Sig.* Gr. divine
fame. *Pron.* thĕ'klä.
(thā'klä), Lat.

Thècle (tā'klĕ), Fr. Thecla

THEOBALD (Theobáldus, i), Her. June 30. R. M.

11 Cent. Count of Champagne, became hermit at
18 years, later joined Order of Camaldolese.
Patron of charcoal-burners. *Sig.* Gr. bold for the
people. *Pron.* thē'ō-bäld.

THEOBALD MONTMORENCY (Bl.), Ab. Jul. 27
   13 Cent.   French noble who became a Cistercian
   monk.
Theobaldo (tā-ō-bäl'dō), Port. Theobald
Theobaldus (thā-ō-bäl'dŭs), Lat. Theobald
Theodericus (thā-ō-dā-rē'kŭs), Lat. Theoderic
Theodor (tā'ō-dōr), Du., Ger., Sw. Theodore

THEODORA (Theodóra, æ), V. M. Apr. 1. R. M.
   2 Cent. Rome.   Martyred with brother St. Hermes.
   Sig. Gr. divine gift. *Pron.* thē-ō-dō'rá.
   (thā-ō-dō'rä), Lat.
   (tā-ō-dō'rä), Ger.

THEODORE (Theodórus, i), B. C. Sept. 19. R. M.
   7 Cent. Greek, Archb. Canterbury.   In art shown
   on horseback or with crocodile under feet.   *Sig.*
   Gr. gift of God.   *Pron.* thē'ō-dōr.
Also Ab. Oct. 29. Priest of Vienne, 6 Cent. R. M.
Also M. Nov. 9. Roman soldier burnt alive in Asia
   Minor. 4 Cent. R. M.
Théodore (tā-ō-dôr'), Fr. Theodore

THEODORET (Theodorétus, i or Theodórus, i), M.
   Oct. 23. R. M. *Pron.* thē-od'ō-rĕt.
Theodoretus (thā-ō-dō-rā'tŭs), Lat. Theodoret

THEODORIC (Theoderícus, i), C. Jul. 1
   6 Cent. Menancourt, disciple of St. Remigius.   *Sig.*
   A. S. powerful among the people.   *Pron.* thē-
   ŏd'ō-rĭk.
Theodoricus (thā-ō-dō-rē'kŭs), Lat. Theodoric
Theodoro (tā-ō-dō'rō), Port. Theodore
Theodorus (thā-ō-dō'rŭs), Lat. Theodore

THEODOSIA (Theodósia, æ), M. May 29. R. M.
4 Cent. Caesarea Philippi. Put to death at 18 years
of age. *Sig.* Gr. gift of God. *Pron.* thē-ō-dō'shȧ.
(thā-ō-dō'sē-ä), Lat.
(tā-ō-dō'sē-ä), Ger.
Also V. M. Apr. 2. 4 Cent.

Théodosie (tā-ō-dō-sē'), Fr. Theodosia

Théodule (tā-ō-dül'), Fr. Theodulus

THEODULUS (Theódulus, i), M. Feb. 17. R. M.
4 Cent. Aged Christian crucified at Caesarea.
Also M., Rome, 2 Cent. May 3. *Pron.* thē-ŏ'dū-lŭs.
(thā-ŏ'dōō-lŭs), Lat.

Theophane Venard (thē'ō-fān vā-när'), *see* John (Bl.)
Sig. Gr. divine manifestation.

Théophane (tā-ō-fän'), Fr. Theophane

Theophanes (thā-ō-fä'nāz), Lat. Theophane

Théophile (tā-ō-fēl'), Fr. Theophilus

Theophilo (tā-ō'fē-lō), Port. Theophilus

THEOPHILUS (Théophilus, i), B. C. Mar. 7. R. M.
9 Cent. Nicomedia. *Sig.* Gr. lover of God. *Pron.*
thē-ŏf'ĭ-lŭs.
(thā-ō'fē-lŭs), Lat.
(tā-ō'fē-lŭs), Ger.

Theresa (tĕ-rē'sȧ), var. of Teresa
(tā-rā'sä), Ger., Port., Sw.

Thérèse (tā-rāz'), Fr. Teresa

Theresia (tā-rā'sē-ä), Du., Ger. Teresa

Thibaut (tē-bō'), Fr. Theobald

Thierry (tyĕ-rē'), var. Theodoric

Thomar (tō-mär'), Port. Thomas

THOMAS (Thómas, æ), Ap. Dec. 21. R. M.
1 Cent. Called Didymus (twin), a Galilean. Doubted Our Lord's Resurrection, preached in Parthia, Apostle of India. In art shown with builder's square or spear. Patron of architects and builders. *Sig.* Heb. twin. *Pron.* tŏm'ăs.
(tō'mäs), Lat.
(tō-mäs'), Port.
(tō-mä'), Fr.

THOMAS ABEL (Bl.), M. Jul. 30
16 Cent. Priest, Doctor of U. of Oxford, hanged at Smithfield.

THOMAS Á BECKET, B. M. Dec. 29. R. M.
12 Cent. Archb. Canterbury, defender of rights of Church. Slain in cathedral by knights of K. Henry II.

THOMAS AQUINAS, C. D. Mar. 7. R. M.
13 Cent. Dominican, called Angelic Doctor, chief exponent of Scholastic philosophy. Composed Office and Mass of Corpus Christi; wrote Summa Theologica; one of greatest theologians; Patron of Catholic schools. In art shown with sun on breast. *Pron.* å-kwī'năs.

THOMAS COTTAM (Bl.), M. May 30
16 Cent. Jesuit martyred at Tyburn.

THOMAS FORDE (Bl.), M. May 28
16 Cent. Priest martyred at Tyburn.

THOMAS OF HEREFORD, B. C. Aug. 25. R. M.
13 Cent. Chancellor of England

THOMAS MORE, M. July 9
   15 Cent. Lord Chancellor under Henry VIII, defender of Papal supremacy, beheaded on Tower Hill.

THOMAS PERCY (Bl.), M. Nov. 14
   16 Cent.   Earl of Northumberland, beheaded at
   York.

THOMAS PLUMTREE (Bl.), M. Feb. 14
   16 Cent. Priest executed at Durham

THOMAS SHERWOOD (Bl.), M. Feb. 7.
   16 Cent. Youth seized while trying to cross from
   England to Douai to become a priest.   Hanged
   and quartered at Tyburn.

THOMAS OF VILLANOVA, B. C. Sep. 22. R. M.
   15 Cent. Castille.   Augustinian, Archb. of Valencia,
   ascetic and mystical writer. In art shown bestow-
   ing alms.

THOMAS WOODHOUSE (Bl.), M. June 19.
   16 Cent. Jesuit priest martyred at Tyburn.
Thomasa (tŏm′á-sà), fem. Thomas
Thomasina (tŏm-à-sēn′à), fem. Thomas.
Thomasine (tŏm′á-sēn), fem. Thomas
Thomaz (tō-mäs′), Port. Thomas
Tibère (tē-bâr′), Fr. Tiberius

TIBERIUS (Tibérius, ii), M. Nov. 10. R. M.
   4 Cent. Montpelier.   *Pron.* tĭ-bē′rĭ-ŭs.
   (tē-bā′rē-ŭs), Lat.
Tiburce (tē-bürs′), Fr. Tiburtius

TIBURTIUS (Tibúrtius, ii), M. Aug. 11. R. M.
   3 Cent. Rome.   *Pron.* tĭ-bûr′sĭ-ŭs.
   (tē-bōŏrt′sē-ŭs), Lat.
   Also M. 3. Cent. with brother Valerian. Apr. 14.

Tiebout (tē′bŏwt), Du. Theobald
Til (tĭl), **Tillie** (tĭl′ĭ), Mathilda
Tilda (tĭl′dȧ), dim. Mathilda
Tim (tĭm), Timothy

TIMON (Tímon, ónis), B. M. Apr. 19. R. M.
  1 Cent. One of first seven deacons. B. of Corinth.
  Pron. tī′mŏn.
  (tē′mŏn), Lat.
Timoteo (tē-mō′tä-ō), It. Timothy
  (tē-mō-tä′ō), Sp.
Timothée (tē-mō-tä′), Fr. Timothy
Timotheo (tē-mō-tä′ō), Port. Timothy
Timotheus (tē-mō′thä-ŭs), Lat. Timothy
  (tē-mō′tä-ŭs), Ger.

TIMOTHY (Timótheus, i), B. M. Jan. 24 and May 9.
  R. M.
  1 Cent. Disciple of St. Paul, who ordained him
  Bishop of Ephesus. Stoned to death. In art shown
  with club or stone. *Sig.* Gr. fearing God.
  Pron. tĭm′ō-thĭ.
  Also M. 4 Cent. at Rome. Aug. 22.
Tish (tĭsh), cor. Letitia
Tite (tēt), Fr. Titus
Tito (tē′tō), It., Port., Sp. Titus

TITUS (Títus, i), B. C. Feb. 6. R. M.
  1 Cent. Ordained by St. Paul and made by him
  Bishop of Crete. *Sig.* Lat. safe. *Pron.* tī′tŭs.
  (tē′tŭs), Lat.
Tobia (tō-bē′ä), It., Sp. Tobias
Tobiah (tō-bī′ȧ), var. Tobias

TOBIAS (Tobías, æ), M. Nov. 2. R. M.
4 Cent. Sebaste. *Sig*. Heb. distinguished of Jehovah.
Pron. tō-bī′ăs.
(tō-bē′äs), Du. Ger., Lat., Sp.
Also holy man of Old Testament whose blindness
was cured by Angel Raphael. Sept. 13.
Tobie (tōbē′), Fr. Tobias
Toby (tō′bĕ), dim. Tobias
Tollie (tŏl′lĭ), dim. Bartholomew
Tom (tŏm), dim. Thomas
Tomas (tō-mäs′), Sp. Thomas
Tomasa (tō-mä′sä), It., Sp. Thomasa
Tomaso (tō-mä′sō), It. Thomas
Tomasz (tō′mäsh), Pol. Thomas
Tommaso (tŏm-mä′sō), It. Thomas
Tommy (tŏm′mĭ), dim. Thomas
Tony (tō′nĭ), dim. Antony

TORQUATUS (Torquátus, i), B. C. May 15. R. M.
1 Cent. Cadiz, consecrated by Apostles. *Sig*. Lat.,
wearing a neck chain. *Pron*. tôr-kwä′tŭs.
(tôr-kwä′tŭs), Lat.
Tracy (trä′sĭ), cor. Teresa

TRANQUILLUS (Tranquíllus, i), Ab. Mar. 14.
6 Cent. Dijon. *Sig*. Lat. calm. *Pron*. trăn-kwĭl′lŭs.
(trän-kwē′lŭs), Lat.
Trix (trĭks), cor. Beatrice
Trudy (trü′dĭ), dim. Gertrude
Tryce (trīs), cor. Beatrice
Tryphæna (trē-fä′nä), Lat. var. Tryphena.
Tryphænes (trē-fä′näz), Lat. Tryphena

TRYPHENA (Tryphæ′nes, is), Jan. 31. R. M.
Cyzicus. Patroness of nursing women and milch
cows. *Sig*. Gr. delicate. *Pron*. trī-fē′nȧ.

TRYPHON (Try'phon, ónis), M. Nov. 10. R. M.
3 Cent. Nicaea. *Sig.* Gr. delicate. *Pron.* trī'fŏn.
(trē'fŏn), Lat.
Tubby (tŭb'ĭ), cor. Thomas
TURIBIUS (Turíbius, ii), B. C. Mar. 23.
17 Cent. Spaniard of Mogrevejo. Archb. Lima, Peru.
Pron. tōō-rĭ'bĭ-ŭs.
(tōō-rē'bē-ŭs), Lat.
TWELVE BROTHERS, MM. Sept. 1.
3 Cent. Benevento. Children of Sts. Boniface and
Thecla.
Tybalt (tĭb'ălt), cont. Theobald

U

UBALD (Ubáldus, i), B. C. May 16, R. M.
12 Cent. Gubbio. *Sig.* Teut. prince of thought. *Pron.*
yōō'bäld.
Ubalde (ü-bäld'), Fr. Ubald
Ubaldo (ōō-bäl'dō), It. Ubald
Ubaldus (ōō-bäl'dŭs), Lat. Ubald
Uberto (ōō-bâr'tō), It., Sp. Hubert
Udalricus (ōō-däl-rē'kŭs), Lat. var. Ulric
Udolfo (ōō-dōl'fō), It. Adolph
Ugo (ōō'gō), It. Hugh
Ugolino (ōō-gō-lē-nō), It. dim. Hugh
Uldaricus (ōōl-dä-rē'kŭs), Lat. var. Ulric
Uliviere (ōō-lē-vē-ä'rä), It. Oliver
Ullie (ŏŏl'lĭ), dim. Ulric

ULRIC (Ulrícus, i), Her. Feb. 20.
12 Cent. Priest at Haselbrough, Dorsetshire. In art
shown holding book. *Sig.* Teut. noble ruler. *Pron.*
ŭl'rĭk.
Also B. C. Jul. 4. R. M.

10 Cent. Augsburg. First formally canonized saint.
Ulrica (ŭl′rĭ-kȧ), fem. Ulric
  (ŏōl-rē′kä), It.
Ulrich (ŏōl′rĭk), Ger. Ulric
Ulricus (ŏōl-rē′kŭs), Lat. Ulric
Ulrike (ŏōl′rē-kē), Ger. Ulrica
Una (yŏō′nȧ), var. Winifred

URANIA (Urȧnia, æ), M. Nov. 7
  (d. u.) Egypt. *Sig.* Gr. heavenly. *Pron.* ū-rā′nĭ-ȧ.
  (ŏō-rä′nē-ä), Lat.
Uranie (ü-rä-nē′), Fr. Urania
Urbaan (ūr′bän), Du. Urban
Urbain (ür-băṅ′), Fr. Urban

URBAN I (Urbȧnus, i), P. M. May 25. R. M.
  3 Cent. Rome. *Sig.* Lat. courteous. *Pron.* ûr′băn.
  (ŏōr′bän), Ger.

URBAN V, P. C. Dec. 19. R. M.
  14 Cent. Benedictine. Transferred Papacy from Avig-
    non to Rome, and later returned. Great canonist.

URBANA (Urbȧna, æ), M. May 19
  (d. u.) Rome. *Sig.* Lat. courteous. *Pron.* ûr-băn′ȧ.
  (ŏōr-bä′nä), Lat.
Urbano (ŏōr-bä′nō), It., Sp. Urban
Urbanus (ŏōr-bä′nŭs), Lat., Ger. Urban
Ursin (ür-săṅ′), Fr. Ursinus
Ursino (ŏōr-sē′nō), It. Ursinus

URSINUS (Ursĭnus, i), B. C. Nov. 9. R. M.
  3 Cent. Bourges, Apostle of Auvergne. *Sig.* Lat.
    bear. *Pron.* ûr-sī′nŭs.
  (ŏōr-sē′nŭs), Lat.
Ursola (ŏōr′sō-lä), Sp. Ursula

URSULA (Ur'sula, æ), V. M. Oct. 21. R. M.
 5 Cent. Put to death with companions by Huns at
 Rhine after fleeing from England. In art shown
 with arrow in breast. *Sig.* Lat. bear. *Pron.* ûr'-
 sū-là.
 (ōōr'sōō-lä), Lat.
Ursule (ür-sül'), Fr. Ursula

V

Vaast (väst), var. Vedast
Val (văl), dim. Valentine

VALENS (Válens, éntis), Dea. M. June 1. R. M.
 4 Cent. Venerable old man said to have been able to
 repeat whole Bible by heart. *Sig.* Lat. valiant,
 healthy. *Pron.* vā'lĕnz.
 (vä'lĕnz), Lat.
Valentijn (vä'lĕn-tīn), Du. Valentine
Valentim (vä-lĕn-tēn'), Port. Valentine
Valentin (vä-lŏn-tăn'), Fr. Valentine
 (vä-lĕn-tēn'), Sp., Sw.
 (fä'lĕn-tēn), Du., Dan., Ger.

VALENTINA (Valentína, æ), V. M. Jul. 25. R. M.
 4 Cent. Caesarea. *Sig.* Lat. healthy. *Pron.* vă-lĕn-
 tī'nà.
 (vä-lĕn-tē'nä), Lat.

VALENTINE (Valentínus, i), M. Feb. 14. R. M.
 3 Cent. Roman priest and physician. In art shown
 bearing sword or holding a sun. *Sig.* Lat. strong,
 healthy. *Pron.* văl'ĕn-tīn.
 (vä-lŏn-tēn'), Fr. Valentina
Valentino (vä-lĕn-tē'nō), It. Valentine
Valentinus (vä-lĕn-tē'nŭs), Lat. Valentine

Valère (vä-lâr′), Fr. Valerius

VALERIA (Valéria, æ), M. Apr. 28. R. M.
1 Cent. Wife of St. Vitalis, mother of Sts. Gervase and Protase. Martyred at Ravenna. *Sig*. Lat. healthy. *Pron*. vä-lē′rĭ-à.
(vä-lä′rē-ä), Lat., It.

VALERIAN (Valeriánus, i), M. Apr. 14. R. M.
3 Cent. Rome. Martyred with brother, St. Tiburtius. Betrothed to St. Caecilia. *Sig*. Lat. healthy. *Pron*. vă-lē′rĭ-ăn.

VALERIANA (Valeriána, æ), M. Nov. 15
(d. u.) Hippo Regius. *Sig*. Lat. healthy. *Pron*. vă-lē-rĭ-ä′nà.
Valeriano (vä-lä-rē-ä′nō), It. Valerian
Valerianus (vä-lä-rē-ä′nŭs), Lat. Valerian
Valérie (vä-lä-rē′), Fr. Valeria
Valerie (vä-lä′rē-ē), Ger. Valeria
Valérien (vä-lä-rē-ăn′), Fr. Valerian
Valerio (vä-lä′rē-ō), It. Valerius

VALERIUS (Valérius, ii), B. C. Jan. 28. R. M.
4 Cent. Saragossa. *Sig*. Lat. healthy. *Pron*. vă-lē′-rĭ-ŭs.
(vä-lä′rē-ŭs), Lat.
Valeska (vä-lĕs′kà), fem. Ladislas, cont. from Vladislavka.
Varfolomei (vär-fōl-ō-mä′ē), Rus. Bartholomew.
Vasilii (vä-sēl′yē), Rus. Basil

VEDAST (Vedástus, i), B. C. Feb. 6. R. M.
5 Cent. Bishop of Arras and Cambrai. Labored with St. Remigius in converting Franks. Also called Vaast, Gaston, Foster. *Pron*. vē′dăst.

Vedastus (vā-däs′tŭs), Lat. Vedast
Veicht (vīkt), Bav. Vitus
Veidl (vī′dl′), Bav. Vitus
Veit (fīt), Ger., Sw. Guy, Vitus
Velimir (vā-lĭ-mĭr), Bulg. Wenceslas
Venance (vā-näṅs′), Fr. Venantius
Venant (vā-näṅ′), Fr. Venantius

VENANTIUS (Venántius, ii), M. May 18. R. M.
    3 Cent. Boy of 15 beheaded near Aneona. *Pron.*
    vĕ-năn′shŭs.
    (vā-nänt′sē-ŭs), Lat.
Venceslav (vĕn′sĕs-låf), Boh. Wenceslas

VENERANDA (Veneránda, æ), V. M. Nov. 14. R. M.
    2 Cent. Gaul. *Sig.* Lat. venerable. *Pron.* vĕn-ĕ-
    rän′då.
    (vā-nä-rän′dä), Lat.
Ventura (vän-tōō′rä) Sp. Bonaventure

VERA (Véra, æ), V. Jan. 24.
    (d. u.) *Sig.* Lat. true. *Pron.* vē′rå.
    (vā-rä), Lat.

VERENA (Veréna, æ), V. M. Sept. 1. R. M.
    4 Cent. Thebes. *Sig.* Gr. sacred wisdom. *Pron.*
    vĕ-rē′nå.
    (vā-rä′nä), Lat.
Vergil (vēr′jĭl), var. Virgil

VERONICA DE JULIANIS (Verónica, æ), V. Jul. 9.
R. M.
    18 Cent. Capuchin abbess at Cittá di Castello, fa-
    vored with visions. Also called Berenice. *Sig.* Gr.
    true image. *Pron.* vĕ-rŏn′ĭ-kå.

(vā-rō′nē-kä), Lat.
(vä-rō-nē′kä), It.

VERONICA OF MILAN, V. Jan. 13. R. M.
15 Cent. Augustinian nun, who led life of penance.
Veronika (vä-rō′nē-kä), Ger. Veronica
Véronique (vä-rō-nēk′), Fr. Veronica
Vest (vĕst), dim. Sylvester
Vester (vĕs′tēr), dim. Sylvester
Vianney (vē-ä-nē′), see St. John Baptist
Viateur (vē-ä-tēr′), Fr. Viator

VIATOR (Viátor, óris), C. Oct. 21. R. M.
4 Cent. Disciple of St. Justus at Lyons. *Pron.*
vī-ā′tŏr.
(vē-ä′tŏr), Lat.
Vibiana (vĭ-bĭ-ăn′à), var. Bibiana
Vicente (vē-thĕn′tä), Sp. Vincent
(vē-sĕn′tä), Port.
Victoire (vēk-twär′), Fr. Victoria

VICTOR (Víctor, óris), M. Mar. 6. R. M.
(d. u.) Nicomedia. *Sig.* Lat. conqueror. *Pron.*
vĭk′tŏr.
(vĭk′tōr), Lat., Ger.
(vēk-tōr′), Fr.

VICTOR, M. Apr. 12. R. M.
4 Cent. Portugal

VICTOR I, P. M. Jul. 28. R. M.
2 Cent. Established date of Easter.

VICTORIA (Victória, æ), V. M. Dec. 23. R. M.
3 Cent. Rome. *Sig.* Lat. victory. *Pron.* vĭk-tō′rĭ-à.
(vĭk-tō′rē-ä), Lat., Ger.

VICTORIAN (Victoriánus, i), M. Mar. 23. R. M.
5 Cent. Pro-consul at Carthage. *Sig.* Lat. victory.
Pron. vĭk-tō'rĭ-ăn.

Victorianus (vĭk-tō-rē-ä'nŭs), Lat. Victorian

VICTORIUS (Victórius, ii), M. Oct. 30. R. M.
4 Cent. Leon, Spain. *Sig.* Lat. victory. *Pron.* vĭk-
tō'rĭ-ŭs.
(vĭk-tō'rē-ŭs), Lat.

Vida (vē'dá), cor. Davida

Viktor (vĭk'tōr), Ger. Victor

Viktoria (vĭk-tō'rē-ä), Ger. Victoria

VINCENT (Vincéntius, ii), Dea. M. Jan. 22. R. M.
3 Cent. Saragossa. In art shown bound to tree.
Sig. Lat. conquering. *Pron.* vĭn'sĕnt.
(văn-sŏṅ'), Fr.

VINCENT FERRER, C. Apr. 5. R. M.
15 Cent. Spanish Dominican, preached Gospel in
France, Spain, Italy, England and Scotland.
Helped to end Great Schism. In art shown with
cardinal's hat or holding sun with I H S in hand.
Pron. fĕr'rĕr.

VINCENT DE PAUL, C. Jul. 19. R. M.
17 Cent. Paris. Founder of Congregation of Mission
(Vincentians) and of Sisters of Charity. Special
patron of all charitable works. In art shown with
infant in arms.

Vincente (vēn-thĕn'tā), Sp. Vincent

VINCENTIA (Vincéntia, æ), M. Nov. 16.
(d. u.) Antioch. *Sig.* Lat. conquering. *Pron.* vĭn-
sĕn'shá.
(vĭn-chĕnt'sē-ä), Lat.

Vincentius (vĭn-chĕnt′sē-ŭs), Lat. Vincent
Vincenz (vēnt′sĕnts), Ger. Vincent
Vincenzio (vēn-chĕn′zē-ō), It. Vincent

VIOLA (Víola, æ), V. M. May 3.
   (d. u.) Verona. *Sig.* Lat. violet. *Pron.* vī (or vē)-
   ō′lả or vī′ō-lả.
   (vē-ō′lä), Ger., It.
   (vē′ō-lä), Lat.
Violante (vē-ō-län′tä), Sp., Port. Viola
Violet (vī′ō-lĕt), var. Viola
Violette (vē-ō-lĕt′), Fr. Viola
Virgie (vĕr′jē), cont. Virginia

VIRGIL (Virgílius, ii), B. C. Nov. 27. R. M.
   8 Cent. Irish missionary in Germany. Bishop of Salz-
   burg. *Sig.* Lat. flourishing. *Pron.* vĕr′jĭl.
Virgile (vēr-zhēl′), Fr. Virgil
Virgilio (vēr-hē′lē-ō), Sp. Virgil
Virgilius (vēr-jē′lē-ŭs), Lat. Virgil
Virginia (vĭr-jĭn′ĭ-à), in honor of virginity of Blessed
   Virgin.
Virginie (vēr-zhē-nē′), Fr. Virginia
Vita (vī′tả), fem. Vitus
Vital (vē-täl′), Fr. Vitalis
Vitale (vē-tä′lä), It. Vitalis

VITALIS OF BOLOGNA (Vitális, is), M. Nov. 4.
   R. M.
   4 Cent. Slave of St. Agricola, with whom he was
   martyred. *Sig.* Lat. of life. *Pron.* vī-tăl′ĭs.
   (vē-tä′lĭs), Lat.

VITALIS OF RAVENNA, M. Apr. 28. R. M.
   1 Cent. Father of Sts. Gervase and Protase.

VITALIS OF ROME, M. Jul. 10. R. M.
One of Seven Holy Brothers.
Vite (vēt), Fr. Vitus
Vitoria (vē-tō'rē-ä), Sp. Victoria
Vittoria (vē-tō'rē-ä), It. Victoria
Vittorio (vē-tō'rē-ō), It. Victorius

VITUS (Vítus, i), M. June 15. R. M.
4 Cent. Child slain with nurse, St. Crescentia, and
her husband, St. Modestus. Invoked against
apoplexy. Also called Guy. *Pron.* vī'tŭs.
(vē'tŭs), Lat.

VIVIAN (Viviánus, i), B. C. Aug. 28. R. M.
5 Cent. Saintes. *Sig.* Lat. lively. *Pron.* vĭv'ĭ-ăn.
Also var. Bibiana
Viviana (vē-vē-ä'nä), It. Bibiana
Vivianus (vē-vē-ä'nŭs), Lat. Vivian
Vivien (vē-vē-ăn'), Fr. Vivian (masc.)
Vivienne (vē-vē-ĕn'), Fr. Vivian (fem.)
Vladislaus (vlä'dĭs-lôs), Rus. Ladislaus

W

WALBURGA (Walbúrga, æ), V. Feb. 25.
8 Cent. daughter of St. Richard, King of England,
sister of St. Willibald. Labored with St. Boniface
for conversion of Germany. Ab. of Hildesheim.
Sig. Teut. strong protection. *Pron.* wäl'bĕr-gȧ.
(wäl-bōōr'gä), Lat.
Walburge (wäl-bürzh'), Fr. Walburga
Waldetrudis (wäl-dä-trōō'dĭs), Lat. Waltrude
Wally (wäl'lĭ), abbr. Walter, Walburga
Walpurgis (väl-pōōr'gēs), Ger. Walburga
Walt (wȧlt), abbr. Walter

WALTER (Gualtérius, ii), Ab. C. Apr. 8.
  11 Cent. Pontoise. *Sig.* Ger. powerful warrior. *Pron.*
  wạl'tẽr.
Walther (wạl'tẽr), Du. Ger. Walter

WALTRUDE (Waldetrúdis, is), Ab. Apr. 9. R. M.
  7 Cent. Noblewoman of France, who led life of self-
  denial. Mons. *Pron.* wäl'trūd.

WARREN (Guarínus, i), B. C. Feb. 6. R. M.
  12 Cent. Canon Regular of Bologna, Cardinal Bishop
  of Palaestrina. *Sig.* Teut. protecting friend. *Pron.*
  wär'rĕn.
Wat (wät), cont. Walter.
Watkin (wät'kĭn), obs. dim. Walter

WENCESLAS, WENCESLAUS (Wencesläus, ái), M.
  Sep. 28. R. M.
  10 Cent. Prague. Duke of Bohemia. *Sig.* great glory.
  Pron. wĕn'sĕs-läs or (lôs).
  (wĕn-sĕs-lä'ŭs), Lat.
Wendalinus (wĕn-dä-lē'nŭs), Lat. Wendelin
Wendel (wĕn'dĕl), form of Wendelin

WENDELIN (Wendalínus, i), C. Oct. 20.
  7 Cent. Patron of swineherds, shepherds, peasants.
  Sig. Teut. wanderer. *Pron.* wĕn'dĕl-ĭn.
Wendolin (wĕn'dō-lĭn), var. of Wendelin.
Wenefrida (wä-nä-frē'dä), Lat. Winifrid
Wenzel (vĕn'tsĕl), Du., Ger., Nor. Wenceslaus

WEREBURGA (Werebúrga, æ), V. Feb. 3.
  7 Cent. Daughter of St. Ermenilda. Mercia. *Sig.*
  strong protection. *Pron.* wä'rĕ-bûr-gà.
  (wä-rä-bōōr'gä), Lat.

WERNER (Wernérus, i), M. Apr. 18
13 Cent. Boy murdered by Jews in Germany. *Sig.*
Teut. protecting army. *Pron.* wĕr′nĕr.
Wernerus (wer-nä′rŭs), Lat. Werner
Wilbrod (wĭl′brōd), form of Willibrord

WILFRED, WILFRID (Wilfrídus, i), B. C. Oct. 12.
8 Cent. Monk of Lindisfarne, Archb. of York,
Apostle of Holland, Sussex and Isle of Wight.
Sig. resolute peace. *Pron.* wĭl′frĕd (or frĭd).
Wilfridus (wĭl-frē′dŭs), Lat. Wilfrid.
Wilhelm (vĭl′hĕlm), Dan., Ger., Sw. William
Wilhelmina (wĭl-hĕl-mē′nȧ), fem. of William
Wilhelmine (vĭl-hĕl-mē′nē), Ger. Wilhelmina
Wilkin (wĭl′kĭn), obs. dim. William
Will (wĭl), dim. William
Willie (wĭl′lē), dim. William
Willebald (wĭl′lē-bäld), var. of Willibald
Willebaldus (wĭl-lä-bäl′dŭs), Lat. Willibald
Willebrord (wĭl′lē-brōrd), var. of Willibrord
Willebrordus (wĭl-lä-brōr′dŭs), Lat. Willibrord
Willem (vĭl′lĕm), Du. William

WILLIAM (Guliélmus, i), Ab. C. June 25. R. M.
12 Cent. Vercelli, near Naples, founder of Williamites
or Hermits of Monte Vergine. In art shown with
wolf at side or with trowel, lily and passion flower.
Sig. Ger. protector. *Pron.* wĭl′yăm.
Also 12 Cent. Archb. York. June 8. R. M.
Also 13 Cent. Archb. Bourges, Cistercian, Jan. 10.

WILLIBALD (Willebaldus, i), B. C. Jul. 7. R. M.
8 Cent. Son of St. Richard, King of England, one of
Apostles of Germany, brother of Sts. Winebald

and Walburga. First B. of Eichstadt. *Sig.* resolute
prince. *Pron.* wĭl'lĭ-bäld.
Willibaldus (wĭl-lĭ-bäl'dŭs), Lat. var. Willibald.

WILLIBRORD (Willébrórdus, i), B. C. Nov. 7. R. M.
    8 Cent. Northumbrian missionary in Holland and
    Belgium. Archb. Utrecht, Apostle of Frisians.
    Pron. wĭl'ĭ-brôrd.
Willibrordus (wĭl-lĭ-brōr'dŭs), Lat. var. Willibrord
Willy (wĭl'lĭ), dim. William
Wilmett (wĭl'mĕt), dim. Wilhelmina
Wilmot (wĭl'mŏt), dim. Wilhelmina
Winefreda (wĭ-nā-frā'dä), Lat. var. Winifrid
Winefride (wĭn'ĕ-frĭd), var. of Winifrid
Winfred (wĭn'frĕd), original name of St. Boniface
Winfrid (vĭn'frĭd), Sw. Winifrid
Winfried (wĭn'frēt), Du. Winifrid
Winifred (wĭn'ĭ-frĕd), var. of Winifrid
    (vē-nē-frĕd'), Fr. Winifrid

WINIFRID (Wenefrída, æ), V. M. Nov. 3. R. M.
    7 Cent. Patron of North Wales, disciple of St. Benno.
    In art shown with book and palm and a head at
    her feet. *Pron.* wĭn'ĭ-frĭd.
Winifride (wĭn'ĭ-frĭd), var. of Winifrid
Winnie (wĭn'nē), dim. Winifrid
Wladislaus (vlä'dĭs-lôs), Pol. Ladislaus

WOLFGANG (Wolfgángus, i), B. C. Oct. 31. R. M.
    13 Cent. Ratisbon. *Pron.* wolf'găng.
Wolfgangus (wōlf-gän'gŭs), Lat. Wolfgang
Wolstan (wōl'stăn), var. of Wulstan
Wolstanus (wōl-stä'nŭs), Lat. var. Wulstan
Wouter (wŏu'tēr), Du. Walter

WULFRAM (Wulfránnus, i), B. C. Mar. 20. R. M.
8 Cent. Archb. Sens., missionary to Friesland. *Pron.*
wŏŏl'frăm.
Wulfrannus (wŏŏl-frä'nŭs), Lat. Wulfram
Wulfstan (wolf'stăn), var. of Wulstan

WULSTAN (Wulstánus, i), B. C. Jan. 19. R. M.
11 Cent. Worcester. *Sig.* Teut. wolf stone. *Pron.*
wŏŏl'stăn.
Wulstanus (wŏŏl-stä'nŭs), Lat. Wulstan

X

Xaverio (zä-vä'rē-ō), It. Xavier
Xaverius (zä-vä'rē-ŭs), Ger., Lat. Xavier
Xavier (zā'vyēr), *see* St. Francis
Xina (zē'nȧ), dim. Christina
Xyste (zēst) Fr. Xystus
Xystus (zĭs'tŭs), Lat. var. of Sixtus

Y

Yakof (yä'kōf), Rus. James
Yekaterina (yä-kä-tä-rē'nä), Rus. Catherine
Yves (ēv), Fr. Ives
Yvette (ē-vĕt'), Fr. Jutta

Z

Zacarias (thä-kä-rē'äs), Sp. Zacharias
Zaccaria (dzäk-kä-rē'ä), It. Zacharias
Zaccheus (zăk-kē'ŭs), var. of Zacheus
Zach (zăk), dim. Zachary, Zacharias
Zachæus (zä-kē'ŭs), Lat. Zacheus
Zachariah (zăk-ȧ-rī'ȧ), var. of Zacharias

ZACHARIAS (Zacharías, æ), Proph. Sep. 6. R. M.
Greatest of minor prophets. *Sig.* Heb. remembered of
Jehovah. *Pron.* zăk-à-rī'ăs.
(zä-kä-rē'äs), Lat. Zacharias or Zachary
Also B. M., 2 Cent. May 26; and P., 8 Cent. Mar. 15
Zacharie (zä-kä-rē'), Fr. Zacharias or Zachary

ZACHARY (Zacharías, æ), Proph. Nov. 5. R. M.
Priest, father of St. John Baptist, beheld vision in
Temple, uttered Canticle Benedictus. *Sig.* Heb.
remembered of Jehovah. *Pron.* zăk'à-rĭ.
Zachée (zä-shä'), Fr. Zacheus
Zacheo (dzä-kä'ō), It. Zacheus

ZACHEUS (Zachæ'us, i), B. C. Aug. 23. R. M.
2 Cent. Jerusalem. *Sig.* Heb. innocent, pure. *Pron.*
(ză-kē'ŭs).
Zander (zăn'dēr), dim. Alexander
Zechariah (zĕk-à-rī'á), var. of Zacharias
Zeke (zēk), dim. Ezechiel
Zelotes (zē-lō'tēz), name given to Apostle St. Simon;
Sig. Zealot.

ZENO (Zéno, ónis), B. M. Apr. 12. R. M.
3 Cent. Verona. *Pron.* zē'nō.
(zā'nō), Lat.

ZENOBIA (Zenóbia, æ), M. Oct. 30. R. M.
4 Cent. martyred with brother Zenobius in Asia
Minor. *Sig.* Aram. father's ornament. *Pron.*
zē-nō'bĭ-à.
(zā-nō'bē-ä), Lat.
Zenobie (zā-nō-bē'), Fr. Zenobia

ZENOBIUS (Zenóbius, ii), B. C. May 25. R. M.
   5 Cent. Friend of St. Ambrose, B. of Florence. *Pron.*
   zĕ-nō′bĭ-ŭs.
   (zā-nō′bē-ŭs), Lat.
Zénon (zā-nöñ′), Fr. Zeno
Zenone (dzā-nō′nā), It. Zeno
Zephaniah (zĕf-à-nĭ′à), var. Sophonias
Zephyrin (zā-fē-rāñ′), Fr. Zephyrinus

ZEPHYRINUS (Zephyrínus, i), P. M. Aug. 26. R. M.
   also Dec. 20.
   3 Cent. *Sig.* Gr. zephyr-like. *Pron.* zĕ-fĭ-rī′nŭs.
   (zĕ-fē-rē′nŭs), Lat.

ZITA (Zíta, æ), V. Apr. 27. R. M.
   13 Cent. Lucca. Patron of servants. In art with
   rosary and large key. *Pron.* zē′tä.
   (zē′tä), Lat.
Zite (zēt), Fr. Zita
Zoa (zō′ä), Lat. var. Zoe

ZOË (Zóë, ës), M. Jul. 5. R. M.
   3 Cent. Wife of Roman official. *Sig.* Gr. life. *Pron.*
   zō′ē.
   (zō′ä), Lat.
Zosimus (zō′sē-mŭs), Lat. var. Zozimus

ZOZIMUS (Zózimus, i), C. Nov. 30. R. M.
   6 Cent. Hermit in Palestine noted for miracles and
   gift of prophecy. *Pron.* zō′zĭ-mŭs.
   (zō′zē-mŭs), Lat.

PATRONS OF COUNTRIES

and Localities

Austria—Blessed Virgin
Bavaria—Blessed Virgin
Belgium—St. Joseph
Borneo—St. Francis Xavier
Brazil—The Holy Cross
Canada—St. Anne, St. George
Chile—St. James
Congo—Blessed Virgin
Cuba—Our Lady of Charity
East Indies—St. Thomas, Ap.
Ecuador—The Sacred Heart
England—St. George
Finland—St. Henry
France—St. Denis
Germany—St. Michael
Holland—St. Willibrord
Hungary—St. Stephen
Ireland—St. Patrick
Lombardy—St. Charles
Lourdes—Our Lady of the Rosary
Mexico—Our Lady of Help, Our Lady of Guadalupe
Naples—St. Januarius
Norway—St. Olaf
Piedmont—St. Maurice
Portugal—St. George
Rome—Sts. Peter and Paul
Russia—St. Andrew, St. Nicholas
Santo Domingo—St. Dominic
Scotland—St. Andrew
Slavs—St. Adalbert
South America—St. Rose of Lima
Sweden—St. Bridget
United States—The Immaculate Conception
Wales—St. David
West Indies—St. Gertrude

PATRON SAINTS

and Those Invoked in Trouble, Sickness, etc.

Actors—Genesius, *M.*, Aug. 25

Altar boys—John Berchmans, *C.*, Aug. 13

Animals—Saturnina, *V.M.*, June 4; Blase, *B.M.*, Feb. 3; Antony, *Ab.*, Jan. 17

Appendicitis—Erasmus, *B.M.*, June 2

Archers—Christina, *V.M.*, Jul. 24; George, *M.*, Apr. 23; Sebastian, *M.*, Jan. 20

Architects—Barbara, *V.M.*, Dec. 4; Thomas, *Ap.*, Dec. 21

Armorers—Dunstan, *B.C.*, May 19; Barbara, *V.M.*, Dec. 4; George, *M.*, Apr. 23

Artillery—Barbara, *V.M.*, Dec. 4

Artists—Luke, *Ev.*, Oct. 18

Automobilists—Christopher, *M.*, Jul. 25

Aviators—Our Lady of Lourdes, Feb. 11

Bakers—Nicholas, *B.C.*, Dec. 6; Wilfrid, *C.*, Oct. 20

Bankers—Matthew, *Ap.,Ev.*, Sept. 21

Barbers—Cosmas and Damian, *MM.*, Sept. 21; Louis, *K.C.*, Aug. 25

Bees—Bernard, *C.D.*, Aug. 20

Beggars—Alexis, *C.*, Jul. 17

Bell founders—Agatha, *V.M.*, Feb. 5

Belt makers—Alexis, *C.*, Jul. 17

Blacksmiths—Dunstan, *B.C.*, May 19

Blindness—Ottilie, *V.*, Dec. 13; Herveus, *C.*, June 17; Thomas, *M.*, Dec. 29

Boatmen—Julian, *M.*, Jan. 9

Bookbinders—John before Latin Gate, May 6

Boys—Aloysius, *C.*, June 21

Boy Scouts—Amand, *C.*, June 18

Breast, diseases of—Agatha, *V.M.*, Feb. 5

Brewers—Arnulph, *C.*, Aug. 19; Nicholas, *B.C.*, Dec. 6; Augustine, *B.C.D.*, Aug. 28; Adrian, *M.*, Sept. 8

Bridges—John Nepomucene, *M.*, May 16

Brush makers—Antony, *Ab.*, Jan. 17

Builders—Thomas, *B.M.*, Dec. 29

Butchers—Antony, *Ab.*, Jan. 17; Luke, *Ev.*, Oct. 18; George, *M.*, Apr. 23; Adrian, *M.*, Sept. 8

Cabinet makers—Anne, Jul. 26

Cancer—Peregrinus, *C.*, Apr. 30; Adelgund, *V.*, Jan. 30

Canonists—Raymund of Pennafort, *C.*, Jan. 23

Captives—Plato, *M.*, Jul. 22

Carpenters—Joseph, *C.*, Mar. 19

Cattle—Bobo, *C.*, May 22; Engelmar, *M.*, Jan. 14

Cavalrymen—George, *M.*, Apr. 23

Cemeteries—Antony, *Ab.*, Jan. 17

Chance, games of—Corona, *M.*, May 14

Charitable societies—Vincent de Paul, *C.*, Jul. 19

Chauffeurs—Fiacre, *C.*, Aug. 30

Children of Mary—Agnes, *V.M.*, Jan. 21 and 28

Cholera—Roch, *C.*, Aug. 16; (Bl.) Bronislava, *V.*, Aug. 30

Circus people—Julian, *C.*, Feb. 12

Coachmen—Fiacre, *C.*, Aug. 30

Cobblers—Crispin and Crispinian, *M M.*, Oct. 25

Coffee-house keepers—Drogo, *C.*, Apr. 16

Colic—Erasmus, *M.*, June 2; Agapitus, *M.*, Aug. 18

Colleges—Thomas Aquinas, *C.*, Mar. 7

Comedians—Vitus, *M.*, June 15

Condemned to death—Dismas, Mar. 25

Contagion—Macarius, *B.C.*, Apr. 9

Cooks—Martha, *V.*, Jul. 29; Owen, *B.C.*, Aug. 24; Lawrence,
        Dea. M., Aug. 10

Coopers—Nicholas, *B.C.*, Dec. 6; Abdon and Sennen, *MM.*,
        Jul. 30

Cramps—Erasmus, *B.M.*, June 2

Cripples—Giles, *Ab.*, Sept. 1

Crossbowmen—Christopher, *M.*, Jul. 25

Danger—Fourteen Holy Helpers

Deafness—Owen, *B.C.*, Aug. 24; Cadoc, *B.M.*, Jan. 23

Death, happy—Joseph, *C.*, Mar. 19
        sudden—Barbara, *V.M.*, Dec. 4; Christopher, M., Jul. 25

Dentists—Cosmas and Damian, *MM.*, Sept. 27; Apollonia,
        V.M., Feb. 9

Desperate cases—Jude Thaddeus, *Ap.*, Oct. 28

Devil, attacks of—Margaret, *V.M.*, Jul. 20

Dizziness—Avertinus, *C.*, May 15

Doctors—Cosmas and Damian, *MM.*, Sept. 21; Luke, *Ev.*,
        Oct. 18; Roch, *C.*, Aug. 16; Pantaleon, *C.*,   Jul. 27
        Blase, *B.M.*, Feb. 3

Dog bite—Hubert, *C.*, Nov. 3; Denis, *B.M.*, Oct. 9

Dogs—Hubert, *C.*, Nov. 3

Drapers—Ursula, *V.M.*, Oct. 21

Drought—Elias, *Proph.*, Jul. 20; Eulalia, *V.M.*, Feb. 12; Odo,
        B.C., Nov. 18; Florian, *M.*, May 4

Drowning—Adjutor, *C.*, Ap. 20

Druggists—Cosmas and Damian, *MM.*, Sept. 21; James, *A p.*,
        Jul. 25

Dying—Joseph, *C.*, Mar. 19; Dismas, Mar. 25

Ear-ache—Polycarp, *B.M.*, Jan. 26

Earthquake—Elias, *Proph.*, Jul. 20; Francis Borgia, *C.*, Oct. 10;
        Rosalia, *V.*, Sept. 4; Agatha, *V.M.*, Feb. 5

Eloquence—Catherine, *V.M.*, Nov. 25

Embroiderers—Clarus, *M.*, Nov. 4

Epidemics—Lucy, *V.M.*, Dec. 13

Epilepsy—Vitus, *C.*, Feb. 5; Valentine, *B.M.*, Feb. 14; Antony,
        A b., Jan. 17

Erysipelas—Antony, *A b.*, Jan. 17

Eucharistic Congresses and societies—Paschal Baylon, *C.*,
        May 17

Eyes—Lucy, *V.M.*, Dec. 13; Ottilie, *V.*, Dec. 13; Clarus, *M.*,
        Nov. 4

Fair weather—Ursus, *C.*, Feb. 1

Families—The Holy Family

Famine—Agatha, *V.M.*, Feb. 5

Farmers—Walstan, *C.*, May 30

Farriers—John the Baptist, *M.*, June 24; Eligius, *C.*, Dec. 1

Fever—Constant, *M.*, Sept. 18; Felix, *B.C.*, Jan. 1, Gertrude,
        V.A b., Mar. 17; Amalberga, *Mat.*, Jul. 10; Sigis-
        mund, *K.M.*, May 1

Fire—Agatha, *V.M.*, Feb. 5; Barbara, *V.M.*, Dec. 4; Lawrence,
        Dea.M., Aug. 10; Florian, *M.*, May 4

Fireworks makers—Barbara, *V.M.*, Dec. 4

First Communicants—(Bl.) Imelda, *V.*, May 13

Fishermen—Andrew, *A p.*, Nov. 30

Fortifications—Barbara, *V.M.*, Dec. 4

Founders—Barbara, *V.M.*, Dec. 4

Foundlings—The Holy Innocents, Dec. 28

Fullers—James, *A p.*, May 1; Anastasius, *M.*, Sept. 7

Gardeners—Dorothy, *V.M.*, Feb. 6; Fiacre, *C.*, Aug. 30; Urban,
        M., May 25; Agnes, *V.M.*, Jan. 21 and 28; Phocas,
        M., Sept. 22

Girls—Ursula, *V.M.*, Oct. 21; Blandina, *V.M.*, June 2; Agnes
　　　V.M., Jan. 21 and 28

Glassworkers—Luke, *Ev.*, Oct. 18

Glaziers—(Bl.) James of Ulm, *C.*, Oct. 12

Goldsmiths—Dunstan, *B.C.*, May 19; Anastasius, *M.*, Jan. 22;
　　　Eligius, *C.*, Dec. 1

Gout—Andrew, *Ap.*, Nov. 30; Maur, *Ab.*, Feb. 15

Grave diggers—Antony, *Ab.*, Jan. 17; Barbara, *V.M.*, Dec. 4

Gravel—Apollinaris, *B.M.*, Jul. 23

Grocers—Michael, *Arch.*, Sept. 29

Hail—Christopher, *M.*, Jul. 25; Mark, *Ev.*, Ap. 25

Hardware workers—Eligius, *C.*, Dec. 1

Harness makers—Crispin and Crispinian, *MM.*, Oct. 25

Hatters—James, *Ap.*, May 1; Clement, *P.M.*, Nov. 23

Headache—Alexander, *M.*, Jul. 10; Catherine, *V.*, Ap. 30;
　　　Denis, *B.M.*, Oct. 9; Peter Damian, *C.*, Feb. 23;
　　　Anastasius, *M.*, Jan. 22

Hernia—Cosmas and Damian, *MM.*, Sept. 21; Peregrinus, *C.*,
　　　Jan. 30; Sigismund, *K.M.*, May 1

Hoarseness—Maur, *Ab.*, Feb. 15

Horses—Eusebius, *C.*, Aug. 14; George, *M.*, Ap. 23

Horse traders—Louis, *K.C.*, Aug. 25

Hospitallers—Camillus, *C.*, Jul. 18; John of God, *C.*, Mar. 8

Hotel keepers—Julian, *C.*, Feb. 12; Theodotus, *M.*, May 18;
　　　Owen, *B.C.*, Aug. 24

Housewives—Anne, Jul. 26; Martha, *V.*, Jul. 29

Hunters—Hubert, *C.*, Nov. 3; Eustace, *M.*, Nov. 3

Hydrophobia—Hubert, *C.*, Nov. 3; Walburga, *V.*, May 1

Impenitence—Barbara, *V.M.*, Dec. 4

Impossible, Saint of—Rita, *Wid.*, May 22

Infantry—Maurice, *M.*, Sept. 22

Infirmities—Macarius, *C.*, Jan. 15

Insane—Dymphna, *V.M.*, May 15, Leonard, *C.*, Nov. 6

Insanity—Florentius, *C.*, Apr. 18

Intestinal troubles—Erasmus, *M.*, June 2

Inundations—Odo, *B.C.*, Jul. 7; Gregory, *B.C.*, Nov. 17

Invalids—Roch, *C.*, Aug. 16

Jewelers—Eligius, *C.*, Dec. 1; Agatha, *V.M.*, Feb. 5

Journalists—Francis of Sales, *B.C.D.*, Dec. 28

Jurists—Catherine, *V.M.*, Nov. 25

Kidney diseases—Walfrid, *Ab.*, Feb. 15

Knights—Michael, *Arch.*, Sept. 29; George, *M.*, Apr. 23

Laborers—Lucy, *V.M.*, Dec. 13

Lace makers—Sebastian, *M.*, Jan. 20

Lawyers—Ives, *C.*, May 19

Letter carriers—Gabriel, *Arch.*, Mar. 24

Lightning—Barbara, *V.M.*, Dec. 4; Mark, *Ev.*, Apr. 25

Locksmiths—Dunstan, *B.C.*, May 19; Eligius, *C.*, Dec. 1; Baldomer, *C.*, Feb. 27

Locust plagues—Gregory, *B.C.*, May 8

Losses—Antony of Padua, *C.*, June 13; Arnulph, *C.*, Aug. 19

Lotteries—Corona, *M.*, May 14

Lumbago—Lawrence, *Dea. M.*, Aug. 10

Marble workers—Clement, *P.M.*, Nov. 23

Mariners—Christopher, *M.*, Jul. 25; Christina, *V.M.*, Jul. 24;
Clement, *P.M.*, Nov. 23; Phocas, *M.* Sept. 22;
Nicholas *B.C.* Dec. 6

Masons—Thomas, *Ap.* Dec. 21

Merchants—Nicholas, *B.C.* Dec. 6; Homobonus, *C.* Nov. 13

Midwives—Raymund, *C.*, Aug. 31

Millers—Arnold, *C.*, Jul. 18; Arnulph, *C.*, Aug. 19; Victor, *M.*,
Jul. 21; Catherine, *V.M.*, Nov. 25; Christina,
V.M., Jul. 24

Miners—Kieran, *B.C.*, Mar. 5

Minstrels—Julian, *C.*, Feb. 12

Missions, Eastern—Francis Xavier, *C.*, Dec. 3
Negro—Peter Claver, *C.*, Sept. 9
Popular—Leonard of Port Maurice, *C.*, Nov. 27
All—Teresa of the Child Jesus, *V.*, Oct. 3

Money affairs—Corona, *M.*, May 14

Mothers—Anne, Jul. 26

Musicians—Cecilia, *V.M.*, Nov. 22; David, *K.*, *Proph.*, Dec. 29;
Dunstan, *B.C.*, May 19; Odo, *B.C.*, Nov. 18

Nail makers—Cloud, *C.*, Sept. 7

Need—Fourteen Holy Helpers

Nervousness—Vitus, *C.*, Feb. 5

Night watchmen—Peter of Alcantara, *C.*, Oct. 19

Noble Guards oɪ Pope—Sebastian, *M.*, Jan. 20

Notaries—Luke, *Ev.*, Oct. 18; Mark, *Ev.*, Ap. 25; Genesius, *M.*,
Aug. 25

Nurses—Agatha, *V.M.*, Feb. 5

Nursing women—Tryphaenes, *M.*, Jan. 31; Bernard, *C.D.*,
Aug. 20; Erasmus, *M.*, June 2; Leonard, *C.*, Nov. 6

Olive trees—Olive, *V.*, Jan. 15

Orators—John Chrysostom, *B.C.D.*, Jan. 27

Organ builders—Cecilia, *V.M.*, Nov. 22

Orphanages—James Emilian, *C.*, Feb. 8

Paper makers—John before Latin Gate, May 6

Paralysis—Martin, *C.*, Nov. 26

Parish priests—John Mary Vianney, *C.*, Aug. 4

Pawnbrokers—Nicholas, *B.C.*, Dec. 6

Peasants—Lucy, *V.M.*, Dec. 13; Wendelin, *C.*, Oct. 20

Penitents—Mary Magdalen, *Pen.*, Jul. 22; Afra, *M.*, Aug. 5

Pestilence—Antony, *A b.*, Jan. 17; Roch, *C.*, Aug. 16; Cyprian, *B.M.*, Sept. 14; Sebastian, *M.*, Jan. 20; Adrian, *M.*, Sept. 8; Florentius, *M.*, June 1

Philosophers—Catherine, *V.M.*, Nov. 25

Piles—Alexander, *M.*, Jul. 10

Pilgrims—Bridget of Sweden, *Mat.*, Oct. 8; James, *A p.*, Jul. 25; Alexis, *C.*, Jul. 17

Plague—Adrian, *M.*, Sept. 8

Poets—Cecilia, *V.M.*, Nov. 22; David, *K.Proph.*, Dec. 29

Poison—Benedict, *C.*, Mar. 21

Poor—Antony of Padua, *C.*, June 13; Lawrence, *Dea.M.*, Aug. 10

Porters—Christopher, *M.*, Jul. 25; James, *A p.*, Jul. 25

Possessed—Margaret, *V.M.*, Jul. 20

Postal employees—Gabriel, *Arch.*, Mar. 24

Potters—Goar, *C.*, Jul. 6; Fiacre, *C.*, Aug. 30

Pregnant women—Margaret, *V.M.*, Jul. 20

Press—Francis of Sales, *C.*, Jan. 29

Printers—Louis, *K.C.*, Aug. 25; Augustine, *B.C.D.*, Aug. 28

Prisoners—Barbara, *V.M.*, Dec. 4; Leonard, *C.*, Nov. 6; Roch, *C.*, Aug. 16; Honorina, *V.M.*, Feb. 27

Propagation of the Faith—Francis Xavier, *C.*, Dec. 3

Purgatory, "Apostle" of—Catherine of Genoa, Sept. 15

Rabies—Denis, *B.M.*, Oct. 9; Hubert, *C.*, Nov. 3

Rain—Aphrodosius, *B.M.*, Mar. 22

Retreats—Ignatius of Loyola, *C.*, Jul. 31

Rheumatism—James, *A p.*, Jul. 25

Rope makers—Paul, *A p.*, June 30; Catherine, *V.M.*, Nov. 25

Saddlers—George, *M.*, Ap. 23; Gualford, *C.*, May 11; Paul, *A p.*, Jan. 25

Sailors—Brendan, *B.C.*, May 16, Peter Gonzales, *C.*, Apr. 14; Cuthbert, *B.C.*, Mar. 20; Nicholas, *B.C.*, Dec. 6; Phocas, *M.*, Sept. 22; Erasmus, *M.*, June 2

Scabies—Ignatius, *B.M.*, Feb. 1

Schools—Thomas Aquinas, *C.*, Mar. 7

Science—Catherine, *V.M.*, Nov. 25

Scrofula—Cadoc, *B.M.*, Jan. 23; Genesius, *M.*, Aug. 25

Servant maids—Zita, *V.*, Ap. 27; Margaret, *V.M.*, Sept. 2

Shepherds—Wendelin, *Ab.*, Oct. 22; Drogo, *C.*, Ap. 16

Sick and attendants—Camillus, *C.*, Jul. 14; John of God, *C.*,
    Mar. 8; Leonard, *C.*, Nov. 6

Silence—John Nepomucene, *M.*, May 16

Silversmiths—Andronicus, *C.*, Oct. 9

Singers—Cecilia, *V.M.*, Nov. 22; Gregory, *P.C.*, Mar. 12

Skin diseases—Antony, *Ab.*, Jan. 17

Slander—John Nepomucene, *M.*, May 16

Smallpox—Bonosa, *V.M.*, Jul. 15

Snakes—Hilary, *B.C.D.*, Jan. 13; Paul, *Ap.*, Jan. 25

Soldiers—Adrian, *M.*, Sept. 8

Sore eyes—Aloysius, *C.*, June 21; Augustine, *B.C.D.*, Aug. 28;
    Lucy, *V.M.*, Dec. 13

Sore throat—Lucy, *V.M.*, Dec. 13; Blase, *B.M.*, Feb. 3; Andrew,
    Ap., Nov. 30; Ignatius, *B.M.*, Feb. 1

Sterility of women—Giles, *Ab.*, Sept. 1; Felicitas, *M.*, Nov. 23

Stomach disorders—Timothy, *M.*, Jan. 24

Stone cutters—Clement, *P.M.*, Nov. 23

Stonemasons—Stephen, *M.*, Dec. 26; Barbara, *V.M.*, Dec. 4;
    Louis, *K.C.*, Aug. 25

Storms—Erasmus, *B.M.*, June 2; Theodore, *M.*, Nov. 9

Students—Catherine, *V.M.*, Nov. 25; Thomas Aquinas, *C.D.*,
    Mar. 7; Aloysius, *C.*, June 21

Surgeons—Cosmas and Damian, *MM.*, Sept. 21

Swine—Antony, *Ab.*, Jan. 17

Swineherds—Wendelin, *Ab.*, Oct. 22

Swiss Guard of Pope—Maurice, *M.*, Sept. 22

Sword cutlers—George, *M.*, Ap. 23

Syphilis—Job, *Pat.*, May 10

Tailors—Clarus, *B.M.*, Feb. 9; John the Baptist, *M.*, June 24

Tax collectors—Matthew, *Ap.*, *Ev.*, Sept. 21

Teachers—Catherine, *V.M.*, Nov. 25; Ursula, *V.M.*, Oct. 21

Tentmakers—Paul, *Ap.*, Jan. 25

Theologians—Augustine, *B.C.D.*, Aug. 28; Thomas Aquinas,
    C.D., Mar. 7

Throat, diseases of—Blase, *B.M.*, Feb. 3

Thunderstorms—Barbara, *V.M.*, Dec. 4; Christopher, *M.*, Jul. 25;
    Agatha, *V.M.*, Feb. 5; Irene, *V.M.*, Ap. 5

Tile makers—Fiacre, *C.*, Aug. 30

Toothache—Apollonia, *V.M.*, Feb. 9

Travelers—Christopher, *M.*, Jul. 25; Raphael, *Arch.*, Oct. 24; Gertrude, *V.Ab.*, Mar. 17

Treasures, hidden—Corona, *M.*, May 14

Turners—Erasmus, *M.*, June 2

Universal Church—Joseph, *C.*, Mar. 19

Universities—Thomas Aquinas, *C.D.*, Mar. 7

Vine dressers—Urban, *P.M.*, May 25

Vineyards—Mitrius, *M.*, Nov. 13

Volcanic eruptions—Januarius, *B.M.*, Sept. 19; Agatha, *V.M.*, Feb. 5

Wagon makers—Catherine, *V.M.*, Nov. 25

War, in—James, *Ap.*, Jul. 25; Valerian, *M.*, May 4

Wax Chandlers—Bernard, *C.D.*, Aug. 20; Nicholas, *C.*, Dec. 6; James, *Ap.*, Jul. 25; Blase, *B.M.*, Feb. 3

Weavers—Anastasia, *V.M.*, Dec. 25; Stephen, *M.*, Dec. 26; Anastasius, *M.*, Jan. 22; Humphrey, *C.*, June 12

Wine makers—Vincent, *M.*, Jan. 22

Woolcombers—Blase, *B.M.*, Feb. 3

Women—Monica, *Mat.*, May 4

Woodcutters—Simon, *Ap.*, Oct. 28

Workmen—Joseph, *C.*, Mar. 19

World—The Sacred Heart, Friday after Octave of Corpus Christi

Yachtsmen—Adjutor, *C.*, Ap. 20

Youth—Aloysius, *C.*, June 21

A CALENDAR OF
FEASTS ACCORDING TO THE DAY OF THE MONTH

JANUARY

1. Circumcision of Our Lord; Fulgence, *B.C.;* Odilo, *Ab.C.;* Euphrosyna, *V.;* Basil, *B.C.D.;* Martina, *V.M.*
2. Macarius, *C.;* Adalhard, *Ab.C.;* Munchin, *B.C.*
3. Genevieve, *V.;* Florentius, *B.M.;* Lucida, *M.;* Bertille, *V.*
4. Dafrose, *M.;* Titus, *B.C.;* (Bl.) Angela of Foligno, *Mat.*
5. Telesphorus, *P.M.;* Simeon Stylites, *C.;* Aemiliana, *V.*
6. Epiphany of Our Lord; Andrew Corsini, *B.C.;* Macra, *V.*
7. Lucian, *Pr.M.,* Aldric, *B.C.;* Canute, *K.M.,* Raymond of Pennafort, *C.*
8. Severinus, *B.C.;* Gudula, *V.;* Albert, *B.C.,* Erhard, *B.C.;* Lawrence Justinian, *B.C.*
9. Julian, *M.;* Marciana, *V.,* Finan, *B.C.*
10. Agatho, *P.C.;* William, *B.C.;* Paul the Hermit, *C;* Gregory X, *P.C.,* Melchiades, *P.M.,* Dermot, *Ab.C.*
11. Hyginus, *P.M.;* Salvius, *B.C.;* Hortense, *B.C.;* Honorata, *V.;* Ethna, *V.;* Balthassar; Egwin, *B.C.*
12. Caesaria, *Ab.;* Arcadius, *M.;* Benedict Biscop, *Ab.C.*
13. Veronica of Milan, *V.;* (Bl.) Jutta, *Wid.;* Allan, *C.;* Remigius, *B.C.*
14. Hilary, *B.C.D.;* Felix of Nola, *Pr.M.,* Kentigern, *B.C.;* Euphrasius, *B.C.,* Macrina, *Wid.;* Malachias, *Proph.*
15. Paul the Hermit, *C.;* Maurus, *Ab.;* Ita, *V.;* Habacuc, *Proph.;* Bonitus, *B.C.;* Micheas, *Proph.*
16. Marcellus, *P.M.;* Accursius, *M.;* Fursey, *C.;* Priscilla, *Mat.*
17. Antony the Great, *Ab.;* Sulpicius, *B.C.;* Leonilla, *M.*
18. Chair of St. Peter at Rome; Paul, *Ap.;* Prisca, *V.M.;* Faustina, *V.*
19. Marius, *M.;* Canute, *K.M.,* Wulstan, *B.C.;* Audifax, *M.;* Abundantia, *V.;* Aldric, Gerontius, *M.,* Martha, *M.;* (Bl.) Peter Julian Eymard, *C.*
20. Fabian and Sebastian, *MM.*
21. Agnes, *V.M.;* Meinrad, *Her.*
22. Vincent, *M.;* Anastasius, *M.,* Enoch, *Pat.*
23. Raymund of Pennafort, *C.;* Emerentiana, *V.M.;* Cadoc, *B.M.;* Ildephonsus, *B.C.*
24. Timothy, *B.M.;* Vera, *V.*

25. Conversion of Paul the Apostle; Peter, *Ap.*; Sigebert, *K.M.*; Artemas, *M.*; Ananias, *B.M.*
26. Polycarp, *B.M.*; Paula, *Wid.*; Gonzales, *B.C.*; Conan, *B.C.*
27. John Chrysostom, *B.C.D.*; Natalis, *Ab.C.*; Angela Merici, *V.*
28. Agnes, *V.M.*; Leonidas, *M.*; Constance, *V.*; Valerius, *B.C.*; Amadeus, *B.C.*;
29. Francis of Sales, *B.C.D.*; Sulphicius Severus, *B.C.*; Constant, *B.M.*
30. Martina, *V.M.*; Hyacintha, *V.*; Adelgund, *V.Ab.*; Bathilda,*Q.*
31. Peter Nolasco, *C.*, Cyrus, *M.*, Felix, *P.C.*, Mark, *Ev.*; Marcella, *Wid.*; John Bosco, *C.*; Tryphena, *M.*

FEBRUARY

1. Ignatius of Antioch, *B.M.*; Bridgid of Kildare, *V.*; Ephrem, *Dea.C.D.*
2. Purification of Blessed Virgin; Candidus, *M.*; Catherine Ricci, *V.*, Cornelius, *B.C.*
3. Blase, *B.M.*; Wereburga, *V.Ab.*; Fillan, *Ab.C.*; Oscar, *B.C.*; (Bl.) John Theophane Venard, *M.*
4. Andrew Corsini, *B.C.*; Gilbert, *C.*; Rembert, *B.C.*, (Bl.) John of Britto, *C.*
5. Agatha, *V.M.*; Philip of Jesus, *M.*
6. Titus, *B.C.*; Dorothy, *V.M.*; Amand, *B.C.*; Vedast, *B.C.*; Warren, *B.C.*
7. Romuald, *Ab.C.*; Chrysolius, *B.M.*; Richard, *K.C.*; (Bl.) Thomas Sherwood, *M.*
8. John of Matha, *C.*; Juventius, *B.C.*; Jerome Aemilian, *C.*
9. Cyril of Alexandria, *B.C.D.*; Apollonia, *V.M.*; Nicephorus, *M.*; Ansbert, *B.C.*
10. Scholastica, *V.*; Irenaeus, *M.*
11. Our Lady of Lourdes; Gregory II, *P.C.*; Adolph, *B.C.*; Calocerus, *B.C.*; Paschal I, *P.C.*; Desiderius, *M.*
12. Seven Holy Founders of Servite Order; Melitius, *B.C.*; Eulalia, *V.M.*; (Bl.) Reginald, *C.*
13. Castor, *C.*; Ermelinda, *Q. Ab.* (Bl.) Beatrice, *V.*; (Bl.) John Theophane Venard, *M.*
14. Valentine, *Pr.M.*, Cyril, *B.C.*; (Bl.) Thomas Plumtree, *M.*
15. Faustinus and Jovita, *MM.*; Sigfrid, *B.C.*; Georgia, *V.*; (Bl.) Jordan, *C.*; (Bl.) Claude de la Columbiere, *C.*
16. Onesimus, *B.C.*; Juliana, *V.M.*
17. Alexis Falconieri, *C.*; Finan, *B.C.*; Fintan, *Ab.C.*, Theodulus, *C.*; (Bl.) John Francis Clet, *M.*

18. Simeon, *B.M.;* Claude, *M.*
19. Mansuetus, *B.C.;* Julian, *M.*
20. Eucherius, *B.C.;* Ulric, *Her.C.*
21. Severian, *B.M.;* Felix, *B.C.;*
22. Chair of St. Peter at Antioch; Paul, *Ap.;* Margaret of Cortona, *Pen.*
23. Peter Damian, *B.C.D.;* Vigil of St. Matthias, *Ap.;* Milburga, *V.;* Polycarp, *B.M.*
24. Matthias, *Ap.;* Ethelbert, *K.C.*
25. Adeltrude, *V.Ab.;* Artemia, *Wid.;* Walburga, *V.Ab.;* Victor, *M.;* Felix, *P.C.*
26. Mechtildis, *V.;* Claudian, *M.*
27. Gabriel of Sorrowful Mother, *C.;* Leander, *B.C.;* Baldomer, *C.*
28. Romanus, *Ab.;* Antoinette, *V.;* Oswald, *B.C.;* Silvan, *Ab.C.*

MARCH

1. Antonia, *M.;* Eudoxia, *M.;* David, *B.C.;* Suitbert, *B.C.;* Seth, *Pat.;* Jared, *Pat.*
2. Aelred, *Ab.C.;* Chad, *B.C.;* Absolon, *M.;* (Bl.) Henry Suso, *C.*
3. Cunegunda, *Emp.;* Aelred, *Ab.C.*
4. Casimir, *K.C.;* Lucius, *IP.M.;* Alberic, *B.C.;* (Bl.) Humbert, *C.;* Romeo, *C.*
5. Carthage, *B.C.;* Marcius, *M.;* Phocas, *M.;* Kieran, *B.C.*
6. Perpetua and Felicitas, *MM;* Colette, *V.;* Fridolin, *C.;* Aleph, *M.;* Victor, *M.;* Chrodegang, *B.C.;* Rose of Viterbo, *V.*
7. Thomas Aquinas, *C.D.;* Theophilus, *B.C.;* Perpetua and Felicitas, *MM.*
8. John of God, *C.;* Felix, *B.C.;* Duthac, *B.C.;* Senan, *B.C.*
9. Frances of Rome, *Wid.;* Catherine of Bologna, *V.;* Gregory of Nyssa, *B.C.D.*
10. Holy Forty Martyrs, Victor, *M.;* Alexander, *M.;* Simplicius, *P.C.*
11. Alberta, *V.M.;* Aengus, *B.C.;* Constantine, *C.;* Eulogius, *Pr.M.;* Sophronius, *B.C.*
12. Gregory the Great, *P.C.D.;* Innocent I, *P.C.*
13. Roderick, *M.,* Patricia, *M.;* Euphrasia, *V.,* Gerald, *B.C.;* (Bl.) Agnellus, *C.*
14. Tranquillus, *Ab.C.,* Eve, *V.;* Diona, *M.;* Mathilda, *Wid.*
15. Silvius, *M.;* (Bl.) Louise de Marillac, *Wid.;* Longinus, *M.,* Clement Hofbauer, *Pr.C.*
16. Herbert, *C.;* Largus and Smaragdus, *MM.;* Cyriac, *Dea.M.*

17. Patrick, *B.C.;* Harold, *M.;* Joseph of Arim., *C.;* Agricola, *B.C.*
18. Cyril of Jerusalem, *B.C.D.;* Narcissus, *B.M.;* Edward, *K.M.;*
    Frigidian, *B.C.*
19. Commemoration of St. Joseph, *Spouse of the Blessed Virgin;*
    Leontius, *C.;* (Bl.) Sibyllina, *V.*
20. Joachim, *Father of Blessed Virgin;* Cuthbert, *B.C.;* Wulfram,
    B.C.; Herbert, *B.C.;* Claudia, *M.*
21. Benedict, *Ab.;* Enda, *Ab.C.*
22. Benvenutus, *B.C.;* Octavian, *M.;* Lea, *Wid.*
23. Turibius, *B.C.;* Victorian, *M.*
24. Gabriel the Archangel; Simon, *M.;* Angelica, *V.;* Macartin,
    B.C.; Romulus, *M.;* Catherine of Sweden, *V.*
25. Annunciation of Blessed Virgin; Irenaeus, *B.M.;* Dismas.
26. Ludger, *B.C.;* Emmanuel, *M.;* Thecla, *M.;* Enna, *B.C.*
27. John Damascene, *C.D.;* Robert Bellarmine, *B.C.D.;* Rupert,
    B.C.; Augusta, *V.M.*
28. John Capistran, *C.;* Guntran, *K.C.;* Gwendoline, *Ab.;*
    Osburga, *V.*
29. Berthold, *C.;* Eustace, *Ab.C.;* Maximin, *B.C.;* Ludolf, *B.C.*
30. John Climacus, *C.*
31. Cornelia, *M.;* Amos, *Proph.;* Balbina, *V.;* Benjamin, *Dea. C.*

APRIL

1. Theodora, *M.;* Venantius, *B.M.;* Hugh, *B.C.*
2. Francis of Paula, *C.;* Mary of Egypt, *Pen.;* Theodosia, *V.M.*
3. Richard of Chichester, *B.C.;* Rosamund.
4. Isidore of Seville, *B.C.D.;* Ambrose, *B.C.D.;* Benedict the
   Moor, *C.*
5. Vincent Ferrer, *C.;* Irene, *V.M.;* (Bl.) Juliana of Cornillon, *V.*
6. Celsus, *B.C.;* (Bl.) Notker, *C.;* William, *A b.C;* Celestine, *P. C.*
7. Hegesippus, *C.;* Rufinus, *M.;* (Bl.) Herman Joseph, *C.;* John
   Baptist de la Salle, *C.*
8. Dionysius, *B.C.;* Concessa, *M.,* Walter, *Ab.C.,* (Bl.) Julia
   Billiart, *V.*
9. Casilda, *V.;* Waltrude, *Ab.;* Monica, *Wid.;* Mary Cleophas
10. Ezechiel, *Proph.;* Terence, *M.*
11. Leo the Great, *P.C.D.;* Alger, *A b.C.*
12. Zeno, *B.C.;* Julius, *P.C.;* Constantine, *B.M.;* Victor, *M.*
13. Hermenegild, *M.;* Justin, *M.*
14. Justin, *M.;* Tiburtius, *M.;* Valerian and Maximus, *MM.;*
    Lidwina, *V.;* Marcia, *M.,* Peter Gonzales, *C.*
15. Basilissa, *M.;* Godwin, *C.;* Octavia, *M.*

16. Benedict Joseph, *C.;* Christiana, *M.;* Engratia, *V.M.;* Magnus, *M.;* Bernadette, *V.;* (Bl.) Archangelo, *C.;* Lambert, *M.;* Celesta, *M.*
17. Anicetus, *P.M.;* Stephen Harding, *B.C.*
18. Perfectus, *Pr.M.;* Laserian, *B.C.;* (Bl.) Mary of the Incarnation, *Mat.;* Werner, *M.*
19. Elphege, *B.M.*, Timon, *B. M.*, Emma, *Mat.*
20. Agnes of Montepulciano, *V.;* Theodore, *C.*
21. Anselm, *B.C.D.;* Felix, *M.*
22. Soter and Caius, *PP.MM.*
23. George, *M.;* Achilleus, *Dea.M.*, Adalbert, *B.M.;* Ivor, *B.C.*
24. Fidelis, *M.;* Egbert, *Pr.C.;* Mellitus, *B.C.;* Bova, *V.M.*
25. Mark, *Ev.;* Ermin, *B.C.;* Floribert, *B.C.;* Callista, *M.*
26. Cletus and Marcellinus, *PP.MM.;* Our Lady of Good Counsel; Clarence, *B.C.*
27. Peter Canisius, *C.D.;* Zita, *V.*, Asicus, *B.C.;* Felicia, *M.*
28. Paul of the Cross, *C.;* Vitalis of Ravenna, *M.;* Prudentius, *B.C.;* (Bl.) Louis Grignon de Montfort, *C.;* Valeria, *M.*
29. Peter of Verona, *M.;* Aemilian, *M.*
30. Catherine of Sienna, *V.;* Marianus, *M.;* Erkenwald (Archibald), *B.C.;* Joseph Benedict Cottolengo, *C.*

MAY

1. Philip and James, *App.;* Sigismund, *K.M.;* Patience, *M.;* Amator, *B.C.;* Asaph, *B.C.;* Brioc, *B.C.;* Jeremias, *Proph.;* Walburga, *V.Ab.*
2. Athanasius, *B.C.D.;* Noe, *Pat.*
3. Finding of Holy Cross; Alexander, *P.M.;* Eventius, *M.;* Juvenal, *B.C.;* Viola, *V.M.*
4. Monica, *Wid.;* Silvan, *B.M.;* Ada, *Ab.;* Antonia, *M.;* Ethelred, *K.C.;* Florian, *M.;* Godard, *B.C.;* (Bl.) Richard Reynolds, *M.*
5. Pius V, *P.C.*
6. John, Ap., before the Latin Gate; Prudence, *V.;* John Damascene, *C.D.*
7. Stanislaus, *B.M.;* Flavia Domitilla, *V.M.*
8. Apparition of St. Michael, *Arch.*
9. Gregory Nazianzen, *B.C.D.;* Beatus, *C.;* Timothy, *B.M.;* Luke, *Ev.;* Pachomius, *C.*
10. Antonine, *B.C.;* Gordian and Epimachus, *MM.;* Alphius, *M.;* Blanda, *M.;* Comgall, *Ab.;* Job, *Pat.;* Cataldus, *B.C.*

11. Francis Jerome, *C.;* Anicia, *M.;* Anthimus, *Pr.M.;* Mamertus, *B.C.*
12. Nereus and Achilleus, *MM.;* Pancratius, *M.;* Flavia Domitilla, *V.M.;* Epiphanius, *B.C.;* (Bl.) Imelda, *V.*
13. Conleth, *B.C.*
14. Boniface, *M.;* Paschal I, *P.C.;* Carthage, *B.C.;* Corona, *M.;*

15. John Baptist de la Salle, *C.;* Achilles, *B.C.;* Dymphna, *V.M.;* Isidore, *M.;* Torquatus, *M.;* Secundus, *Pr.C.*
16. Ubald, *B.C.;* John Nepomucene, *Pr.M.;* Honoratus, *B.C.;* Simon Stock, *C.;* Peregrine, *M.;* Brendan, *B.C.;* (Bl.) Mary Anne of Jesus, *V.;* Adam, *Ab.C.*
17. Paschal Baylon, *C.*
18. Venantius, *M.;* Felix of Cantalicio, *C.;* Alexandra, *V.M.;* Eric, *K.M.*
19. Peter Celestine, *P.C.;* Pudentiana, *V.;* Pudens, *M.;* Ives, *C.;* (Bl.) Alcuin, *Ab.C.;* Dunstan, *B.C.;* Urbana, *M.*
20. Bernardine, *C.;* Basilla, *V.M.;* Alfreda, *V.*
21. Adalric, *M.*
22. Rita, *Wid.*
23. John Baptist dei Rossi, *C.;* Desiderius, *M.*
24. Our Lady Help of Christians; Our Lady of the Way; Afra, *M.;* Edgar, K.C.
25. Gregory VII, *P.C.;* Urban I, *P.M.;* Aldhelm, *B.C.;* Madeleine Sophie, *V.;* Zenobius, *B.C.*
26. Philip Neri, *C.;* Eleutherius, *P.M.;* Zacharias, *B.M.*
27. Bede, *C.D.;* John I, *P.M.*
28. Augustine of Canterbury, *B.C.;* Germanus, *B.C.;* Emil, *M.;* (Bl.) Thomas Forde, *M.;* (Bl.) Margaret Pole, *M.;* (Bl.) Robert Johnson, *M.*
29. Mary Magdalen of Pazzi, *V.;* (Bl.) Richard Thirkill, *M.;* Theodosia, *V.M.;* Maximin, *B.C.*
30. Felix I, *P.M.;* Ferdinand III, *K.C.;* Joan of Arc, *V.;* (Bl.) Thomas Cottam, *M.;* Macrina, *Wid.*
31. Angela Merici, *V.;* Petronilla, *V.*

JUNE
1. Crescentinus, *M.;* Pamphilus, *Pr.M.;* Valens, *Dea.M.;* Fortunatus, *C.*
2. Peter and Marcellinus, *MM.;* Erasmus, *M.;* Alcibiades, *M.;* Sanctus, *Dea.M.;* Blandina, *M.;* Eugene, *P.C.*
3. Clotilda, *Q.;* Kevin, *Ab.C.;* Olive, *V.*

4. Francis Caracciolo, *C.;* Optatus, *B.C.;* Saturnina, *V.M.*
5. Boniface, *B.M.;* Dorotheus, *Pr.M.;* Sanctius, *M.*
6. Norbert, *B.C.;* Claude, *B.C.;* Jarlath, *B.C.;* Paulina, *M.*
7. Robert, *A b.C.;* Colman, *B.C.*
8. Médard, *B.C.;* William, *B.C.*
9. Primus and Felician, *MM.;* Columba, *B.C.*
10. Margaret of Scotland, *Q. Wid.;* (Bl.) Diana, *V.;* Landry, *B.C.;* (Bl.) Amata, *V.*
11. Barnabas, *A p.;* Rembert, *B.C.;* Gregory Ñazianzen, *B.C.*
12. John of St. Facundo, *C.;* Basilides, *M.;* Christian, *B.C.;* Cyrinus, *M.;* Humphrey, *C.;* Antonia, *M.;* Nabor, *C.;* Nazarius, *M.*
13. Antony of Padua, *C.*
14. Basil, *B.C.D.;* Eliseus, *Proph,*
15. Vitus, *M.;* Crescentia, *V.M.;* Modestus *M.;* Germana, *V.*
16. Aurelian, *B.C.;* John Francis Regis, *C.;* Benno, *B.C.;* Cyr, *C.;* Lutgarde, *V.;* Roland, *M.*
17. Avitus, *Pr.C.;* Botulph, *A b.C.;* Emma, *Mat.;* Solomon, *K.*
18. Ephrem, *C.D.;* Mark and Marcellian, *MM.;* Alena, *V.M.;* Constance, *V.M.*
19. Juliana Falconieri, *V.;* Gervase and Protase, *MM.;* (Bl.) Thomas Woodhouse, *M.;* Romuald, *A b.C.*
20. Silverius, *P.M.;* Deodatus, *B.C.;* Florentina, *V.;* Novatus, *C.*
21. Aloysius, *C.;* Demetria, *V.M.;* Ralph, *B.C.;* Alban, *M.*
22. Paulinus, *B.C.;* Flavius, *M.;* Everard, *B.C.*
23. Vigil of St. John the Baptist; Etheldreda, *Q.;* Josias, *K.;* John Fisher, *B.M.*
24. Nativity of St. John the Baptist; Agilbert, *M.*
25. William, *A b.C.;* Adelbert, *C.;* Febronia, *V.M.;* Prosper, *B.C.*
26. John and Paul, *MM.*
27. Our Lady of Perpetual Help; Crescent, *B.M.;* Ladislas, *K.C.*
28. Irenaeus, *B.M.;* Vigil of Sts. Peter and Paul; Benignus, *B.M.;* Serenus, *M.;*
29. Commemoration of Sts. Peter and Paul, *A pp.;* Alexia, *V.;* Benedicta, *V.;* Salome, *V.;* (Bl.) Angelina of Spoleto, *V.*
30. Commemoration of St. Paul the Apostle; Theobald, *Her.C.*

JULY

1. The Most Precious Blood; Rumold, *B.M.;* Aaron, *Pr.;* Julius, *M.;* Theodoric, *C.*
2. Visitation of Blessed Virgin, Processus and Martinian, *MM.;* Otto, *B.C.;* Swithin, *B.C.*

3. Leo II, *P.C.;* Bertram, *B.C.;* Anatole, *B.C.;* Thomas, *Ap.;*
   Eulogius, *C.*
4. Aggeus, *Proph.;* Bertha, *Ab.;* Odo, *B.C.;* Osee, *Proph.;*
   Martin of Tours, *B.C.;* Flavian, *B.C.;* Ulric, *B.C.*
5. Antony M. Zac., *C.;* Cyrilla, *M.;* Grace; Zoe, *M.;* Blanch, *V.M.*
6. Dominica, *V.M.;* Isaias, *Proph.;* Dion, *M.;* Palladius, *B.C.*
7. Cyril and Methodius, *BB.CC.;* Ethelburga, *V.,* Willibald,
   B.C.; Hedda, *B.C.;*
8. Elizabeth of Portugal, *Q. Wid.;* Adrian, *P.C.;* Alethius, *M.;*
   (Bl.) Edgar, *K.C.;* Kilian, *B.M.*
9. Veronica de Julianis, *V.;* Anatolia, *V.M.;* Everilda, *V.;*
   Thomas More, M.; Grace, *V.M.*
10. Seven Holy Brothers; Secunda, *V.M.;* Rufina, *V.M.;* Martial,
    M.; Amalburga, *V.;* Vitalis of Rome, *M.*
11. Pius I, *P.M.;* Olga, *Mat.;* Aleth, *C.;* (Bl.) Oliver Plunkett,
    M.; Sigisbert, *C.*
12. John Gualbert, *Ab.;* Nabor and Felix, *MM.*
13. Anacletus, *P.M.;* Silas, *C.;* Mildred, *V.;* Esdras, *Proph.,*
    Joel, *Proph.,* Nehemias, *Proph.*
14. Bonaventure, *B.C.D.;* Camillus, *C.;* Francis Solano, *C.*
15. Henry, *Emp.;* Baldwin, *Ab.C.;* Bonosa, *V.M.;* Donald, *C.;*
    Rosalia, *V.*
16. Our Lady of Mt. Carmel; Mary Magdalen Postel, *V.;*
    Eustathius, *B.C.;* Faustus, M.; Helier, *M.;* Ceslas, *C.*
17. Alexis, *C.;* Generosa, *M.;* Generosus, *M.;* Marina, *V.;*
    Kenelm, *C.*
18. Camillus, *C.;* Symphorosa, *M.;* Frederick, *B.M.;* Arnold, *C.;*
    Arnulph, *B.C.*
19. Vincent de Paul, *C.;* Arsenius, *Dea.C.;* Epaphras, *B.M.*
20. Jerome Aemilian, *C.;* Margaret of Antioch, *V.M.;* Cassia,
    M.; Elias, *Proph.*
21. Praxedes, *V.;* Julia, *V.M.;* Daniel, *Proph.;* (Bl.) Angelina of
    Corbara, *Mat.*
22. Mary Magdalen, *Pen.;* Salvian, *Pr.C.;* Lawrence of Brindisi, *C.*
23. Apollinaris, *B.M.;* Liborius, *B.C.;* Melchior.
24. Vigil of St. James; Christina, *V.M.;* Declan, *B.C.;* Romanus
    (Boris), *M.*
25. James the Greater, *Ap.;* Christopher, *M.;* Florence, *M.*
    (male); Valentina, *V.M.*
26. Anne, *Mother of Blessed Virgin;* Erastus, *B.M.*
27. Pantaleon, *M.;* Camilla, *V.;* (Bl.) Rudolph, *M.;* (Bl.)
    Theobald Montmorency, *Ab.C.*

28. Nazarius and Celsus, *MM.;* Victor I, *P.M.;* Innocent I, *P.C.;* Ezechias, *K.;* Sampson, *B.C.;* Eustathius, *M.*
29. Martha, *V.;* Felix, *M.;* Seraphia, *V.M.;* Seraphina, *V.;* Beatrice, *M.;* Simplicius, *M.;* Olaf, *K.M.;* Lucilla, *M.*
30. Abdon and Sennen, *MM.;* Julitta, *M.;* (Bl.) Richard Featherstone, *M.;* (Bl.) Thomas Abel, *M.*
31. Ignatius of Loyola, *C.;* Fabius, *M.*

AUGUST

1. St. Peter's Chains; Commemoration of St. Paul, *Ap.;* Holy Machabees, *MM.* Electa, *V.M.;* Faith, Hope, Charity, *VV. MM.* Eleazar, *M.;* Eusebius, *B.M.*
2. Alphonsus Liguori, *B.C.D.;* Stephen I, *P.M.*
3. Relics of St. Stephen, *First M.;* Cyra; Nicodemus, *M.;* Gamaliel, *C.;* (Bl.) Peter Julian Eymard, *C.;* Lydia.
4. Dominic, *C.;* Agabius, *B.C.*
5. Our Lady of the Snow; Cassian, *B.C.;* Afra, *M.;* Emigdius, *B.M.;* Oswald, *K.M.*
6. Transfiguration of Our Lord; Felicissimus, *M.;* Sixtus, II, *P.M.;* Agapitus, *Dea. M.;* Hormisdas, *P.C.*
7. Cajetan, *C.;* Donatus, *B.M.;* Claudia, *Wid.*
8. Cyriac, *Dea.M.;* Largus and Smaragdus, *MM.;* Altmann, *B.C.*
9. Vigil of St. Lawrence; Romanus, *M.;* John Baptist Vianney, *Pr.C.;* Domitian, *B.C.;* Nathy, *B.C.;* (Bl.) Peter Faber, *C.*
10. Lawrence, *M.;* Agilberta, *V.;* Blane, *B.C.*
11. Tiburtius and Susanna, *MM.;* Philomena, *V.M.;* Attracta, *V.;* Lelia, *V.*
12. Clare of Assisi, *V.;* Columbinus, *C.;* Hilaria, *M.;* Phineas; Muredach, *B.C.*
13. Hippolytus and Cassian, *MM.;* John Berchmans, *C.;* Felim, *B.C.;* Radegund, *Q.*
14. Vigil of Assumption; Eusebius, *C.;* Athanasia, *Wid.*
15. Assumption; Stanislaus Kostka, *C.;* Tarcisius, *M.;* (Bl.) Alfred, *B.C.;* Napoleon, *M.;* Macartin, *B.C.*
16. Joachim, *Father of Blessed Virgin;* Diomede, *M.;* Eleanor, *V.M.;* Roch, *C.;* Serena, *Mat.*
17. Hyacinth, *C.;* Clare of Cross, *V.;* Isaac, *Pat.;* Liberatus, *M.;* Myron, *Pr.M.*
18. Agapitus, *M.;* Firmin, *B.C.;* Helen, *Emp.*
19. John Eudes, *C.;* Sarah; Louis, *B.C.*   [Ronald, *M.*
20. Bernard, *Ab.;* Oswin, *K.M.;* Philibert, *Ab.;* Samuel, *Proph.;*
21. Jane Frances, *Wid.;* Cyriaca, *Wid.M.*

22. Timothy, *M.;* Symphorian, *M.;* (Bl.) Richard Kirkman, *M.*
23. Philip Benizi, *C.;* Vigil of St. Bartholomew; Eugene, *B.C.;* Zacheus,*B.C.*
24. Bartholomew, *Ap.;* Jovian, *M.;* Owen, *B.C.;* Rose of Lima, *V.*
25. Louis IX, *K.C.;* Elmer, *B.C.;* Lucilla, *V.M.;* Genesius, *M.;* Thomas,*B.C.*
26. Zephyrinus, *P.M.;* Rose of Lima, *V.*
27. Joseph Calasanctius, *C.;* Gebhard,*B.C.;* Caesarius,*B.C.*
28. Augustine, *B.C.D.;* Hermes, *M.;* Jacob, *Pat.;* Vivian, *B.C.* Méderic, *Pr.C.*
29. Beheading of John the Baptist; Sabina, *M.;* Adelphus, *B.C.*
30. Rose of Lima, *V.;* Felix and Adauctus, *MM.;* Fiacre, *C.;* (Bl.) Bronislava, *V.*
31. Raymond Nonnatus, *C.;* Aristides, *C.;* Aidan,*B.C.;* Isabel

SEPTEMBER

1. Giles, *Ab.;* Twelve Brothers, *M.M.;* Constant,*B.C.;* Gedeon; Verena, *V.M.;* Josue, *Pat.;* Ruth
2. Stephen of Hungary, *K.C.*
3. Erasma, *V.M.;* Albertinus, *C.;* Macanisius, *B.C.;* Phoebe
4. Rose of Viterbo, *V.;* Rosalia, *V.;* Candida, *Mat.;* Ida, *Mat.;* Moses, *Proph.*
5. Lawrence Justinian, *B.C.;* Bertin, *Ab.C.*
6. Beata, *V.M.;* Hieronyma, *V.M.;* Zacharias, *Proph.*
7. Cloud. *C.;* Regina, *V.M.;* Humbert,*B.C.*
8. Nativity of Blessed Virgin; Adrian, *M.;* Nestor, *M.;* Peter Claver, *C.*
9. Gorgonius, *M.;* Kiernan, *Ab.C.*
10. Nicholas of Tolentino, *C.;* Pulcheria, *V.Emp.*
11. Protus and Hyacinth, *MM.;* (Bl.) John Gabriel Perboyre, *M.*
12. Holy Name of Mary; Aloysia, *V.M.;* Juventius,*B.C.*
13. Amatus,*B.C.;* Nothburga, *V.;* Tobias.
14. Exaltation of Holy Cross; John Chrysostom, *B.C.D.;* Crescentius, *M.;* Judith
15. Seven Dolors of Blessed Virgin; Nicomedes, *M.;* Catherine of Genoa, *Wid.;* Achard, *Ab.C.;* Albinus,*B.C.*
16. Cornelius and Cyprian, *MM.;* Euphemia, *V.M.;* Abundius, *Pr.M.;* Abundantius, *Dea.M.;* Ninian, *B.C.;* (Bl.) Evangelist, *Pr.C.;* Edith, *V.;* Geminianus, *M.;* Lucy, *M.*
17. Stigmata of St. Francis of Assisi, *C.;* Hildegard, *V.;* Lambert,*B.M.;* Ariadne, *V.M.*
18. Joseph of Cupertino, *C.*
19. Januarius, *M.;* Theodore,*B.C.*

20. Eustace, *M.;* Vigil of St. Matthew; Fausta, *V.;* Philippa, *M.*
21. Matthew, *Ap.;* Jonas, *Proph.*
22. Thomas of Villanova, *B.C.;* Maurice, *M.;* Digna, *V.M.;* Drusilla, *V.M.*
23. Linus, *P.M.;* Thecla, *V.M.;* Adamnan, *Ab.C.*
24. Our Lady of Ransom; Pacificus, *C.*
25. Cleophas, *M.;* Finbar, *B.C.*
26. Cyprian and Justina, *MM.;* Zephyrinus, *P.M.;* Nilus, *C.;* Isaac Jogues, *Pr.M.;* John de Brébeuf, *Pr.M.;* John Lalande, *M.;* Noël Chabanel, *Pr.M.;* René Goupil, *M.* Antony Daniel, *Pr.M.;* Charles Garnier, *Pr.M.;* Gabriel Lalemant, *Pr.C.*
27. Cosmas and Damian, *MM.;* Hiltrude, *V.;* Caius, *B.C.*
28. Wenceslas, *M.;* Lioba, *V.;* Baruch, *Proph.*
29. Dedication of St. Michael, *Arch.*; Alaric.
30. Jerome, *Pr.C.D.;* Gregory Illuminator, *B.M.;* Honorius, *B.C.;* Sophia, M.; Francis Borgia, *C.*

OCTOBER

1. Remigius, *B.C.*
2. Holy Guardian Angels; Thomas of Hereford, *B.C.;* Leodegar, *B.M.*
3. Teresa of Child Jesus, *V.;* Alvin, *B.C.;* Ewald, *M.*
4. Francis of Assisi, *C.;* Quentin, *M.;* Berenice, *V.M.;* Crispus, *C.*
5. Placid, *M.;* Aimard, *C.*
6. Bruno, *C.;* Junius, *Dea.C.;* John Leonard, *C.*
7. Most Holy Rosary; Mark, *P.C.;* Marcellus, *M.;* Sergius, *M.;* Apuleius, *M.;* August, *Pr.C.;* Bacchus, *M.*
8. Bridget of Sweden, *Wid.;* Melania the Elder; Reparata, *V.M.;* Demetrius, *M.;* John of Bridlington, *C.;* Keyna, *V.;* Laurentia, *M.;* Pelagia, *Pen.*
9. Denis, *B.M.;* Louis Bertrand, *C.;* Abraham, *Pat.;* Gunther, *Her.C.;* Rusticus, *M.;* Andronicus, *C.*
10. Francis Borgia, *C.;* Malo, *M.*
11. Canice, *Ab.C.;* Placidia, *V.*
12. Edwin, *K.M.;* Maximilian, *B.C.;* Seraphinus, *C.;* Wilfrid, *B.C.*
13. Edward, *K.C.;* Congan, *Ab.C.;* Angelus, *M.*
14. Callistus I, *P.M.;* Fortunata, *V.M.;* Burchard, *B.C.*
15. Teresa of Jesus, *V.;* Aurelia, *V.*
16. Florentine, *B.C.;* Gall, *Ab.;* Gerard Majella, *C.;* Lullus, *B.C.*
17. Hedwig, *Wid.;* Margaret Mary Alocoque, *V.*

18. Luke, *Ev.;* Paul of Cross, *C.*
19. Peter of Alcantara, *C.;* Frideswide, *V.*
20. John Cantius, *Pr.C.;* Wendolin, *C.*
21. Hilarion, *Ab.;* Urusla, *V.M.;* Angelina, *V.M.;* Celina, *V.;* Viator, *C.;* Condedus, *C.*
22. Alodia, *M.;* Cordelia, *V.M.;* Mary Salome; Mark, *B.M.*
23. Ignatius of Constantinople, *B.C.;* John Capistran, *C.;* Gratian, *M.;* Theodoret, *M.*
24. Raphael, *Arch.;* Maglorius, *B.C.*
25. Chrysanthus and Daria, *MM.;* Crispin and Crispinian, *MM.;* Dorcas, *Wid.;* Gaudentius, *B.C.;* John of Beverly, *B.C.*
26. Evaristus, *P.M.*
27. Vigil of Sts. Simon and Jude; Otteran, *B.C.*
28. Simon and Jude, *App.;* Eunice, *M.*
29. Eusebia, *V.M.*
30. Victorius, *M.;* Arilda, *V.M.;* Lucan, *M.;* Serapion, *B.C.;* Xenobia, *M.*
31. Vigil of All Saints; Alphonsus Rodriguez, *C.;* Wolfgang, *B.C.;* Lucilla, *V.M.*
    Last Sunday in October: Our Lord Jesus Christ the King.

NOVEMBER

1. All Saints; Harold, *K.C.*
2. All Souls; Tobias, *M.;* Cumgar, *Ab.C.*
3. Hubert, *B.C.;* Malachy, *B.C.;* Sylvia, *Mat.;* Winifred, *V.M.*
4. Charles Borromeo, *B.C.;* Vitalis and Agricola, *MM.;* Felix of Valois, *C.;* Clair, *Pr.M.;* Emeric, *C.;* Bertille, *Ab.*
5. Zachary, *Pr.Proph.;* Elizabeth, *Wid.*
6. Illtyd, *Ab.C.*
7. Ernest, *M.;* Rufus, *B.C.;* Urania, *M.;* Willibrord, *B.C.;* Engelbert, *B.M.;* Carina, *M.*
8. Four Crowned Martyrs: Severus, Severian, Carpophorus and Victorinus; Godfrey, *B.C.;* Adeodatus (Deusdedit), *P.C.*
9. Dedication of Archbasilica of Our Savior; Theodore, *M.;* Orestes, *M.;* Ursinus, *B.C.*
10. Andrew Avellino, *C.;* Tryphon, *M.;* Florence, *M.* (female); Justus, *B.C.;* Nympha, *V.M.;* Respicius, *M.;* Tiberius, *M.*
11. Martin of Tours, *B.C.;* Mennas, *M.*
12. Martin I, *P.M.;* Aurelius, *B.M.;* Livinus, *B.M.;* Renatus, *B.C.*

13. Didacus, *C.*; Homobonus, *C.*; Brice, *B.C.*
14. Josaphat, *B.M.*; Dubritius, *B.C.*; Erkonwald (Archibald), *B.C.*; Lawrence O'Toole; *B.C.*; (Bl.) Thomas Percy, *M.*; Veneranda, *V.M.*
15. Gertrude, *V.*; Albert the Great, *B.C.D.*; Valeriana, *M.*; Baruch, *Proph.*; Leopold, *C.*; Malo, *B.C.*
16. Margaret, *Q. Wid.*; Othmar, *Ab.*; Edmund Rich, *B.C.*; (Bl.) Agnes of Assisi, *V.Ab.*
17. Gregory Thaumaturgus, *B.C.*; Hugh, *B.C.*; Alpheus, *M.*; Gregoria, *M.*; Hilda, *V.*
18. Dedication of Basilica of Sts. Peter and Paul; Frigidian, *B.C.*; Odo, *Ab.*
19. Elizabeth of Hungary, *Q.Wid.*; Pontianus, *P.M.*; Abdenago; Abdias, *Proph.*
20. Felix of Valois, *C.*; Edmund, *K.M.*; Octavius, *M.*
21. Presentation of Blessed Virgin; Albert, *B.M.*; Columban, *Ab.*; Gelasius, *P.C.*; Fergus, *B.C.*
22. Cecilia, *V.M.*; Philemon, *C.*
23. Clement I, *P.M.*; Felicitas, *M.*; Lucretia, *V.M.*; Adela, *Wid.*
24. John of Cross, *C.*; Chrysogonus, *Pr.M.*; Colman, *B.C.*; Crescentian, *M.*; Flora, *V.M.*
25. Catherine of Alexandria, *V.M.*; Jucunda, *V.*
26. Sylvester, *Ab.*; Peter of Alexandria, *B.M.*; Leonard of Port Maurice, *C.*; Conrad, *B.C.*
27. Severinus, *C.*; Virgil, *B.C.*
28. Sosthenes, *C.*; Gregory, III, *P.C.*
29. Vigil of St. Andrew; Saturninus, *M.*; (Bl.) Cuthbert Mayne, *M.*
30. Andrew, *Ap.*; Zozimus, *C.*; (Bl.) Blanche, *Q.*

DECEMBER

1. (Bl.) Edmund Campion, *M.*; Elegius, *B.C.*; Nahum; *Proph.*, Natalia, *Wid.*; (Bl.) Richard Whiting, *Ab.M.*
2. Bibiana, *V.M.*; Adria, *M.*; Theodoret, *M.*
3. Francis Xavier, *C.*; Birinus, *B.C.*
4. Peter Chrysologus, *B.C.D.*; Barbara, *V.M.*; Osmund, *B C.*; Ada, *Ab.*
5. Sabbas, *Ab.*; Crispina, *M.*; Lucius, *C.*
6. Nicholas of Myra, *B.C.*; Tertius, *C.*; Dionysia, *M.*; Leontia, *M.*
7. Ambrose, *B.C.D.*; Anianus; Vigil of the Immaculate Conception.
8. Immaculate Conception; Elfrida, *V.M.*; Eucharius, *B.C.*; Lucilla, *V.M.*

9. Delphina, *V.;* Leocadia, *V.M.;* Peter Fourier, *C.*
10. Melchiades, *P.M.*
11. Damasus, *P.C.*
12. Our Lady of Guadalupe; Synesius, *M.;* Epimachus, *M.:* Finian, *B.C.*
13. Lucy, *V.M.;* Ottilia, *V.;* Jane Frances, *Wid.;* Aubert, *B.C.;* John Bosco, *C.*
14. Spiridion, *B.C.;* Agnellus, *Ab.;* John of Cross, *C.*
15. Octave of the Immaculate Conception.
16. Eusebius, *B.M.;* Adelaide, *Wid.Emp.;* Bean, *B.C.;* Ado, *B.C.;* Albina, *V.M.;* Ananias, Azarias and Misael; (Bl.) Urban, *P.C.*
17. Begga, *Wid.;* (Bl.) Cherubinus, *C.;* Lazarus, *B.C.;* Ignatius of Antioch, *B.M.*
18. Salvator, *M.;* (Bl.) Mary of Angels, *V.*
19. Flannan, *B.C.;* Anastasius, *P.C.;* Darius, *M.*
20. Vigil of St. Thomas; Esther
21. Thomas, *Ap.*
22. Flavian, *M.;* Ischyrion, *M.*
23. Dagobert, *K.M.;* (Bl.) Hartman, *C.;* Victoria, *V.M.*
24. Vigil of Nativity; Delphinus, *B.C.;* Irmina, *V.;* John Cantius, *Pr.C.*
25. Nativity; Anastasia, *M.;* Eugenia, *V.M.*
26. Stephen, *First Martyr*
27. John the Evangelist; Alvin, *B.C.*
28. Holy Innocents; Abel; Domna, *V.M.;* Francis of Sales, *B.C.D.*
29. Thomas à Becket, *B.M.;* (Bl.) Gaspar del Bufalo, *C.;* David, *K. Proph.;* Jesse; Nathan, *Proph.;* Crescent, *B.C.*
30. Anysia, *M.;* Egwin, *B.C.;* Jucundus, *B.C.;* Roger, *B.C.;* Sabinus, *B.M.;* Alfreda, *V.*
31. Sylvester, *P.C.;* Donata, *M.;* Melania the Younger.

PRINTED BY BENZIGER BROTHERS, NEW YORK

Printed in the United States
126994LV00001B/50/A